Nonmedication Treatments for Adult ADHD

Nonmedication Treatments for Adult ADHD

Evaluating Impact on Daily Functioning and Well-Being

J. Russell Ramsay

American Psychological Association • Washington, DC

Published by
American Psychological Association
750 First Street, NE
Washington, DC 20002
www.apa.org

To order
APA Order Department
P.O. Box 92984
Washington, DC 20090-2984
Tel: (800) 374-2721; Direct: (202) 336-5510
Fax: (202) 336-5502; TDD/TTY: (202) 336-6123
Online: www.apa.org/books/
E-mail: order@apa.org

In the U.K., Europe, Africa, and the Middle East, copies may be ordered from
American Psychological Association
3 Henrietta Street
Covent Garden, London
WC2E 8LU England

Typeset in Goudy by Circle Graphics, Columbia, MD

Printer: Maple-Vail Books, York, PA
Cover Designer: Mercury Publishing Services, Rockville, MD
Technical/Production Editor: Jeremy White

The opinions and statements published are the responsibility of the authors, and such opinions and statements do not necessarily represent the policies of the American Psychological Association.

Library of Congress Cataloging-in-Publication Data

Ramsay, J. Russell.
 Nonmedication treatments for adult ADHD : evaluating impact on daily functioning and well-being / J. Russell Ramsay.
    p. cm.
 Includes bibliographical references and index.
 ISBN-13: 978-1-4338-0564-6
 ISBN-10: 1-4338-0564-2
 1. Attention-deficit disorder in adults—Treatment. I. Title.

RC394.A85R364 2010
616.85'89—dc22

                                                        2009014261

British Library Cataloguing-in-Publication Data

A CIP record is available from the British Library.

Printed in the United States of America
First Edition

For my daughters, Abigail and Brynn

CONTENTS

ACKNOWLEDGMENTS

In the interests of full disclosure, I would like to first inform readers about potential conflicts of interest that could be perceived as affecting my review of various treatments for adult attention-deficit/hyperactivity disorder (ADHD). My hope is that by being transparent about these potential sources of conflicts, I will have enabled readers to make informed judgments about any possible bias in my reviews and conclusions. I served as a consultant on the McNeil Pediatrics National Adult ADHD Steering Committee in 2007. I have no other commercial or financial conflicts of interest. I am also involved as a researcher on some of the nonmedication treatments for adult ADHD reviewed or mentioned in this book, that is, cognitive–behavioral therapy (chap. 2; Ramsay & Rostain, 2007a; Rostain & Ramsay, 2006a) and the family-based treatment program mentioned in chapter 5. The project is mentioned as a study in progress. I received support for this study from a Comprehensive Neuroscience Center award from the University of Pennsylvania School of Medicine, as well as from a University Research Foundation grant from the University of Pennsylvania for a study of mindfulness meditation training (chap. 7; Z. B. Rosen et al., 2008).

I would like to thank many individuals, without whom the development and completion of this book would not have been possible. First, the original idea for the book came during a discussion with Lansing Hays, then with American Psychological Association (APA) Books. Although the seed of the idea was planted then, it blossomed with the persistence of Susan Reynolds, also of APA Books, who encouraged me to take on and complete the project, and with the support of the editorial staff at APA, who helped carry the project through to completion.

I thank my colleagues in the Department of Psychiatry at the University of Pennsylvania (PENN) School of Medicine, under the direction of its chairman, Dwight L. Evans. I am fortunate to work in a department in which the clinical and research objectives promote the development and use of evidence-supported models, the training of future clinicians, and the helping of patients who entrust us with their care.

In particular, I cannot sufficiently express my gratitude for having had the opportunity to collaborate with Anthony ("Tony") Rostain over the past decade. Tony first envisioned PENN's Adult ADHD Treatment and Research Program, which we cofounded in March 1999 and continue to operate. Tony is a world-class clinician, researcher, and teacher, whose winning personality is infectious to those who spend even a brief time around him. I often joke that there are two types of people in the world: those who know Tony and those who are about to know Tony. I am ever thankful to be numbered among the former, and I cherish our collaboration and friendship.

I also would like to express my thanks to the current staff of the PENN Adult ADHD Treatment and Research Program, many of whom provided helpful feedback on early drafts of the book: Bruce Berg, Katie Buek, Bridget Callaghan, Michele Cepparulo, Andrea Fabricatore, Lofton Harris, Meghan Leahy, Ambreen Naeem, Parin Patel, Brad Rosenfield, and Rosellen Taraborelli. Past staff members and those who provided crucial administrative and organizational support deserve acknowledgment and thanks for the important role they each played at various times in the growth of the program: Sarah Charlesworth, Lanre Dokun, Jennifer Elliott, Marissa Fernandez, Stacey Garfield, Caitlin Howarth, Tina Inforzato, Melissa Kahane, Hollie Levy-Mack, Lisa Mimmo, and Stacey Oppelman.

A number of professional colleagues who have collaborated with our program on various clinical and research projects over the years deserve acknowledgment: Ted Brodkin; Mary Riggs Cohen; Myrna Cohen; William Culbertson; Amishi Jha and her lab; John Listerud; Paul Moberg; Edward Moss; Tracey Rush; John Schureman; James J. Stone; Roberta Waite; and members of the Children's Hospital of Philadelphia's (CHOP's) Center for the Management of ADHD, including Nathan Blum, Josephine Elia, Tom Power, Stephen Soffer, and Peter Wiley. Elizabeth Utsch and Seth Laracy of CHOP have been instrumental in establishing the CHOP–PENN ADHD conference as an annual event.

One of the rewarding aspects of being a psychologist working with adults with ADHD is witnessing the therapeutic effects of healthy, supportive relationships with others. In my personal and professional lives, I have benefited firsthand from connections and bonds with many friends and colleagues, and I treasure these relationships.

I also acknowledge all the researchers whose work is reviewed herein. Although a project centered on the review of clinical outcome research demands a rigorous critique of the researchers' empirical studies, their labors were dedicated to the betterment of clinical services available for individuals with ADHD. Clinician–researchers start their work as seekers, but with the publication of their studies become beacons for others. Thus, all the researchers whose hard work provides the basis for this book have my profound respect.

I have had the benefit of wonderful education and training throughout my professional development. Anita L. Greene and Leonard I. Jacobson were my graduate and undergraduate mentors, respectively. I also received wonderful training during my predoctoral internship at CPC Behavioral Healthcare in Red Bank, New Jersey, and my postdoctoral fellowship at the Center for Cognitive Therapy at PENN. I continue as a clinical staff member at the Center for Cognitive Therapy, under the direction of my mentor and friend Cory Newman, where I am fortunate to work with skilled and dedicated clinicians who also happen to be wonderful people.

I would not have been able to complete this project or any of my professional roles without the loving support through the years of my grandmother, Harvena Felty; my parents, Mary Ann Ramsay and the late J. Roger Ramsay; and my sister, Jennifer Ramsay.

Finally, my immediate family deserves special acknowledgment and thanks, as they have made sacrifices to allow me to perform the work of a psychologist. Although I regard myself as a serviceable writer (at least on my good days), I remain incapable of conveying the feelings of love and esteem I have for my daughters, Abigail and Brynn. I am filled with awe and wonder as I watch them grow up, and I am immeasurably proud to be their father. Finally, my wife, Amy, has been a steadfast and loving partner over the years, and I could not have completed this book without her support.

Nonmedication Treatments for Adult ADHD

INTRODUCTION

Let me be crystal clear at the outset: This book is not an antimedication book.

As a clinical psychologist specializing in the assessment and treatment of adults with attention-deficit/hyperactivity disorder (ADHD), and one whose closest professional colleague and collaborator is a psychiatrist with the same specialty, I have borne witness to many individuals whose lives have been changed for the better as a result of an accurate diagnosis and treatment with medications for ADHD. Symptoms and associated impairments that had previously seemed overwhelming to those affected are lessened, allowing them to experience marked improvements in central domains of their lives.

ADHD is currently understood as a neurodevelopmental syndrome with symptoms that are highly heritable and neurobiological in their origin. Pharmacotherapy stands alone as the single most efficacious treatment for ADHD for individuals of all ages. Medications, psychostimulants in particular, are effective in reducing the core symptoms of inattention, hyperactivity, and impulsivity.

Despite the effectiveness of pharmacotherapy for ADHD, however, adequate treatment often requires more than mere symptom reduction. It is the cascading negative effects of ADHD symptoms on various aspects of daily life that create distress for which people seek relief. This is not to minimize the importance of symptom relief provided by medications. On the contrary, in most cases pharmacotherapy provides a foundation for the treatment of ADHD in patients of all ages. However, adult patients usually rate their treatment progress in terms of their ability to fulfill personal roles and perform tasks rather than in terms of symptom reduction.

The insidiousness of ADHD, particularly for adults, is that it thwarts individuals' ability to handle the common demands of daily life and pursue reasonable goals. Many of the domains of life affected by ADHD are those from which people derive a sense of competence, industry, connection with others, and consequently, sense of self. Thus, emerging research indicates that rather than being a mild disorder characterized by "nuisance" symptoms, ADHD is among the most chronically, pervasively, and severely impairing disorders in psychiatry.

As sinister as the negative effects of untreated ADHD are the corrosive psychological effects of growing up with the disorder, particularly if it has gone unrecognized. Hidden within data demonstrating that ADHD impairs functioning in most, if not all, activities of adult life, are the underappreciated issues related to heightened sense of hopelessness, self-denigration, shame, and pessimism that affect many adults with ADHD. Thus, adults with ADHD face a double whammy of dealing with more and greater difficulties managing daily affairs than people without ADHD and having lower levels of optimism and resilience with which to take on these challenges.

The first step in getting help is to identify that there is a problem and to determine whether chronic difficulties fit a developmental profile consistent with ADHD. Observing ADHD is akin to looking for the wind—it can be felt (e.g., breeze against face), its effects can be observed (e.g., branches moving, leaves blown across the ground), but it can never actually be seen, although it is undeniably present. Moreover, wind ranges in strength from a light breeze to gale-force winds. It is similarly difficult to directly observe ADHD, although it has clear and negative effects that fall along a continuum of severity. Individuals usually present for treatment with obvious symptoms and functional impairments that can be discerned by experienced mental health professionals using comprehensive assessment methods. To extend the earlier metaphor, the claim that "everyone has ADHD" is comparable to a person who is recovering from the effects of a hurricane and another person who lost some papers in a stiff breeze being considered as similar because both encountered problems associated with wind.

Once the diagnosis of adult ADHD has been established, attention turns to treatment. Because of the documented effectiveness of medications, they are considered the first line of treatment for ADHD in patients of all ages. Pharmacotherapy often provides a degree of symptom relief that is also associated with positive functional outcomes, such as improved academic or occupational performance, improved follow-through on tasks, safer driving behaviors, better interpersonal skills, and so on. It is not that the medications imbue individuals with new skills—"pills do not teach skills." Rather, medications improve functioning in regions of the brain associated with self-management, thereby reducing the unseen barriers that had interfered with the implementation of the adaptive coping skills.

Despite the documented effectiveness of medications for ADHD, symptom improvements provided by medications do not inexorably lead to improvements in coping behaviors and functioning in most adults with ADHD. Although many individuals experience global improvements in functioning with effective medication treatment for ADHD, a greater number require additional modes of treatment to adequately address areas of functional impairment. Moreover, many patients may not have a positive response to medications, either not obtaining hoped-for therapeutic effects or suffering intolerable side effects that require discontinuation of treatment. In rare cases, adverse events or medical contraindications might obviate the use of medications. Finally, some individuals might simply decline the option of using medications, preferring instead to seek alternative coping options. Examining the adjunctive treatment options for individuals fitting these scenarios provided the impetus for writing this book.

From a personal standpoint, the motivation for taking on the challenge of writing this book was the result of the desire to answer many questions I had about various treatments available for adults with ADHD. Although I considered myself well versed in my area of professional interest, namely psychosocial treatments for adult ADHD, over the years I have fielded many questions about other treatment options and heard anecdotal accounts of the benefits of different approaches, such as neurofeedback training, ADHD coaching, various complementary and alternative treatments, and so on. I was relatively informed and up to date on some of these treatments; in most cases, I had only a cursory understanding of them, relying on second-hand information. Thus, this book represents the fulfillment of a personal goal to forge through the clinical outcome literature on nonmedication treatments for adult ADHD, to evaluate the research support for these treatments, and to present them in a manner that will be informative and useful to interested clinicians and researchers.

The overarching purpose of the present volume is to review the status of nonmedication interventions currently available for adults with ADHD. Although there is an empirical foundation for multimodal treatments for children with ADHD, such an evidence base does not currently exist for adults with ADHD. Thus, the twofold goal of this book is to (a) introduce and describe the various nonmedication treatment options available for adult ADHD and (b) review the extant clinical outcome studies (or, in several cases, the lack thereof) of their efficacy to determine those adjunctive treatment options with the highest likelihood of providing help to the greatest number of adults with ADHD.

I anticipate that the primary audience for this book will be practicing mental health clinicians who are looking for an accessible and instructive source of information about available nonmedication treatments for adult ADHD. However, practicing professionals in other areas of health care, advanced graduate or medical students, or anyone interested in the topic will, I hope, find the information herein understandable, informative, and helpful. Finally, I hope that clinical researchers may be inspired to fill in the gaps in the evidence base for the treatments discussed in the chapters that follow to establish empirically supported and clinically relevant treatment guidelines that will make a positive difference in the lives of adults living with ADHD. Although providing an overview and descriptions of various treatments, the book was not designed to be a treatment manual. Hence, although various clinical issues and treatments relevant for adults with ADHD are discussed, assessment strategies are only briefly reviewed and specific case examples are not included. However, copious references and resources are provided for individuals seeking additional information about the treatments reviewed.

Chapter 1 is an introduction to adult ADHD, including an overview of the current, and possible future, incarnation of the diagnostic criteria. This first chapter also reviews the developmental course and life outcomes of individuals with ADHD, including the types of problems that lead them to seek help. A brief overview of the components of a comprehensive diagnostic assessment is presented, as is a summary of the research support for pharmacotherapy as a first-line treatment of adult ADHD.

Each of the following six chapters provides a review of a different category of nonmedication treatment. Each chapter describes the treatment, its applicability for use with adults with ADHD, and available clinical outcome research. Chapter 2 focuses on individual and group psychosocial treatments for adult ADHD. The existing treatment options reflect psychotherapy models that will be familiar to practicing psychotherapists but that have been modified to target common functional problems reported by adults with ADHD, which may be less familiar to most therapists. This chapter also includes a discussion of what is called "ADHD coaching," which is a growing specialty increasingly mentioned in the clinical literature for adult ADHD.

Chapter 3 reviews academic support and accommodations for individuals with ADHD enrolled in postsecondary educational programs, although many of the approaches are relevant for any learning situation encountered by adults, such as a software certification course or a continuing education class. The effects of ADHD on academic performance are discussed, and the manner in which educational support services and academic accommodations are used in colleges and graduate schools to address learning difficulties is examined, including three preliminary studies of the effects of academic support, or coaching, for college students with ADHD.

Chapter 4 focuses on issues related to workplace problems faced by individuals with adult ADHD. Similar to the difficulties faced by postsecondary students with ADHD, workers with ADHD report many difficulties related to their symptoms of poor time management, disorganization, and procrastination. This chapter also deals with issues related to career counseling and the process of finding jobs that are good fits for individuals with ADHD. Informal workplace accommodations also are discussed.

Chapter 5 examines the wide-ranging effects of adult ADHD on relationship functioning, primarily in terms of its impact on marriages and committed relationships, family life, and overall social skills. Although it is increasingly appreciated that ADHD negatively affects social functioning, this topic is only starting to receive its due attention in the clinical and research literatures on adults with ADHD.

Chapter 6 provides an overview of the various neurofeedback and neurocognitive training technologies that have been developed for ADHD, probably one of the more contentious topics within the field of ADHD treatment. Although primarily studied in children, these technologies have also been used with adults. Despite having been available in various forms for many years, these treatment approaches have not yet gained widespread acceptance as a mainstream treatment option for ADHD, even though proponents avow the existence of compelling anecdotal and research support for its use. These anecdotal and empirical claims; the history of the controversies about neurofeedback; and new directions in neurocognitive training, specifically working memory training, are discussed.

Chapter 7 explores various complementary and alternative treatments, such as the use of meditation training, dietary supplements, food restriction programs, and other nonstandard treatments. In some cases, preliminary findings indicate that a complementary approach might provide some small benefit to some adults with ADHD as an adjunct to a standard treatment protocol, and these findings deserve follow-up study; in most cases, however, these treatments have not been shown to be beneficial in the treatment of adult ADHD. The purported rationale for these treatments and extant research (or anecdotal) support are reviewed to provide a complete overview of the types of treatments marketed for adult ADHD.

Finally, chapter 8 provides an overview of the implications for clinicians of the current state of the field of nonmedication treatments for adult ADHD.

Directions and challenges for future research are discussed, and final thoughts on the topic are offered.

The appendixes provide references for publications and Web sites for individuals interested in more information about the types of treatment reviewed, as well as for reputable publications and international ADHD organizations.

I performed comprehensive computerized searches of clinical databases using relevant search terms to identify clinical outcome studies of nonmedication treatments for adult ADHD. I also cross-referenced existing published research as well as the clinical literature, including professional and trade books on adult ADHD, to identify outcome studies and commonly recommended treatment approaches that may not yet have been subjected to study, such as marital therapy for adults with ADHD. Although the state of nonmedication treatments for adult ADHD is not at a point at which definitive clinical guidelines based on empirical evidence of effectiveness can be offered, I hope that this book helps readers make informed decisions about the potential usefulness of available treatment options. More specifically, the review of clinical research findings helps readers to differentiate those treatments that are likely to be helpful to adult patients with ADHD from those that are not likely to be helpful on the basis of the particular difficulties for which they are seeking help.

1

ADHD IN ADULTHOOD

Attention-deficit/hyperactivity disorder (ADHD) is one of, if not the most, controversial of the diagnostic categories in psychiatry and psychology. On the one hand, it is dismissed by skeptics as a 21st century disorder, a diagnosis du jour, or as a uniquely American disorder, the implication being that ADHD is not a valid disorder worthy of classification and formalized treatment. On the other hand, it is the most prevalent psychiatric disorder of childhood in the United States, with roughly similar prevalence rates found in international samples. What is more, it is increasingly recognized that affected children do not invariably "grow out of it," despite comforting bromides to the contrary. In fact, ADHD may well be considered one of the more impairing psychiatric conditions in terms of its pervasive effects on important life domains.

One of the reasons the topic of ADHD is so contentious is that many individuals have only a cursory understanding of the diagnostic criteria (including the requirement that symptoms directly cause clinically significant impairment), the competent assessment strategies, and the range and severity of negative effects ADHD has on people's lives. It is a challenging topic even for seasoned mental health professionals because most of them have not received formalized training in the assessment and treatment of ADHD in children and adolescents, much less in adults.

The purpose of this chapter is to provide an overview of ADHD in adults. More specifically, this chapter briefly reviews the evolution of the diagnostic criteria and the relatively recent acknowledgement that clinically significant symptoms of ADHD persist into the adulthood years for a majority of affected children. The developmental course of ADHD from childhood to adulthood also is discussed, backed with research on the persistence and prevalence rates of ADHD. Next, and key to the aim of this book, the many psychological, behavioral, and functional impairments associated with ADHD for which adult patients may seek assessment and treatment are presented. There is a brief discussion of the components of a competent assessment for adult ADHD as well as an overview of the empirical evidence supporting the efficacy of pharmacotherapy for adult ADHD. The discussion of medications sets the stage for the review of adjunctive treatments designed to address the myriad difficulties faced by adults with ADHD that constitutes the central focus of this book.

EVOLUTION OF THE DIAGNOSTIC CRITERIA FOR ADHD

ADHD is currently thought of as a dimensional disorder, which means that it is not a simple matter of making a diagnosis based on the presence of atypical symptoms or on test results, such as can be done for appendicitis or hepatitis. Rather, the symptoms of ADHD are thought to represent the extreme end of a continuum of a set of cognitive processes, deemed the *executive functions*, that collectively generate people's ability to regulate themselves and their actions (Barkley, 1997a, 1997b; Brown, 2005, 2006). Most people fall in the middle, average range of the distribution of these cognitive processes. Some people fall at the end of the dimension that represents unusually strong executive functioning, the types of people who are particularly organized and reliably follow through on tasks. At the opposite end of the continuum, executive dysfunction is associated with an assortment of difficulties, such as poor impulse control, inattention and distractibility, physical restlessness, disorganization, inefficient memory, and many other symptoms that are considered features of ADHD. Of course, these examples of executive dysfunction can be associated with symptoms of other psychiatric disorders, such as depression or schizophrenia. The individual symptoms of ADHD are akin to a fever to the extent that it is a nonspecific symptom that is a feature of different medical problems, such as influenza, infection, or malaria, for which more information is required to make an accurate diagnosis. However, the ADHD syndrome has a distinctive developmental and symptom profile that can be identified through thorough assessment.

Consequently, rather than being a disorder of the 21st century, ADHD is an ageless syndrome, likely having been present ever since there has been a human brain. In fact, Barkley (2001) posited that the executive functions emerged in the course of evolution as an adaptation that confers survival value insofar as it allows social species to handle increasingly complex social networks and issues of reciprocity. Many aspects of contemporary society, such as compulsory classroom education and the modern workplace, do not cause ADHD but rather increase the likelihood that symptoms of ADHD will be more readily noticed by observers. In fact, the same skills valued in our modern, technologically loaded society—impulse control, organization, planning and follow-through, and self-discipline—are valued in agrarian societies, hunter–gatherer cultures, and countless other environments. Conversely, impairments in these skill domains cause diverse functional problems in a wide range of settings. Thus, although ADHD is not an environmentally caused disorder (e.g., Barkley, 2006a; Nigg, 2006), it is an environmentally bound disorder, inasmuch as it is associated with significant problems functioning in various domains of life (Wakefield, 1992).

Although it is tempting to discern features of ADHD in historical figures and literary characters, the first formal clinical identification of the combination of hyperactivity, impulsivity, and inattention as a distinct syndrome is credited to pediatrician George Still (1902/2006). Still provided a clinical report on a group of 20 children (out of a larger sample of 43 children) with no history of organic brain disorders or injuries but who nevertheless exhibited significant symptoms of impulsivity and poor self-control. He made the prescient observation that the difficulties appeared to be dispositional, and therefore hereditary, rather than resulting from environmental causes (i.e., poor parenting). Still's observation of disinhibited behaviors commonly seen in children with a history of brain damage led subsequent clinician researchers to look for possible organic etiologies for these behavioral manifestations.

Although Still's (1902/2006) work represents the first clinical observations of ADHD, a recently uncovered chapter written by the physician Alexander Crichton (1798/2008) places the introduction of the notion of an ADHD-related syndrome in the 18th century. Crichton described the faculty of attention as "the parent of all our knowledge" (p. 200), conjecturing on different ways attention problems can be disordered. Although not explicitly drawing on clinical observations in the manner of Still's work, Crichton noted a similar association of attention problems and functional impairments.

In the 1930s, pediatrician Charles Bradley stumbled upon the benefits of stimulant medications for reducing impulsivity and improving behavioral self-control in young patients exhibiting the difficulties first noted by Crichton and Still (Conners, 2000; Pliszka, 2003). Using stimulants as a means for reducing headaches associated with a common x-ray technique of the day, Bradley noted that typically overactive children responded to the treatment by evidencing improved behavior. In fact, teachers of hyperactive children treated by Bradley dubbed the medications the "math pills," owing to the improvements in the children's academic and behavioral functioning in school. Pharmacotherapy using psychostimulants remains the most researched, best supported treatment for ADHD in all age groups, with stimulants being the most widely studied of all medications prescribed for children (American Academy of Child and Adolescent Psychiatry [AACAP], 1997; Greenhill, 2001).

Although what came to be known as ADHD was a subject of clinical interest and study among those interested in childhood behaviors, it did not appear in the official diagnostic criteria as set down in the *Diagnostic and Statistical Manual of Mental Disorders* (DSM) of the American Psychiatric Association until its second edition (*DSM–II*) in 1968. It was named "hyperkinetic reaction of childhood (or adolescence)" and was considered relatively benign, with its symptoms thought to lessen by the teenage years: "This disorder is characterized by overactivity, restlessness, distractibility and short attention span, especially in young children; the behavior usually diminishes in adolescence" (p. 50). Subsequent years saw interest in the syndrome expand from the behavioral manifestations of hyperactivity to include the cognitive deficits (e.g., short attention span) and their influence on learning problems (Douglas, 1999, 2005).

The third edition of the *DSM* (*DSM–III*; American Psychiatric Association, 1980) reflected the aforementioned shift in emphasis with a name change to Attention Deficit Disorder (ADD) and demarcation of two subtypes: ADD with Hyperactivity (ADD+H) or ADD without Hyperactivity (ADD–H). The ADD moniker was retained in the revised edition (*DSM–III–R*; American Psychiatric Association, 1987), but it was defined by a single list of 14 symptoms. In 1994, the diagnosis was renamed Attention-Deficit/Hyperactivity Disorder and the use of subtypes was restored. The revised subtype list included ADHD Predominantly Hyperactive-Impulsive Type, ADHD Predominantly Inattentive Type, and ADHD Combined Type, with the last category reflecting individuals with prominent symptoms of both subtypes (American Psychiatric Association, 1994). Although the symptom list reflected clinical problems relevant for children and adolescents, criteria suggested that adults could exhibit symptoms of ADHD, which had previously been deemed *residual symptoms*. The category ADHD, Not Otherwise Specified (NOS) was added to capture clinical difficulties encountered by individuals who did not fulfill diagnostic thresholds for ADHD but nonetheless warranted clinical attention. These categories have been preserved in the most recent, fourth edition, text revision, of the *DSM* (*DSM–IV–TR*; American Psychiatric Association, 2000).

The development of the fifth edition of the *DSM* (*DSM–V*) is particularly interesting for clinicians interested in adult ADHD. As of the writing of this book, the work groups charged with making the relevant revisions have already had preliminary meetings, with a projected publication date of 2011 or 2012. There are many issues to be debated, such as the use of distinct subtypes (Barkley, 2007; Loo & Smalley, 2008; Solanto et al., 2007), clarifying the definition of *impairment,* and reviewing the extant symptoms (Barkley, 2007).

As was mentioned earlier, the extant diagnostic criteria were based on research on children and adolescents between the ages of 4 and 17 years. Thus, the use of strict *DSM* criteria alone is inadequate for the assessment of adult ADHD because symptoms manifest differently in individuals at different ages. More recently, Barkley and colleagues (Barkley & Murphy, 2006b; Barkley, Murphy, & Fischer, 2008) published an empirically derived set of diagnostic criteria for adult ADHD that may be a template for inclusion of adult-specific criteria in the *DSM–V.*

Barkley et al. (2008) administered a structured interview to 352 adults using a pool of 91 new symptoms reflecting executive dysfunction in adulthood. A single list of nine symptoms (with endorsement of at least six symptoms considered as the diagnostic threshold) that adequately differentiated adults with ADHD from both clinical (i.e., those without ADHD) and community control groups emerged, with overall classification accuracy of adult ADHD of 78%. Moreover, the researchers proposed that the age of onset for emergence of symptoms causing impairment be raised to 16 years old from the current age of onset criterion of 7 years old, which had not been empirically derived (Barkley, 2007; McGough & Barkley, 2004). In addition to the symptoms reflecting differences in the manifestation of ADHD in adults, the proposed age-of-onset criterion change pointed out that many individuals experience unremitting symptoms of ADHD from an early age but do not suffer impairment until the normative demands of the environment exceed their executive functioning abilities.

The relationship of environmental demands and individual development is important in the assessment of ADHD. That is, the symptoms of ADHD, although chronic and unremitting into adulthood in the majority of cases, change in important ways with ongoing brain development and maturation. Likewise, the responsibilities and situations faced by adults with ADHD are very different than they are for children. Consequently, it is important to consider the developmental course of ADHD and its associated impairments at various points in life.

DEVELOPMENTAL COURSE OF ADHD

ADHD is currently understood as a neurodevelopmental syndrome that stems from neurobiological processes affecting downstream capacities, such as behavioral inhibition and foresight. These capacities create the foundation for self-control and self-regulation. The preponderance of scientific evidence indicates that there is a genetic predisposition for ADHD, as it has been found to be highly heritable (Barkley, 2006a; Nigg, 2006). That is to say, the symptoms of ADHD are primarily biological in origin and are not the result of environmental factors such as diet, poor parenting, or too much television. These deficits make it difficult for individuals to handle the diverse demands of life, regardless of one's age. However, as was mentioned earlier, the symptoms manifest themselves differently at different points in development and, in turn, different contextual demands associated with different points in development. What follows is a discussion of the developmental course of ADHD.

ADHD in Childhood

Many parents of children diagnosed with ADHD, particularly the hyperactive-impulsive and combined types, observe that their children were "active," "always moving," "driven by a motor," or "all over the place" when they were toddlers. In fact, hyperactivity is the iconic symptom for the diagnosis of ADHD. Although these features are more prominent among children diagnosed with ADHD, the purely hyperactive-impulsive type is the least prevalent subtype (Millstein, Wilens, Biederman, & Spencer, 1997; Wilens, Biederman, & Spencer, 2002).

It is not surprising that these sorts of hyperactive behaviors, particularly when they are disruptive, draw the attention of others. This is particularly so when children enter regimented social or academic settings, such as group day care, preschool, or elementary school. Highly structured environments with externalized reminders of rules and consistent, positive reinforcement can be helpful for children with ADHD. It is not that these children do not understand the rules for conduct in these settings, but rather that they lack the self-control to follow these rules at the *point of performance*, or the moment they are relevant (Barkley, 1997a; Douglas, 2005).

An especially troubling comorbidity pattern is ADHD paired with conduct disorder (CD) (ADHD+CD). Children with ADHD+CD are at greater risk than children with ADHD only and control groups without ADHD for having additional lifetime psychiatric, substance use, and behavioral problems (Barkley et al., 2008). The behavioral disruptions associated with the Hyperactive-Impulsive and Combined Types result in these children as a group experiencing higher levels of emotional and behavioral difficulties in all stages of life than the Predominantly Inattentive Type (Fischer, Barkley, Smallish, & Fletcher, 2002; Satterfield & Schell, 1997; Satterfield et al., 2007; Wilens et al., 2002).

As was mentioned before, the purely Hyperactive-Impulsive subtype is seen in only a minority of cases of ADHD. When there are signs and symptoms of developmentally inappropriate impulsivity and overactivity, they most often coincide with attention and information-processing difficulties, or the attention deficit side of ADHD. In fact, the notion of "attention deficit" is a misnomer, as it is the effortful allocation and maintenance of attention that is difficult for these children rather than an insufficient quantity of attention. Hence, many parents and teachers will cite examples of a child with ADHD being very attentive during a favorite video game or activity as possible evidence of intact attention. Rather, it is the inability to initiate and sustain attention in the absence of immediate reinforcement that is a primary source of concentration problems associated with ADHD.

Whereas children with hyperactivity and impulsivity are likely to be noticed by parents, teachers, and child care workers, children with the Predominantly Inattentive Type are not disruptive and therefore may not be identified at an early age. Inattentive children may be described as "spacey," "daydreamers," "in another world," or "zoning out" because they are distracted from a task by competing stimuli, such as watching construction workers outside a classroom window instead of doing a worksheet in class. There may also be difficulties related to memory for day-to-day routines (e.g., having to repeat things several times), losing things, making "stupid mistakes" on school work, disorganization, and a poor sense of time, often resulting in the perception that the child is "not fulfilling his or her potential."

Within ADHD, Predominantly Inattentive Type, a subset of individuals is described as daydreamy, anxious, and somewhat sluggish and languid in terms of energy level. Further, these individuals seem to have problems related to social functioning, tending to be withdrawn and exhibiting fewer externalizing behaviors compared with other individuals with ADHD. This collection of symptoms, deemed *sluggish cognitive tempo* (SCT), is associated with a similar level of impairment as the more familiar manifestations of ADHD but does not seem to respond as well to treatment with stimulant medications (Barkley, 2006a; Carlson & Mann, 2002; Hartman, Willcutt, Rhee, & Pennington, 2004). Children with SCT commonly experience anxiety and might respond better to psychosocial treatments targeting anxiety than other children with ADHD. SCT continues to be explored as a potentially distinct subtype of ADHD.

The most common subtype of ADHD, composing well over half of all identified cases, is the Combined Type, in which individuals exceed symptom thresholds for both Hyperactive-Impulsive and Inattentive Types (Millstein et al., 1997; Nigg, 2006; Wilens et al., 2002). Because there is much overlap of the behavioral problems experienced by individuals with the Combined Type and the Hyperactive-Impulsive Type, these groups are commonly combined in research and in terms of conceptual understanding for clinical practice. In fact, the presence of hyperactivity and impulsivity in childhood appears to predict the later development of Combined Type features in adolescence and adulthood (Barkley, 2006a; Barkley et al., 2008). The combination of prominent difficulties related to information processing and behavioral disinhibition associated with the Combined Type is associated with the highest level of impairment among the ADHD subtypes (Wilens et al., 2002).

Children with relatively mild symptoms may navigate primary school and other novel settings with relatively minor, if any, difficulties. For children diagnosed with ADHD, these initial transitions are often much more difficult. The developmental trajectory into adolescence, however, involves increasing demands for independent functioning and self-control. The next section looks at ADHD in adolescence.

ADHD in Adolescence

In a telephone survey of adults with ADHD, the median age at which respondents were diagnosed was 12 years old, meaning that 50% of the sample was diagnosed before reaching adolescence (Biederman et al., 2006). Thirty-five percent of the same sample was first diagnosed with ADHD in adulthood (e.g., age 18 years or older), leaving only 15% of the sample diagnosed during their teen years. One of the factors that might contribute to the drop-off in the incidence of new diagnoses of ADHD in adolescents is that the overt, observable signs of physical hyperactivity wane with increased chronological age and cortical maturation (Barkley, 2006a; Loo & Smalley, 2008; M. Weiss, Murray, & Weiss, 2002; Wilens et al., 2002).

Children with the most prominent symptoms of ADHD are most likely to be identified and receive treatment at an early age. Many other children, however, may function adequately enough to float under the radar through elementary school. Even if conspicuous problems in adolescence are present, the level of impairment may be relatively mild, without a "crisis" (e.g., failing a class, suspension), or the problems are attributed to "typical teenage issues." Finally, some families may be skeptical of ADHD or simply may not have access to services.

Adolescent ADHD is complicated by the fact that adolescence is a very dynamic period of cognitive, emotional, and physical development, with progressively greater expectations for maturity. Increased incidence of mood and anxiety disorders also occur during the adolescent years when compared with childhood (Jamison, 1999). Nadeau and Quinn (2002) hypothesized that many of the physiological changes associated with puberty may exacerbate symptoms of ADHD, particularly for girls, who may experience symptom fluctuation associated with their menstrual cycles. School becomes more challenging, with increasing expectations of personal organization and responsibility throughout middle and high school. Peer relationships and nonfamily activities become increasingly important to teens and compete with family time.

Adolescence is the developmental stage at which some children with ADHD who had exhibited oppositional behaviors when they were younger may display more severe conduct problems. Adolescents with the ADHD+CD combination are at greater risk of facing increasingly severe consequences to their actions, including detentions, suspensions, and in severe cases, expulsions from school, not to mention facing legal entanglements for their conduct (including substance abuse) in the community.

Comparatively few new cases of ADHD are recognized during adolescence, perhaps because other issues (e.g., mood, conduct problems, family conflict) may mask the symptoms. Because these teens were not identified during childhood, it could also be the case that their symptoms have not yet been associated with enough functional impairment to draw attention. Many adolescents may resist their families' efforts to pursue assessment or treatment, resulting in a strategy of toughing it out to get through high school and looking forward to a fresh start in college or in a job that will not have the same demands of school. Teens who had been diagnosed with ADHD in childhood may have already received treatment, including a stable medication regimen that has provided sufficient symptom improvement. Moreover, their families may have already implemented coping regimens at home that will support their teen with ADHD and guide them until he or she assumes an adult role.

However, rather than being liberating, the demands of adult life are even more difficult for many individuals than the demands of the school years. Hence, the next section provides a thorough review of issues related to ADHD in adulthood.

Overview of Adult ADHD

Evidence of features of ADHD in samples of young adults can be found in research published about 40 years ago. However, there has been a great deal of research conducted over the past 10 to 15 years that has provided important information on the persistence and prevalence of adult ADHD, as well as the life outcomes of individuals diagnosed with the disorder, which are reviewed in the following sections.

Persistence of Adult ADHD

As was reflected in the *DSM II*, professional consensus used to suggest that children and teens with ADHD would eventually and invariably "grow out of it." Indeed, studies have documented a decrease in the number of *DSM*-defined symptoms of ADHD endorsed by individuals followed from childhood to young adulthood, resulting in decreased incidence of the full disorder or decreased syndromatic persistence (Barkley, 2002a; Biederman et al., 2006; Biederman, Mick, & Faraone, 2000; Faraone & Biederman, 2005b; Faraone, Biederman, & Mick, 2006; Mick, Faraone, & Biederman, 2004).

However, closer review of the data indicates that this decrease is not a significant reduction of overall symptoms, as one would expect in a remission of a condition, but rather is primarily accounted for by fewer symptoms of hyperactivity and impulsivity (Wilens et al., 2002). If the syndromatic persistence of ADHD is defined as exceeding the symptom count established in the *DSM*, then reduction in a few symptoms could result in an individual being deemed subthreshold. That is, if a child exhibited seven of nine symptoms of inattention required for ADHD but as a young adult exhibited four or five of the same nine symptoms, he or she might be considered to not have ADHD.

A recently published longitudinal study compared children with and without ADHD using neuroimaging technology to track their brain development, namely, cortical thickness (P. Shaw et al., 2007). The researchers observed that cortical maturation was significantly delayed among children with ADHD but that its developmental trajectory was the same across groups, a finding that was promoted in the media as evidence that ADHD is a developmental delay. However, research comparing adults with ADHD and those without ADHD indicates ongoing differences in cortical thickness (Makris et al., 2007).

Some longitudinal studies have reported low rates of persistence of ADHD. Hill and Schoener's (1996) review of nine longitudinal studies suggested that ADHD decreases by 50% every 5 years, resulting in a persistence rate of 0.8% by the age of 20 years old and 0.2% by age 30 years old. Similarly, a study of adult outcome in a primary care setting indicated only 5.5% of a sample of children diagnosed with ADHD continued to fulfill diagnostic criteria when reassessed as adults (McCormick, 2004). However, there are several methodological flaws in the Hill and Schoener study (as reviewed in Barkley, 1998) that likely led to an underrepresentation of the true persistence of ADHD. The McCormick study was conducted in a primary care setting and may not have included individuals with severe symptoms and impairment for which specialized psychiatric care was required. Moreover, only adults (ages 18–26 years old) meeting full *DSM* criteria were considered as unremitting cases, and residual symptoms were not considered evidence of persistence. Research has indicated that *DSM* thresholds for ADHD in children are not sufficient for adults with ADHD, with endorsement of four symptoms sufficient to differentiate adults with ADHD from control samples (Barkley et al., 2008). Although data on the average length of stimulant treatment were provided, the medication status of individuals at follow-up was unclear; that is, it is possible that ongoing treatment resulted in fewer endorsed symptoms.

In an analysis of longitudinal diagnostic data from a standpoint of functional status, such as identifying the persistence of at least five *DSM*-defined symptoms of ADHD and at least moderate impairment in daily life, the symptomatic persistence of ADHD in young adulthood was reported as 90% (Biederman et al., 2000). Many other studies have examined the persistence of ADHD from childhood to adulthood. Despite differences across studies in the definition of persistence and types of assessments used, research has generally found that ADHD persists into adulthood for at least 50% of childhood cases, although the persistence of residual symptoms causing some form of functional impairment more often falls in the range of 65% to 75% (Barkley et al., 2008; Loo & Smalley, 2008; Mannuzza & Klein, 1999; Rasmussen & Gillberg, 2000; G. Weiss & Hechtman, 1993; Wilens et al., 2002).

ADHD was included in the National Comorbidity Study Replication, a massive survey of psychiatric comorbidity in a representative sample of adults ages 18 to 44 years ($N = 3,197$) in the United States (Kessler, Adler, Barkley, et al., 2005). The results of the survey indicated that 36.3% of individuals diagnosed with childhood ADHD continued to meet full *DSM–IV* (American Psychiatric Association, 1994) criteria as adults. The best predictors of persistence were severity of childhood symptoms and having received treatment for ADHD in childhood, which are equivalent indicators of ADHD severity. The authors noted that this percentage is likely an underestimation of the true persistence of symptoms because of the limitations of *DSM* criteria for assessing adults.

A recent review of numerous follow-up studies of children with ADHD reported a range of persistence from 36% to 86% when using criteria for "partial remission" or persistence of "residual" symptoms (Faraone et al., 2006). The persistence rates fell as low as 4% when *persistence* was defined as "full diagnostic criteria." The take-home point from these studies of persistence is that falling below threshold for the full *DSM* diagnosis in adulthood should not necessarily be construed as remission in terms of level of functioning.

The aforementioned studies of the persistence of ADHD have been crucial in establishing that ADHD is truly a life span disorder characterized by developmentally inappropriate levels of inattention, hyperactivity, and impulsivity. However, research on the persistence of ADHD from childhood to adulthood, although vitally important, is representative of individuals first diagnosed in childhood. As previously indicated, 35% of individuals surveyed are first diagnosed with ADHD in adulthood. Therefore, it is important to review studies that establish the prevalence of adult ADHD.

Prevalence of Adult ADHD

Studies of children show variability in the prevalence rates of ADHD, stemming from the use of different operational definitions of the diagnosis, including different editions of the *DSM*. The *DSM–IV–TR* establishes the prevalence of ADHD in the United States at about 3% to 7% of the school-age population. Barkley's (2006a) review of a variety of studies that share the use of established diagnostic criteria for ADHD in children indicates prevalence rates ranging from 2% to 9.5% (average = 4.9%) of children and adolescents when using *DSM–III* criteria and 1.4% to 13.3% (average = 5.9%) when using adults' ratings of *DSM–III–R* criteria. Although cultural and other diversity issues remain understudied (Gingerich, Turnock, Litfin, & Rosén, 1998), ADHD is evident in all populations studied, regardless of grouping by nation, ethnicity, gender, or income group.

Before the past few years, a handful of studies had indicated that the prevalence rate of adult ADHD was around 4% of the adult population; these researchers surveyed college students in the United States (Heiligenstein, Conyers, Berns, & Smith, 1998) and in other countries (DuPaul et al., 2001), as well as adults renewing their driver's license (K. R. Murphy & Barkley, 1996b). More recently, extensive scientific surveys conducted around the world have supported the aforementioned 4% prevalence rate of adult ADHD. The results of a telephone survey indicated a 2.9% prevalence of strictly defined ADHD in adulthood, although reanalysis of the data, allowing for subthreshold ADHD criteria, yielded a 16.4% prevalence rate (Faraone & Biederman, 2005b). A recent national survey estimated that 4.4% of adults in the United States between 18 and 44 years old fulfill diagnostic criteria for adult ADHD, representing about 8 million American adults (Kessler et al., 2006). A subsample of U.S. workers surveyed indicated a 4.2% prevalence rate of ADHD, with 4.9% of working men and 3.3% of working women exceeding diagnostic thresholds (Kessler, Adler, Ames, Barkley, et al., 2005). A similar international survey of adults in the Americas, Europe, and the Middle East revealed an international prevalence rate for adult ADHD of 3.4%, ranging from 1.2% to 7.3% (Fayyad et al., 2007). Countries with higher per capita income rates also reported higher rates of adult ADHD (4.2% vs. 1.9%) than countries with lower income rates.

Thus, it is increasingly clear, if not downright established, that ADHD is not a diagnosis du jour contained within the geographical boundaries of the United States or the sociohistorical boundaries of the late 20th and early 21st centuries (Biederman & Faraone, 2004; Faraone, 2005; Faraone, Sergeant, Gillberg, & Biederman, 2003; Loo & Smalley, 2008). What is more, it is not the mere presence of symptoms that compels individuals to seek assessment and treatment for ADHD but rather the recurring problems and impairments in their daily lives. The next section discusses the life outcomes of adults with ADHD.

Life Outcomes

Although individuals may share a diagnosis of ADHD, there is great variability regarding the threshold at which they experience impairment. As was noted earlier, 35% of individuals with ADHD were not diagnosed until reaching adulthood. Overall, longitudinal and cross-sectional studies indicate that when their life circumstances are compared with control groups without ADHD, adults with ADHD report lower levels of educational attainment, a higher incidence of psychiatric comorbidity, increased risk of substance abuse, greater relationship discord, poorer driving records, and not surprisingly, more negative outlooks and higher levels of pessimism (Barkley, Fischer, Smallish, & Fletcher, 2006; Barkley et al., 2008; Biederman & Faraone, 2005; Biederman et al., 2006; K. R. Murphy & Barkley, 1996a; G. Weiss & Hechtman, 1993; Wilens et al., 2002).

Regarding educational outcomes, individuals with ADHD diagnosed in childhood who are tracked into adulthood are less likely to complete high school than control participants without ADHD and are more likely to receive special education services (Barkley et al., 2008). Individuals first diagnosed with ADHD in adulthood, on the other hand, have comparable high school graduation rates and performance on standardized tests to control participants without ADHD but report higher rates of academic impairment (e.g., homework, school behavior) and low grades. ADHD students are also more likely than control participants to fail a class, to be held back a grade, and to receive disciplinary actions (including expulsion).

Individuals with ADHD attend college at rates lower than the national average and are less likely to be graduated (Barkley, 2002a; Barkley et al., 2006, 2008; Wolf, 2001). Postsecondary schools are increasingly providing support services for students with ADHD beyond the requirements of the Americans With Disabilities Act (1990). Although college students with ADHD tend to have a combination of relatively mild symptoms (compared with individuals with ADHD who do not attend college), intact intellectual functioning, and other positive prognostic indicators, academics are more difficult for them than they are for students without ADHD.

In fact, Brown (2005) reported that 42% of a sample of adults with ADHD interrupted their postsecondary education at least once in their lives. Individuals with ADHD, on average, simply do not get as far in their educational pursuits and, thus, earn lower incomes than individuals without ADHD. These findings are not presented to imply that degree status and income are markers of well-being and happiness, as there are diverse paths to personal fulfillment. However, it is important to recognize that many adults with ADHD may be frustrated in their attempts to complete necessary and reasonable education or training programs because of a treatable condition.

Surveys of adult workers with ADHD indicate that the difficulties they encountered handling the demands of school carry over to the workplace. Workers with ADHD earn lower salaries, have greater conflict with supervisors, are less punctual, produce lower quality work, have lower scores on ratings of work performance, and are more likely to be disciplined by superiors than both clinical and community samples (Barkley et al., 2006, 2008). Adults with ADHD report greater rates of underemployment and being in the position of currently seeking work, lower rates of full-time employment (regardless of academic attainment), less productivity, and more frequent job changes than matched control participants without ADHD (Barkley et al., 2008; Biederman & Faraone, 2005; Biederman et al., 2006; Kessler, Adler, Ames, Barkley, et al., 2005).

More recently, Barkley et al. (2008) completed a massive study of the occupational functioning of adults with ADHD compared with both clinical control and community control samples without ADHD. Both clinician and employer ratings indicated that clinic-referred adults exhibited more symptoms of inattention and poorer follow-through on tasks and expectations associated with their jobs (e.g., projects, punctuality, time management) when compared with workers without ADHD. Adults with ADHD change jobs more frequently, including as a result of being fired or quitting from boredom, than do control participants without ADHD. These trends are more pronounced among individuals identified with ADHD in childhood who are tracked into adulthood.

Recent studies have looked at the economic impact of ADHD for individual households as well as for the overall economy in the United States. Of course, the economic costs of ADHD are a downstream effect of many associated problems, such as low education attainment, underperformance on the job, health care costs, and so on. Although the toll ADHD exacts on personal well-being provides adequate evidence of the need for comprehensive diagnostic assessment and treatment approaches, financial data usually capture the attention of even the most hardened skeptics of the disorder.

Statistical analyses performed under the assumption that the reported differences in educational attainment and achievement are fully attributable to ADHD symptoms indicate that the estimated annual income loss associated with a diagnosis of ADHD for the United States is over $70 billion. The estimated annual income loss for households affected by adult ADHD falls in the range of $10,300 to $15,400 (Biederman & Faraone, 2005; Biederman et al., 2006).

Societal costs are associated with underperformance of adults with ADHD in the workplace. Workers with ADHD in the United States were surveyed, and it was estimated that the disorder was associated with 7 weeks annual lost productivity through a combination of absenteeism (13.6 days of missed work) and "presenteeism" (21.6 days of underperformance on the job), amounting to 120.8 million lost workdays per year (Kessler, Adler, Ames, Barkley, et al., 2005). The annual salary-equivalent loss associated with ADHD was calculated at $5,661 per worker with ADHD, with the projected impact on the U.S. labor force estimated to be a salary-equivalent cost of

$19.6 billion. Similar results were obtained from a study of international samples of adult workers with ADHD (de Graaf et al., 2008).

Birnbaum et al. (2005) studied the administrative health care claims of a large corporation during 2000 to compare health care costs and lost productivity in workers whose households were affected by ADHD with control households without ADHD. The findings were extrapolated to the population of the United States on the basis of available prevalence rates of ADHD. The findings indicated an estimated excess cost of ADHD at $31.6 billion accounted for through a combination of health care costs for the worker with ADHD, family members with ADHD, lost productivity at work, and ADHD treatment. It is important to note that direct treatment of ADHD accounted for only 5% of the excess cost, begging the question of whether increased investment in providing effective, evidence-based treatment programs would ultimately decrease costs.

Research also points out ADHD's negative effects on personal health and physical well-being. The emerging findings from the Milwaukee Study, one of the largest longitudinal studies of a sample of individuals with ADHD compared with matched community control participants, are providing shocking information about health-related outcomes (Barkley et al., 2006, 2008). Within the sample of children with ADHD followed into young adulthood, there was a 38% teen pregnancy rate compared with 4% in the control sample. It is not surprising that there was four times the incidence of sexually transmitted disease among the ADHD sample, owing to poor safe sex practices. Related cross-sectional research comparing young adult men with a lifetime history of ADHD with control participants without ADHD indicated that ADHD predicts earlier initiation of sexual activity, a greater number of sexual partners, more incidents of casual sex, and a greater frequency of partner pregnancies (Flory, Molina, Pelham, Gnagy, & Smith, 2006).

Issues related to diminished self-control, poor planning, and problems thinking through the long-range consequences of actions (or inaction) that are characteristic of ADHD may also lead to negative outcomes related to physical health and financial planning. Longitudinal and cross-sectional studies of adults with ADHD suggest a pattern of poor health behaviors, such as nicotine use, sedentary lifestyle, lack of exercise, poor diet, and so on, that would predict various health risks later in life. Likewise, adults with ADHD were less likely than control participants to save money, to save money in a retirement fund, and to resist impulse purchases (Kaufman-Scarborough & Cohen, 2004) and were more likely to experience problems related to non-payment of bills (e.g., utilities turned off; Barkley et al., 2006, 2008).

A sizable foundation of research shows that automobile drivers with untreated ADHD exhibit poorer driving behaviors than do control participants without ADHD. On the basis of both reviews of personal driving records and performance on driving simulation tasks, individuals with ADHD have a greater number of, and more severe, driver-caused accidents; are more likely to be involved in an driver-caused accident resulting in physical injury; incur a greater number of moving violations; and exhibit more erratic and unsafe driving behaviors (e.g., speeding) than control participants without ADHD (Barkley, 2006b; Barkley & Cox, 2007; Barkley, Murphy, DuPaul, & Bush, 2002; Barkley et al., 2008; Fried et al., 2006; A. L. Thompson, Molina, Pelham, & Gnagy, 2007). In fact, the performance of drivers with ADHD who have not taken medication has been found to be equivalent to the levels of impairment seen in drivers without ADHD whose blood alcohol levels would have them be considered legally intoxicated (Weafer, Camarillo, Fillmore, Milich, & Marczinski, 2008). Moreover, although alcohol impairs driving performance for all drivers, it has greater negative effects on drivers with ADHD who are not treated with medication.

Finally, several studies indicate that individuals with ADHD incur greater health care costs than do control participants, even when the costs of psychiatric care are controlled (Barkley, 2002a). The health care costs for childhood ADHD were found to be no different from those for asthma (Kelleher, 2002), and children with ADHD have more outpatient, inpatient, and emergency room visits than control participants without ADHD, resulting in ADHD being associated with twice the total health care costs incurred by control participants (Leibson, Katusic, Barbaresi, Ransom, & O'Brien, 2001).

In reviewing the aforementioned studies of life outcomes of adults with ADHD, it is clear that there is virtually no area of life that is unaffected by the disorder. In addition to functional impairments in myriad life domains, ADHD is associated with a high rate of psychiatric comorbidity among affected adults. The next section reviews the comorbidity patterns commonly observed in adults with ADHD.

Psychiatric Comorbidity

Comorbidity is clearly the rule rather than the exception in adult ADHD; witness the fact that about 70% to 75% of clinic-referred adults with ADHD have at least one coexisting psychiatric disorder (Barkley, 2006a; Biederman, 2004; Fischer et al., 2002; McGough et al., 2005; Montes, García, & Ricardo-Garcell, 2007; Safren, Lanka, Otto, & Pollack, 2001; Schatz & Rostain, 2006; Sobanski, 2006). The most commonly reported disorders are anxiety (24%–60%), depression (major depression: 16%–31%; dysthymic disorder: 19%–37%), and substance abuse (32%–53% alcohol abuse, 8%–32% other substance abuse), with obsessive–compulsive disorder reported to a lesser degree (4%–14%). The rates of mood and anxiety symptoms are comparable with those found in childhood ADHD samples and occur more frequently than would be predicted by chance. The prevalence of substance use disorders among patients with ADHD is double that found in the general population (Barkley, 2006a; Biederman, Wilens, Mick, Faraone, & Spencer, 1998; Biederman, Wilens, Mick, Spencer, & Faraone, 1999; McGough et al., 2005). A review of personality disorders among a sample of adults with ADHD indicated that they report significantly higher rates of Cluster B and Cluster C Axis II disorders when compared with a control group (Miller, Nigg, & Faraone, 2007).

The results of a controlled, 10-year follow-up study in which youths both with and without ADHD were tracked into young adulthood (i.e., mean age of 21 years) and were assessed for the lifetime prevalence of psychopathology reinforce the high comorbidity rate associated with ADHD (Biederman et al., 2006). The sample was originally obtained from both psychiatric and pediatric samples, with no reported differences between participants drawn from these different referral sources on a wide range of functional domains (e.g., Busch et al., 2002), thus increasing the generalizability of the results. Individuals with ADHD were significantly more likely than control participants to report a lifetime history of major psychopathology, anxiety disorders, antisocial disorders, developmental disorders, and substance dependence disorders. When controlling for baseline psychopathology, the study showed that individuals with ADHD remained at significantly elevated risk of lifetime history of major depression, bipolar disorder (BD), separation anxiety, oppositional-defiant disorder, conduct disorder, antisocial personality disorder, tics/Tourette's disorder, and nicotine dependence.

Considering the fact that many clinicians may not be well versed in screening for symptoms of adults with ADHD, it is important to consider that many individuals may initially seek treatment for other problems, with ADHD issues identified only later in treatment. Thus, there is a new trend to look for "reverse comorbidity" of ADHD (Wilens, 2007) in studies of other disorders. Alpert et al. (1996) assessed a sample of patients in treatment for depression and found that 16% had a history of significant symptoms of ADHD in childhood, with 12% of the sample reporting persistent difficulties related to these symptoms in adulthood. Kessler et al. (2006) found that the prevalence of ADHD in U.S. adults with major depression is 9.4%, and among adults with dysthymia, that 22.6% have coexisting ADHD.

Clinical interviews conducted with nonpsychotic adult outpatients and healthy community control participants in Mexico revealed prevalence rates for ADHD of 16.8% and 5.37%, respectively (Montes et al., 2007). The severity of psychopathology among individuals with ADHD was higher than for individuals without ADHD. A study of 1,000 patients in treatment for BD revealed a lifetime prevalence of coexisting ADHD for nearly 10% of the sample (Nierenberg et al., 2005). Individuals with the BD+ADHD combination report earlier onset of mood problems, shorter periods of wellness, more depressive periods, and more psychiatric comorbidity than individuals with BD alone. Reviews of other studies of BD and ADHD indicate the coexistence of these two disorders is in the range of about 5% to 47% (Moyer, 2007a; Wingo & Ghaemi, 2007).

There are many understudied populations in which the symptoms of ADHD may affect functioning. Considering the effects of ADHD on impulse control and its comorbidity with CD and antisocial personality disorder, it would seem that a subgroup of individuals with ADHD would be at risk for a history of interaction with the legal system (P. J. Hurley & Eme, 2004; Satterfield et al., 2007). Data suggest that a diagnosis of ADHD increases risk for antisocial behavior and incarceration in adolescence (Teplin, Abram, McClelland, Dulcan, & Mericle, 2002) and adulthood (Mannuzza, Klein, Bessler, Malloy, & LaPadula, 1998; Mannuzza, Klein, Konig, & Giampino, 1989). A study of a juvenile detention center found that 11.2% of boys and 16.4% of girls had ADHD (Teplin et al., 2002). A cross-sectional study of a randomly selected group of 55 adult male inmates seeking psychiatric services in an Irish prison revealed 9% fulfilled diagnostic criteria for ADHD (Curran & Fitzgerald, 1999). Incidence rates of ADHD in prison populations of 25% (Eyestone & Howell, 1994) and 46% (Rasmussen, Almvik, & Levander, 2001) have been reported in the published literature, prompting emerging interest in developing specific treatment programs for this population (Appelbaum, 2008).

Kennemer and Goldstein (2005) performed a chart review of the incidence of ADHD among adults with severe mental health problems for which they received inpatient psychiatric treatment. Their review revealed that 2.1% of patients received a diagnosis of ADHD at discharge, with substance abuse and personality disorders being the most common comorbid diagnoses. Although all aforementioned patients diagnosed with ADHD were treated with medications, none were prescribed stimulant medications.

Finally, there is little information about the effects of aging on the symptoms of ADHD after middle age and the potential interaction with cognitive changes observed in older adults (da Silva & Louza, 2008). Although they can be difficult to differentiate, symptoms of ADHD in some middle-age and older adults might be misattributed to "normal aging."

Although there has been mounting evidence of the functional impairments associated with adult ADHD, their psychological effects have been less documented. The next section reviews the extant research on how living with adult ADHD can have toxic effects on outlook, attitude, and self-esteem.

Psychological Effects

In addition to the difficulties encountered by adults with ADHD in myriad life domains, a psychological toll is also associated with these struggles. What is more, because ADHD is a developmental disorder affecting functioning over time and across life domains, the negative psychological effects experienced by many adults with ADHD are likely cumulative and corrosive. It may be that the negative effects on self-efficacy and hope are, in fact, the most pernicious features of ADHD insofar as they erode individuals' sense of self and their resilience.

Adults with ADHD have been found to have recollections of growing up that are more negative than recollections reported by adults without ADHD (Biederman et al., 2006). More specifically, adults with ADHD report being significantly less likely to have had cultural and educational experiences outside the household or to have participated in extracurricular activities and organized sports, dated, or spent free time with friends or family. It is not surprising that adults with ADHD rate their childhoods more negatively than do control participants, are more likely to have childhood memories that remain disturbing, and state that their past experiences have continued negative effects on their current sense of self.

The same study examined current attitudes and found that adults with ADHD were significantly less likely than control participants to report strong satisfaction in the areas of family life, relationships with loved ones, social life, health and fitness, career, and overall sense of achievements in life. Finally, adults with ADHD endorse current life outlooks that are significantly more likely to indicate low levels of self-acceptance; lack of optimism about the future; high levels of negative mood; and the occurrence of more frequent negative or angry thoughts, impulsive actions, and social mistakes than were control participants without ADHD.

Females with ADHD, although experiencing many of the same symptoms and functional impairments as males with ADHD (Barkley et al., 2008), may have some distinctive experiences (see, e.g., Ramsay & Rostain, 2005b; Solden, 1995). Girls have been underrepresented in studies of clinic-referred studies of ADHD children because girls are less likely to exhibit disruptive behaviors in the classroom or to have specific learning disabilities (Biederman, Mick, et al., 2002).

That said, the same line of research indicates that boys and girls with ADHD report comparable levels of ADHD-associated impairment, a finding also obtained in studies of nonreferred children with ADHD (Biederman, Kwon, et al., 2005) and clinically referred adults with ADHD (Barkley et al., 2008; Biederman, Faraone, Monuteaux, Bober, & Cadogen, 2004). Young adults with ADHD are at increased risk of sexual impulsivity (e.g., unsafe sex) and, consequently, at increased risk for unplanned pregnancy and contracting a sexually transmitted disease. Moreover, less than half of these young adult parents with ADHD have custody, with the children being raised by the mother's family, put up for adoption, or placed in foster care (Barkley, 2002a). Furthermore, women with ADHD, when compared with women without ADHD, report lower ratings on self-esteem measures; a greater sense of not being able to exert influence on outcomes (i.e., "learned helplessness"); higher levels of stress, anxiety, and depressive symptoms; a greater reliance on emotion-focused (vs. task-focused) coping strategies, and more negatively rated memories about childhood events (Rucklidge & Kaplan, 1997, 2000).

The effects of ADHD cut across many domains of life, including academic and occupational functioning, relationship satisfaction, family functioning, and personal well-being, as is discussed in more detail in later chapters. Ironically, the wide range of types and severity of symptoms and impairments associated with ADHD also makes it very difficult for many mental health professionals to diagnose it accurately. It may be difficult to differentiate symptoms of ADHD and other disorders, such as depression, anxiety, or bipolar spectrum disorders that may mimic the symptoms of ADHD. Many medical disorders also have symptom profiles that overlap with ADHD, such as sleep disorders or thyroid dysfunction. Finally, in cases involving complex patterns of comorbidity, even if ADHD is not the primary diagnosis contributing to functional difficulties, the effects of undiagnosed secondary ADHD may result in an incomplete response to treatment that may heighten risk of symptom relapse or discontinuation of treatment.

The accurate assessment of ADHD is important to minimize the likelihood of misdiagnosis, either wrongly diagnosing the presence (i.e., false positive) or absence of ADHD (i.e., false negative), as well as to identify comorbid disorders that could affect treatment outcome. The next section offers a brief review of the components of a comprehensive diagnostic assessment for adult ADHD. A comprehensive review of diagnostic assessment protocols is beyond the purview of this book. More extensive reviews of assessment protocols, inventories, and related issues are available in Barkley and Murphy (2006a), Davidson (2008), K. R. Murphy and Gordon (2006), Ramsay and Rostain (2008a), Reilly (2005), Resnick (2000), and Tuckman (2007).

ASSESSMENT OF ADULT ADHD

As desirable as it would be to have a quick and easy diagnostic tool for ADHD, there are no shortcuts to making the diagnosis. The diagnosis is arrived at through a combination of procedures for gathering relevant clinical information. A competent assessment for ADHD includes a thorough diagnostic interview (including review of presenting complaints); a comprehensive developmental history (including detailed accounts of academic, occupational, and interpersonal functioning); review of personal and family psychiatric and medical histories, and at least the screening, if not the full testing, of neurocognitive functioning.

ADHD symptoms are assessed throughout the interview process. Targeted assessment of *DSM*-defined ADHD symptoms in childhood and adulthood involves both self- and observer reports and review of corroborative other information when possible, such as school records or job performance ratings (e.g., Barkley & Murphy, 2006a). Several respected inventories have been designed for the assessment of ADHD in adults, including the Conners' Adult ADHD Rating Scales (CAARS; Conners, Erhart, & Sparrow, 1999); the Brown Attention Deficit Disorder Scale for Adults (Brown, 1996); and the 18-item Adult Symptom Rating Scale developed through the World Health Organization (Kessler, Adler, Ames, Demler, et al., 2005), of which a 6-item version has proven to be an effective screening tool (Kessler, Adler, Gruber, Spencer, & Van Brunt, 2007).

The assessment process relies a great deal on the descriptions of symptoms and impairment provided by patients. Although it is possible for individuals to exaggerate symptoms or "fake bad" (i.e., malinger) to secure a secondary gain, such as academic accommodations (A. G. Harrison, 2006; A. G. Harrison, Edwards, & Parker, 2007), the issue is no different than it is for other psychiatric disorders, considering that clinical interviews rely on accounts provided by patients. Although malingering to secure secondary gains must be considered in certain situations, thorough assessment strategies help decrease the likelihood of deception.

It is useful to invite individuals who are in a position to observe the daily functioning of a patient seeking assessment for ADHD to participate in the interview (with the patient's expressed knowledge and permission). Soliciting other persons' observations helps guard against misdiagnosis. Research supports the reliability of reports by patients with ADHD (P. Murphy & Schachar, 2000), particularly once they reach their late 20s or early 30s (Barkley et al., 2008), although one study indicated that parents' reports of symptoms and impairments were more accurate than self-reports provided by their young adult children with histories of ADHD (Barkley, Fischer, Smallish, & Fletcher, 2002).

In addition to the focus on ADHD, it is important to assess for the presence of other disorders, such as depression or anxiety. In fact, it may be symptoms of these disorders that finally compel individuals with ADHD to seek help. Individuals with a confirmed diagnosis of ADHD might also have coexisting psychiatric symptoms that need to be addressed in treatment planning. For some individuals, ADHD might be a secondary or tertiary clinical issue, but one that could influence outcomes for the primary condition being treated, such as depression. Many people who think they have ADHD, however, might find that their difficulties are better explained by other diagnoses, particularly as attention and concentration problems are one of the most common symptoms observed among psychiatric disorders.

In some cases, additional neuropsychological or psychoeducational testing, or both, might be performed to identify some functioning and learning deficits that could negatively affect academic or workplace functioning. Although these tests may help to identify specific areas of difficulty and are often required when an individual seeks formal academic or standardized testing accommodations, ADHD remains a clinical diagnosis based on the assessment of symptoms and functional impairment. Testing has not been found to be helpful in the diagnostic assessment of ADHD, although quantitative electroencephalography may be a useful tool, when combined with the aforementioned evaluation strategies, in making the differential diagnosis of ADHD (S. M. Snyder et al., 2008; discussed in more detail in chap. 6, this volume).

The end goal of the assessment process is to determine whether an individual's symptoms and impairments fit a profile consistent with ADHD, to assess for comorbid disorders, and to identify areas of impairment. This information is then used to inform a review of treatment options, which is the focus of the next section.

TREATMENT PLANNING

It could be said that an accurate diagnosis of ADHD for an adult patient represents the first clinical intervention. That is, the diagnosis represents a modified psychological framework for understanding what had heretofore seemed to be uncontrollable behaviors or evidence of poor character, rightfully recasting these difficulties as the downstream result of disordered neurobiological processes (Ramsay & Rostain, 2008a).

After the diagnosis is confirmed, attention turns to figuring out how to deal with it. A first step for many individuals with ADHD is psychoeducation. Although such education is empowering regardless of the specific psychological or medical condition, it holds special importance for adults with ADHD. Such education helps patients realize in personal terms the manner in which ADHD affects their day-to-day lives. Information about the genetic and neurobiological causes of ADHD helps individuals recognize that their difficulties are not reflective of poor character or laziness. Despite its biological underpinnings, however, responsibility for one's actions and coping with ADHD lies with the individual. To this end, many treatments are available for adults with ADHD that can help them find a newfound measure of control in their lives.

The most widely used intervention for ADHD in all age groups is pharmacotherapy. Considering the unequivocal empirical support for their effectiveness for ADHD, medication options should be discussed with all patients. The next section reviews the extant empirical support for pharmacotherapy for adult ADHD. (See Appendix B for lists of medications commonly prescribed for adult ADHD.)

PHARMACOTHERAPY FOR ADULT ADHD

Currently, five medications have been approved by the U.S. Food and Drug Administration (FDA) for the treatment of ADHD in adults. These medications include the stimulants Adderall XR (mixed salts of a single-entity amphetamine; Weisler et al., 2006), Concerta (methylphenidate hydrochloride; Berry et al., 2007; Medori et al., 2008), Focalin XR (dexmethylphenidate hydrochloride; Spencer et al., 2007), Vyvanse (lisdexamfetamine dimesylate; Adler et al., 2007), and the nonstimulant Strattera (atomoxetine; Chamberlain et al., 2007; Michelson et al., 2003). A wider assortment of medications has been approved for the treatment of children and adolescents with ADHD, including all the aforementioned preparations (Spencer, Biederman, & Wilens, 2004a, 2004b). As long as a medication has FDA approval, it can be prescribed at the discretion of a physician. Thus, medications with FDA approval for the treatment of childhood ADHD and other approved medications, such as some antidepressants, may be used to treat ADHD in what is known as *off-label* use.

The stimulants stand out as the most effective pharmacological agent for the treatment of ADHD for patients of all ages (Prince, Wilens, Spencer, & Biederman, 2006). Most of the FDA-approved medications for ADHD represent different preparations of methylphenidate- or amphetamine-based compounds, which differ mainly with regard to their delivery system, speed of onset, and duration of therapeutic effects (Dodson, 2005). Practice guidelines (designed for children and teens) dictate starting pharmacotherapy with the use of a psychostimulant unless there is evidence of a medical contraindication, comorbidity contraindication (e.g., substance abuse), or past nonresponse to stimulants (AACAP, 2002, 2007; American Academy of Pediatrics, 2001). There is no evidence of preferential effects of different stimulant preparations on particular subtypes of ADHD, although individuals exhibiting features of SCT do not seem to respond as positively as other individuals with ADHD to stimulants.

Vyvanse is one of the two medications (along with Concerta) that received FDA approval in 2008 as treatments for adult ADHD (Shire Pharmaceutical, 2008b). Vyvanse is a long-acting stimulant that is somewhat different from other medications in that class. That is, the chemical compound of Vyvanse is inactive in capsule form before oral ingestion. Once ingested and absorbed from the gastrointestinal tract, natural enzymatic processes convert the molecules to *d*-amphetamine, thus activating the stimulant effects in an extended release manner (Adler et al., 2007; Shire Pharmaceutical, 2008a).

Various reviews of medication studies have established that the positive response to stimulants in the treatment of adult ADHD falls in the range of 50% to upwards of 80%, with large effect sizes. Positive response rates are improved if a second stimulant is prescribed successively if there is not a positive response to the first stimulant. Normalization rates are lower than clinical improvement rates, generally falling in the 50% to 60% range. Studies of the effectiveness of medications for ADHD adults are more limited than they are for children, and adults tend to have more variable responses to them than children. However, even if there is not a positive response to the first stimulant medication prescribed, there is a high likelihood of positive response to another medication within this class (AACAP, 2002; Dodson, 2005).

Despite different preparations, delivery systems, and mechanisms of action, stimulants work by increasing the availability of the neurotransmitters norepinephrine (NE) and dopamine (DA) at the synaptic level. Methylphenidate increases the availability of these neurotransmitters by operating as a time-limited reuptake inhibitor. In addition to acting as a reuptake inhibitor, amphetamine also accelerates the release of these transmitters into the synaptic cleft (Ramsay & Rostain, 2008a). Response rates to different stimulant preparations roughly follows the so-called rule of thirds, with a meta-analysis of studies of the treatment of children indicating that 37% of patients responded better on amphetamine, 26% responded better on methylphenidate, and 37% responded equally well to both medications (Greenhill, Abikoff, Arnold, & Cantwell, 1996). Treatment guidelines suggest that there be a nonresponse (or lack of robust response) to at least one methylphenidate preparation and at least one amphetamine preparation before prescribing a second-tier medication (AACAP, 2002, 2007).

Second-tier medications generally have more modest response rates than stimulants, and effect sizes fall in the medium range (AACAP, 2007; Dodson, 2005; Michelson et al., 2003, Prince et al., 2006). Strattera is currently the sole nonstimulant medication with FDA approval specifically for the treatment of adult ADHD, and it has been found to be safe and effective (Adler, Spencer, Williams, Moore, & Michelson, 2008). Effect sizes obtained in studies of Strattera fall in the moderate range, but positive response rates for stimulant-naive cases are about 75% (as opposed to 55% for cases already tried on stimulants). Strattera may also be helpful in cases of comorbid anxiety as well as in cases of SCT. Strattera acts by blocking the reuptake of both NE and DA at the synaptic level. A longer duration of action is reported with Strattera, with 24-hour symptom coverage achieved once a therapeutic dose has been established. A recent double-blind, placebo-controlled study indicated that once-daily Strattera is efficacious in the treatment of adult ADHD at 10 weeks and 6 months after the initiation of treatment (Adler et al., 2009). Because of the slower onset of therapeutic effects, however, some patients may underestimate its positive effects because they do not feel the medication "kick in." Careful monitoring of functioning and input from significant others helps track response, including improvements in emotional regulation (Reimherr et al., 2005). Adults generally tolerate Strattera less well than do children, with common side effects for adults including nausea, dry mouth, decreased appetite, and erectile dysfunction.

Wellbutrin (bupropion), an antidepressant with some stimulating effects, has produced favorable effects for adults with ADHD, particularly those with depressed mood, nicotine dependence, or both. Controlled studies indicate a 50% response rate for adults with ADHD (Wender & Reimherr, 1990; Wilens et al., 2001, 2005), and it may be particularly helpful as part of a combined medication treatment for comorbid mood disorders (Wilens et al., 2001). Another antidepressant, Effexor (venlafaxine), also has shown some promising anti-ADHD effects (Prince et al., 2006).

Tricyclic antidepressants are an effective treatment option, with studies reporting positive response rates over 65% (J. J. Ratey, Greenberg, Bemporad, & Lindem, 1992; Wilens, Biederman, Mick, & Spencer, 1995; Wilens et al., 1996). These medications, particularly desipramine and imipramine, previously had been widely prescribed for ADHD but are not often used now because of their side effects, most notably risk for cardiac arrhythmias, sleepiness, dry mouth, and toxicity risk with overdose.

Provigil (modafinil) is a stimulant medication approved for the treatment of narcolepsy (Kumar, 2008). Despite some early promise in a small study of adults with ADHD (Taylor & Russo, 2000), controlled follow-up studies did not find it to be consistently effective (Cephalon, Inc., 2006; Dodson, 2005).

It should be noted that Cylert (pemoline) falls in the stimulant class with the desirable feature of being longer acting than methylphenidate or amphetamine (Dodson, 2005). However, studies of Cylert indicated that it produced lower response rates and less robust therapeutic effects as well as requiring up to 3 weeks for therapeutic effects (Wilens, 2003). What is more, the risk of possible rare but potentially fatal liver failure has relegated it to being a seldom-used, tertiary-level medication.

Recent research has focused on medications targeting the nicotinic receptors in the brain as a potentially useful treatment for ADHD symptoms in adults. This line of research has also been of interest because cigarette use among individuals with ADHD is considered, in part, self-medication to improve attention (Ohlmeier et al., 2007; Wilens & Decker, 2007). A small ($N = 11$) randomized, double-blind, placebo-controlled, crossover pilot study indicated that a neuronal nicotinic receptor (NNR) partial agonist was significantly superior to placebo in reducing symptoms of adult ADHD (Wilens, Verlinden, Adler, Wozniak, & West, 2006). No significant safety issues or side effects were reported. A larger ($N = 221$) randomized, double-blind, placebo-controlled crossover study provided further evidence that the NNR was well tolerated and outperformed placebo (Abi-Saab et al., 2008). However, the clinical improvements, as measured by the CAARS, although statistically significant, were generally mild.

NONMEDICATION TREATMENTS FOR ADULT ADHD

Despite the impressive and important positive effects achieved with medications for ADHD, many adult patients need and seek additional therapeutic support to improve their daily functioning, even with effective pharmacotherapy (e.g., Gualtieri & Johnson, 2008). Adjunctive treatments are most often pursued in combination with medications but in some cases—by choice or necessity—are carried out without medications. Although the number of nonpharmacological treatments designed to help improve the functioning of adults with ADHD is growing, they do not yet have a research foundation approaching that supporting pharmacotherapy.

Nevertheless, the need for adjunctive treatments for adults with ADHD is pressing. Many individuals with mild to moderate symptoms of ADHD in relatively uncomplicated situations (e.g., no comorbid psychiatric or learning problems, good interpersonal support, stable job) may experience sufficiently improved functioning with symptom improvements afforded by medications. However, some individuals with mild symptoms might initially choose to pursue nonpharmacologic coping methods. Furthermore, a significant number of ADHD patients on prescribed medications require additional help to develop and implement effective coping strategies or to address complicating issues. These issues include severity of ADHD symptoms, the presence of comorbid psychiatric diagnoses (including substance abuse), and severity of impairment in different life domains. Finally, some individuals may not be able to take medications for ADHD because of side effects or medical contraindications, with some individuals simply declining pharmacotherapy options, thus leaving them to seek another treatment approach.

Hope is an essential intervention for adult ADHD that is implicit in all nonmedication treatment approaches reviewed, however strong or weak the evidence for their benefits. ADHD is a pernicious syndrome that corrodes one's sense of confidence in managing many essential domains of life. Consequently, living with ADHD, particularly when it has gone unidentified until adulthood, can slowly erode one's sense of self, particularly as it interferes with many aspects of life from which people construct identity, such as work, school, and relationships.

Hope can come in many forms. The accurate diagnosis of ADHD, understanding that its difficulties are the result of a neurobiological syndrome rather than laziness and recognizing its effects on one's daily life, is an important first step. A positive relationship with a clinician or other supportive individuals who understand the challenges of managing adult ADHD provides an important foundation. Medications may provide the hope of symptom improvement.

Central to the focus of this book, hope can come in the form of a plan for change that promises to improve day-to-day life for an adult with ADHD. However, hope is an investment that helps individuals engage in the change process, with the ultimate dividend of this investment being the experience of improvements and development of coping strategies that empower adults with ADHD to take increasing control of their lives. Consequently, clinical outcome research of the efficacy of various treatments helps identify the approaches most likely to help these patients.

Subsequent chapters review specific adjunctive nonmedication treatments and support services that have been designed for adults diagnosed with ADHD. The goal of these chapters is to provide readers with an understanding of each of the different nonmedication treatment options and the rationale for their use with adults with ADHD. The extant research literature examining the effectiveness of different treatments is also reviewed and discussed. Treatments reviewed were selected because of either published outcome studies of their efficacy or their common appearance in the clinical or popular literature as recommended approaches for adult ADHD, in some cases despite limited or nonexistent research support. By erring on the side of overinclusion, I hope that this book will provide clinicians, researchers, students, and interested consumers with a useful overview of the current state of adjunctive clinical services for adults with ADHD to help them make informed decisions about treatment options and to wisely invest their hope for change.

2

PSYCHOSOCIAL TREATMENTS

Despite the fact that medications have been established as the best single treatment available for individuals with attention-deficit/hyperactivity disorder (ADHD) of all ages, there has been an ongoing search for adjunctive treatments to further improve psychosocial functioning. In fact, many of the treatment approaches delivered to children with ADHD in the early 20th century focused on environmental and educational modifications to reduce potential sources of what was termed excessive stimulation before the advent of stimulant medications (Barkley, 2006a). Despite the understandable focus on the neurobiological etiology of ADHD and the benefits of pharmacotherapy, interest in the development of psychosocial treatments targeting the impairments associated with ADHD has continued.

The psychosocial treatments for children with ADHD that have proven most effective are parent and teacher training in principles of behavioral management to establish consistency in responding to targeted behaviors, including the importance of positive reinforcement for adaptive behaviors (Antshel & Barkley, 2008; Barkley, 2002b; Chronis, Jones, & Raggi, 2006; Pelham, Wheeler, & Chronis, 1998; Root & Resnick, 2003). Direct contingency management, involving intensive behavioral shaping in a number of environmental settings, has also been found to be effective (Pelham et al.,

2000; Wells et al., 2000). The combination of parent and teacher training and direct contingency management in the context of a summer treatment program made up the behavioral treatment module of the Multimodal Treatment Study of Children with ADHD (MTA; Jensen et al., 2007; MTA Cooperative Group, 1999).

When ADHD in adults gained public notoriety in the mid-1990s, however, there was no such scientific basis from which to fashion or choose psychosocial treatments for this clinical population. In fact, treatment guidelines for ADHD published by the American Academy of Child and Adolescent Psychiatry (AACAP; 1997) noted that the psychosocial treatment literature for adults with ADHD was based entirely on clinical anecdote. Although it seemed the notion of ADHD in adulthood arose de novo, clinicians versed in ADHD had long recognized its features in adults and endeavored to devise effective treatments, including the use of psychosocial treatments (J. J. Ratey, Greenberg, Bemporad, & Lindem, 1992; Wender, 1975; Wender, Reimherr, & Wood, 1981; Wood, Reimherr, Wender, & Johnson, 1976). As clinicians encountered more patients with adult ADHD, the starting point for developing psychosocial treatments involved the modification of standard psychotherapy approaches to meet the unique clinical needs of these patients.

REVIEW OF PSYCHOSOCIAL TREATMENT APPROACHES FOR ADULT ADHD

Although no clinical outcome research was conducted on psychosocial approaches until about a decade ago, clinicians started to identify some important adaptations to psychotherapy to address the needs of adult patients with ADHD. The next sections review how different models of psychotherapy address adult ADHD.

Early Psychoanalytic Conceptualizations

Psychoanalytic perspectives on what would currently be viewed as childhood ADHD focused on issues related to the latency period of mental development (Rafalovich, 2001). On the one hand, restlessness and fidgetiness were ascribed to anxiety representing inherent psychosexual processes; inattention or daydreaminess, on the other hand, was viewed as a compulsion neurosis manifested as introversion (or at least disengagement from the environment) despite intact intelligence and logic. Subsequent conceptualizations suggested that the features of ADHD indicated the dynamics of a *fragmented ego,* that is, a mercurial relationship between the internal and external worlds manifested by inconsistent functioning.

According to this paradigm, the differences between child and adult symptomatology of "adult brain dysfunction" were interpreted as resulting from increased ego maturation imparting adults with greater measures of internalized control and self-awareness than are experienced by children (Bellak, 1977; Mann & Greenspan, 1976). The biological symptoms of ADHD, such as distractibility and restlessness, and personality development were seen as intertwined (Bellak, 1977; Bemporad & Zambenedetti, 1996; Mann & Greenspan, 1976). The interaction of the biological and developmental is consistent with ADHD being akin to the notion of temperament insofar as its symptoms affect most developmental experiences and therefore influence the development of a core belief network (Ramsay & Rostain, 2003, 2008a).

Although acknowledging the biological underpinnings of ADHD and the effectiveness of pharmacotherapy, psychoanalysts saw the increased attention and concentration provided by medications as opening the way for long-term psychotherapy to treat the functional disorders of adulthood in terms of personality structure. Indeed, a pitfall of misattributing all the patient's problems as stemming from ADHD was that it would "invariably support the patient's defensive rationalizations against self-inquiry and further convince him of the reality of his often unconscious negative self-image" (Mann & Greenspan, 1976, p. 1016). Conversely, therapists were also cautioned not to prematurely attribute to unconscious processes (e.g., resistance, conflict) behaviors that could be better explained as resulting from the core features of ADHD (e.g., arriving late to sessions, forgetfulness), echoing suggestions made in the recent clinical literature (Hallowell, 1995; Ramsay & Rostain, 2005a).

Contemporary Psychoanalytic Conceptualizations

Contemporary psychoanalysts provide case examples to illustrate how their model makes accommodations for the needs of adults with ADHD (Carney, 2002; Gilmore, 2000; Wright, 2006; Zabarenko, 2002). Carney (2002) conceptualized ADHD "as a deficit in the neurological substrate that complicates and colors the development of self- and interactive regulation" (p. 356), stating that psychoanalysis is well suited as a treatment for this sort of deficit, although no research supports this claim. The regulatory function is attributed to the ego: "We can usefully consider AD/HD as a disturbance in the synthetic, organizing, and integrative function of the ego" (Gilmore, 2000, p. 1260). The description of the ego's organizing role is compatible with Barkley's (1997a, 1997b) model of executive dysfunction (driven by behavioral disinhibition) as the defining feature of ADHD. That is, the role of the *ego* (i.e., adaptive self-control or reality driven) as the arbiter between the *id* (i.e., prepotent response or instinctual pleasure) and *superego* (i.e., rule-governed conduct or moral aspirations) in the structural theory of psychoanalysis (Kahn, 2002) is similar to the role of executive functions (i.e., self-regulation) to mediate the tension between prepotent impulses and environmental demands. Consequently, the executive functions could, in part, be viewed as functions of the ego in the psychoanalytic model; on the other hand, ego development and maturation could be viewed as contingent upon executive functioning.

Anecdotal case studies suggest that psychoanalysis for ADHD is more effective with concurrent pharmacotherapy (Carney, 2002; Wright, 2006; Zabarenko, 2002). For example, once prescribed a psychostimulant, Carney's (2002) adult patient with ADHD was thereafter better able to experience and express painful affect (without derailing his train of thought), recognize his defensive patterns, and face complicated transference issues. It is interesting that the patient's obsessive thinking and magical thinking in sessions were at once interpreted as defenses and compensations. These patterns were defenses insofar as they separated the patient from strong affect associated with the danger he presumably experienced in his daily life because of his erratic behavior. They were compensations in that they allowed the patient to slow down his actions and to have some basis for decision making, however imperfect (see Zabarenko, 2002, for similar clinical examples of distancing behaviors). Wright (2006) formulated an adult female analysand's inconsistent medication compliance as a transference issue, with the patient becoming more dependent, withdrawn, and disconnected from her internal emotional state when not medicated. Conversely, Wright (2006) noted the case of a young girl with ADHD whose analysis was more productive during a period in which she was unmedicated. Finally, Seitler (2008) suggested that the symptoms of ADHD, particularly hyperactivity in children, are actually manifestations of agitation operating as a defense against depression.

Although the fragmented ego conceptualization of ADHD parallels neurobiological models, it does not necessarily follow that traditional therapeutic approaches, such as being nondirective, the use of free association, and so on, are helpful for adults with ADHD. Moreover, many behaviors exhibited by adults with ADHD, such as missing or arriving late to appointments or poor follow-through on therapeutic tasks, might be wrongly misinterpreted as "resistance" or "passive aggression." It became increasingly clear that traditional models of psychotherapy would have to be modified for adults with ADHD to derive benefit from them (Hallowell, 1995; J. J. Ratey et al., 1992; M. Weiss, Hechtman, & Weiss, 1999). Consequently, the 1990s saw a discussion of modified psychosocial interventions for this clinical population.

Transtheoretical Clinical Approaches

J. J. Ratey et al. (1992) performed a naturalistic review of adult patients presenting for treatment with unrecognized ADHD. Sixty adult patients who had been deemed treatment "failures" by their previous psychotherapists were reassessed and determined to fulfill diagnostic criteria for ADHD. The authors found that previous traditional conceptualizations of patients' presenting symptoms, such as resistance, defense mechanisms, or low self-esteem provided little benefit in terms of treatment formulation, and more often served to lower patients' already fragile self-images. All patients were prescribed a low dose of desipramine for 1 month. Those patients who did not respond to desipramine were switched to methylphenidate.

J. J. Ratey et al. (1992) used a coping model of therapy, including psychoeducation, emphasizing the neurobiological nature of ADHD, a focus on developing coping skills, and building up patients' existing strengths and capabilities. All patients were judged as being significantly improved by the end of treatment, although these improvements were based on clinical impressions without the use of formal outcome measures. However, the study shed light on the issue of unrecognized adult ADHD in clinical practice and introduced a combined treatment model integrating a transtheoretical psychosocial component.

Hallowell and J. J. Ratey (Hallowell, 1995; Hallowell & Ratey, 1994; J. J. Ratey, Hallowell, & Miller, 1997) further reformulated the ground rules for psychotherapy for adult ADHD by suggesting that the traditional therapeutic neutrality maintained by therapists be exchanged for a more active, exhortative stance likened to that of a coach. This sort of active, directive approach, using concrete feedback and encouragement, presumably kept patients focused on the content of sessions. Although not abandoning psychotherapy process issues, the authors noted that clinicians must consider resistant behaviors as extensions of the deficits associated with ADHD. Hallowell (1995) encouraged clinicians to adopt a humanistic stance in which patients' neurobehavioral difficulties did not divert attention from their emotional experiences, stating that a positive alliance with, and feeling understood by, a therapist is beneficial for patients with ADHD.

Multimodal Treatments

Drawing from both the popular and professional literatures, clinicians in recent years have devised treatment programs designed specifically for adults with ADHD. A multimodal treatment (MMT) approach has been touted as the most logical overarching model for treating a disorder with pervasive effects on functioning, following the approach set forth in the MTA Cooperative Group (1999) study of the treatment of ADHD in children. The most commonly cited modes of treatment in the adult ADHD clinical literature are an accurate diagnosis, patient education about ADHD, environmental restructuring, psychosocial therapy, ADHD coaching, and pharmacotherapy (see AACAP, 1997; Attention Deficit Disorder Association [ADDA], 2006b; Brown, 2000; Hallowell, 1995; K. R. Murphy, 2005; Ramsay & Rostain, 2005a, 2007b; J. J. Ratey et al., 1997; Tuckman, 2007; M. Weiss, Murray, & Weiss, 2002). Many clinicians also extol the benefits of group therapy and support groups (e.g., Brown, 2000; Hallowell & Ratey, 1994; Kelly, 1995; Morgan, 2000) and targeted services for specific difficulties (e.g., academic support, vocational counseling; Nadeau, 2005). Although an MMT approach makes intuitive sense, such comprehensive treatment may be difficult for many people to afford, not to mention that MMT in adults with ADHD has not yet been systematically studied in the manner it has been studied in children with ADHD.

A garden-variety recommendation that psychotherapy helps adults with ADHD is no longer sufficient. Psychosocial treatments that have been designed specifically for adults with ADHD are reviewed in the following sections.

Cognitive Remediation and Cognitive Rehabilitation Approaches

C. S. Weinstein (1994) promoted the use of an adjunctive cognitive remediation approach, which is equated with coaching. Cognitive remediation targets specific coping tools and strategies the ADHD adult needs to promote behavior change and improve adaptive daily functioning. A treatment plan is derived from an assessment of the patient's relative neuropsychological strengths and weakness, and includes attention strategies, memory-enhancing strategies, and problem-solving skills (including stress and anger management). C. S. Weinstein (1994) cautioned against falling prey to the tendency of simply telling patients what to do and ignoring the emotional experience of patients as they practice these coping skills.

Drawing from this model, other clinicians have focused on clinical applications of various forms of modular cognitive remediation programs (CRPs). Jackson and Farrugia (1997) suggested a therapeutic approach pinpointing the various deficits typically reported by adults with ADHD. Modular therapy fosters attention management skills using pragmatic strategies such as developing an awareness of the timing of one's attention span, nondefensively asking someone to repeat a point missed in a conversation, and breaking down tasks into manageable portions. The construct of "self-control" is parsed into three therapeutic components: self-awareness of personal strengths and weaknesses; self-monitoring to track one's behavioral tendencies; and self-reinforcement to reward desired behavior. Social skills interventions (including group therapy) are used to help patients establish and maintain healthier relationships, whereas stress and anger management skills enhance emotional control and improve problem-solving skills.

Sohlberg and Mateer (2001) tailored the cognitive rehabilitation techniques used to retrain attentional skill deficits stemming from acquired brain injury into techniques for adults with ADHD. This rehabilitation model for treating attention problems is composed of diverse approaches including environmental modification, focused attention training exercises, self-management strategies, external coping aids, and psychosocial support. There are no data on the effectiveness of the cognitive rehabilitation model for adults with ADHD, although its use with children with ADHD has tentative support (Riccio & French, 2004).

At the other end of the rehabilitation spectrum, Wasserstein and Lynn (2001) put forward a metacognitive rehabilitation approach, which has been adapted for use with college students with ADHD (Wedlake, 2002). This approach represents an integration of existing intervention treatment models (cognitive–behavioral, psychodynamic, and neuropsychological) that targets the functional disconnection between the anterior (expressive systems) and posterior (receptive systems) higher cortical regions, as opposed to dysfunction in corticostriatal pathways affecting the relationship between frontal and prefrontal lobes. The contribution of this model to an MMT program is that it welds patients' problematic behavior patterns or issues with personally relevant, emotionally evocative metaphors that capture the essence of their struggles. As such, the metaphor serves both as a signal (e.g., activating self-monitoring) so that patients are better able to implement coping skills in a timely manner and as an intervention point for developing new behaviors or coping strategies.

Finally, Aviram, Rhum, and Levin (2001) focused on treating the unique therapeutic needs of ADHD adults with comorbid psychoactive substance use disorders, thereby responding to the heightened risk of comorbid substance abuse among adults with ADHD. The authors pointed out that the issue of relapse prevention, with its focus on impulse control and distress tolerance, is relevant for the management of both urges to use substances and the core symptoms of ADHD. The structure and regularity of therapy sessions provide a sense of stability for patients. The authors added that although ambivalence and resistance must be considered when patients miss or are tardy for appointments, these behaviors more often reflect features of ADHD or drug relapse behavior. In addition to developing healthier coping strategies, patients can benefit from "self-talk," a therapeutic focus to foster an awareness of the connections among the patients' thoughts, feelings, and actions.

Modern Psychodynamic Approaches

As was mentioned earlier in the chapter, psychoanalysts view the traditional symptom picture of ADHD as resulting from a core disturbance in ego integration (e.g., Gilmore, 2000). Bemporad (2001) and Bemporad and Zambenedetti (1996) suggested that although many adult patients with

ADHD respond well to pharmacotherapy and psychoeducation, many individuals struggle with dysfunctional personality characteristics from having grown up with ADHD. Thus, modern psychodynamic therapists target the defenses that adults with ADHD habitually use to deal with painful affect associated with upsetting developmental experiences (Bemporad & Zambenedetti, 1996; Carney, 2002; Zabarenko, 2002). These defenses may come to the forefront in therapy with the aid of medications that increase the patient's ability to focus on them and to decrease the tendency to escape into actions.

There are two primary triggers for the therapeutic resistance seen in adults with ADHD (Bemporad & Zambenedetti, 1996). First are the novel levels of introspection and emotional processing, which could be simultaneously bewildering and painful. The second trigger is the patient's desire to recapture some aspects of his or her ADHD behaviors that provide the experience of living on the edge. The patient may compensate for these defenses by self-medicating via chronic substance abuse, thrill-seeking behaviors, or nonconformist pursuits.

What is more, these resistant behaviors are purported to mask two recurring therapeutic themes (Bemporad & Zambenedetti, 1996): a sense of anger and sadness over failed opportunities, and a ubiquitous sense of low self-esteem. Although working through the first issue is akin to working through grief, modifying low self-esteem is thought to be central to psychotherapy for adult ADHD. It is thought to crop up in various transferential reenactments, such as the "charming and likable patient" who tries to avoid rejection and the "naughty child" who is frequently apologetic or frantic when late for appointments. Dream analysis typically reveals themes of frustration, failure, and abandonment that likely reflect the sum of past relationships with significant others. Psychodynamic psychotherapy presumably heightens awareness of how these patterns are replayed in the patient's daily life and helps restructure dysfunctional personality characteristics, although these models are based on clinical anecdote.

Cognitive–Behavioral Therapy Approaches

Although many of the interventions suggested in the aforementioned treatments for adult ADHD have correlates in cognitive–behavioral therapy (CBT), only in the past decade have comprehensive CBT models and conceptualizations of adult ADHD been introduced (McDermott, 2000, 2009; Ramsay & Rostain, 2003, 2008a; Rostain & Ramsay, 2006a; Safren, Perlman, Sprich, & Otto, 2005). Adapted from Beck's (1976) traditional cognitive model, CBT focuses on the interplay of thoughts, emotions, and behaviors through understanding individuals' beliefs about, and interpretations of, their experiences. This is not to say that thoughts precede and cause all emotions and behaviors but rather that these cognitions play a pivotal role in one's experience and provide an important and effective intervention point. Similar to Bemporad's (2001) emphasis on the fit between one's environmental demands and one's temperament, CBT explores this fit in terms of the particular belief systems the individual constructs about himself or herself, the world, and the future—Beck's (1976) cognitive triad.

Of course, one's neurobiology, beliefs, emotions, and behaviors form a braided cord of experience and personal meaning. These experiences contribute to the development of one's most central beliefs about the world and one's place in it, the *schema* (Ramsay & Rostain, 2003, 2008a). Adults with ADHD often describe experiences of recurring frustrations and failures in several important life domains. These experiences contribute to the development and subsequent maintenance of negative schemata such as "inadequacy" or "failure" that may be experienced in the form of idiosyncratic core beliefs such as "I'm a loser." Over time, these beliefs become overgeneralized and give rise to many seemingly self-defeating behaviors, or *compensatory strategies*. These compensatory strategies make sense in terms of the underlying belief system (e.g., "[Because I'm a loser . . .] studying in advance of the exam won't improve my grade. I'll just study the night before the exam."), but they insidiously reinforce the maladaptive belief system (e.g., poor grade on the exam because of insufficient preparation). These negative beliefs conspire with the chronic deficits associated with ADHD to wear away an individual's sense of efficacy. Left unchallenged and untreated, these beliefs unnecessarily limit an individual's potential coping and life options. Although ADHD is not the result of negative thoughts, cognitive and behavioral modification often open the way for patients to implement new coping skills and gain new experiences that promote new outlooks on themselves and new coping options (Ramsay, 2007; Safren, 2006). What is more, CBT is an effective treatment for comorbid disorders commonly seen in cases of adult ADHD, primarily depression and anxiety.

Miscellaneous Psychotherapies

Various other therapeutic approaches have been modified to address the unique difficulties faced by adults with ADHD, including gestalt therapy (e.g., Root, 1996) and logotherapy (Schulenberg, Melton, & Foote, 2006). Eclectic approaches in which intervention plans are based on the particular functional problems reported by patients, selecting from supportive, CBT, and interpersonal interventions, also have been proposed (e.g., Gentile, Atiq, & Gillig, 2006). However, similar to traditional psychotherapies, these miscellaneous approaches are based on limited clinical anecdote and have not yet been tested in studies of adult ADHD.

ADHD Coaching

The notion of "coaching" for adult ADHD was originally used as a metaphor for the need to adopt a more interactive, directive therapeutic alliance than is seen in traditional therapy (Hallowell & Ratey, 1994). The field of ADHD coaching arose as a profession designed to help adults with ADHD develop the necessary organization, time management, and other skills to handle the challenges of daily life (National Resource Center on AD/HD [NRC], 2003a). ADHD coaching is not a psychosocial treatment per se, to the extent that it is not a traditional psychological treatment; does not require a degree or credentialing in a mental health profession; and does not involve the comprehensive assessment and treatment of various cognitive, emotional, behavioral, developmental, and personality factors. Instead, it is a targeted support service that uses various cognitive and behavior modification principles to promote the use of adaptive coping skills. Thus, a discussion of ADHD coaching fits in this chapter.

ADHD coaching is a specialty that is an outgrowth of life and executive coaching movements (Berman & Bradt, 2006; Neenan & Dryden, 2002). ADHD coaching builds on the foundation of positive psychology (Seligman & Csikszentmihalyi, 2000), a wellness model that emphasizes factors involved in healthy development, the acquisition of adaptive living skills, and the notion that individuals can be encouraged to discover solutions to their problems (The ADDA Subcommittee on AD/HD Coaching, 2002; International Coaching Federation, 2008; N. A. Ratey, 2008). In effect, ADHD coaching is a personal education approach, focusing on recognizing and using psychological strengths, and making use of existing aptitudes and talents, rather than directly focusing on problem reduction (N. A. Ratey, 2008).

The established niche for ADHD coaching seems to be helping generally well-functioning adults with ADHD who experience role-specific underfunctioning, such as poor productivity in the workplace, academic underperformance resulting from poor study skills and procrastination, or disorganization and inefficiency in managing the recurring demands of running a household. ADHD coaching provides personalized education about the effects of ADHD on the performance of day-to-day roles and offers timely support, encouragement, and ongoing accountability as clients attempt to execute their objectives. Coaching sessions may occur in any number of settings and modalities, including in the coach's office, group settings, traditional office visits, home or workplace visits, online, or via telephone (NRC, 2003a).

Specific models of ADHD coaching have been recently introduced. For example, N. A. Ratey (2002, 2008) conceptualized coaching as a three-legged stool made from a collaborative partnership, the development of internal and external structure focused on client strengths, and the process of guided exploration and learning to the benefit of the client. Behavioral analyses and review of negative thoughts related to difficulties following through with personal goals are used to help individuals develop a better understanding of themselves and their coping priorities. Coaching interventions involve pragmatic problem solving with the end goal of helping clients to implement their behavioral plans, such as reducing procrastination at work, keeping up with assigned reading at college, or organizing and paying bills at home. Said differently, ADHD coaching strives to bridge the gap between ability and performance (J. L. Young & Giwerc, 2003). N. A. Ratey (2002) proposed that five main ways ADHD coaching is helpful are by maintaining arousal, modulating emotions, maintaining motivation and providing immediate reward, serving as the "executive secretary of attention" (i.e., keeping sight of the big picture), and supporting the client's ability to carry out self-directed actions and change behavior patterns. Considering difficulties ADHD adults have with implementing coping plans, ADHD coaching appears to be helpful for many individuals, particularly for individuals whose ADHD symptoms are reasonably managed and who do not experience coexisting complications.

ADHD coaching differs from psychosocial treatments. Psychosocial treatments often involve comprehensive assessments and in-depth case conceptualizations that take into account a wide array of psychological factors that affect functioning. Patients seeking psychosocial treatment enter a formal professional relationship governed by the professional and ethical standards of the practitioner's field (e.g., psychiatry, psychology, clinical social work) and in which their privileged communications are protected by law. Licensed mental health professionals have training backgrounds that emphasize the assessment and diagnosis of psychiatric disorders, including review of potential medical conditions that could contribute to symptoms, and are well versed in psychological treatments. Although some therapists include elements of coaching in their practices, either as a distinct professional role or as a component of integrative treatment (e.g., Tuckman, 2007), ADHD coaches are not required to earn a degree or have training in psychology or mental health–related fields.

ADHD coaching is still developing and defining its professional and ethical standards (see The ADDA Subcommittee on AD/HD Coaching, 2002; N. A. Ratey, Maynard, & Sleeper-Triplett, 2007). ADHD coaching is not currently considered as a treatment protected by confidentiality laws. The less formal relationship is thought to allow ADHD coaches to be more actively encouraging of their clients to recognize their strengths and follow through on plans (J. L. Young & Giwerc, 2003). However, licensed mental health professionals who also act as coaches in their practices may still be bound by the professional, ethical, and legal standards of their professional license (Koocher, 2008).

Although seeming to have a niche in an MMT approach for adult ADHD, coaching is a relatively new field, and the lines between coaching and therapy remain somewhat ambiguous (e.g., Knouse, Cooper-Vince, Sprich, & Safren, 2008). Several formal training programs lead to certification in ADHD coaching, but there are currently no degree requirements for participants or accreditation requirements for the training programs. However, several organizations have been launched during the past few years to establish certification standards for ADHD coaches. The Institute for the Advancement of AD/HD Coaching has set up a two-level certification: Certified AD/HD Coach and Senior Certified AD/HD Coach, requiring a minimum of 2 and 5 years of professional experience, respectively. The Professional Association of ADHD Coaches is reportedly compiling its certification standards. ADHD coaching as a field will have to continue to develop its professional and ethical guidelines and to provide research evidence of its effectiveness to understand its mechanisms of change (Goldstein, 2005).

Moving From Clinical Anecdote to Clinical Research

All of the therapies reviewed above acknowledge the neurobiological underpinnings of the self-regulation problems characteristic of ADHD and, therefore, can be considered theoretically congruent with prevailing models of ADHD. However, although anecdotal accounts of the aforementioned treatments are encouraging, empirical support is the gold standard for establishing their efficacy. The next section reviews the results of outcome studies of psychosocial treatments for adult ADHD.

RESEARCH EVIDENCE FOR PSYCHOSOCIAL TREATMENTS FOR ADULT ADHD

As of the writing of this book, a computerized literature search of psychosocial treatment studies for adult ADHD, augmented by cross-referencing the published literature as well as tracking down various research papers presented at conferences, yielded a total of 17 clinical outcome studies (including the J. J. Ratey et al., 1992, study reviewed in an earlier section). It should be noted that a recent review of published outcome studies was composed of eight of these studies (Ramsay & Rostain, 2007b). Thus, there have been five additional publications (as well as an account of an ongoing outcome study) and several other conference abstracts that have been included in the current review, indicating growing research activity on psychosocial treatments for adults with ADHD.

The extant studies used a variety of different methodologies and treatment objectives, although it is fair to classify most, if not all of them, as falling under the CBT umbrella. For clarity of review, the studies are grouped according to the format in which they were delivered: (a) individual treatment approaches, (b) group treatment approaches, (c) a self-directed treatment, and (d) ADHD coaching.

Individual Treatment Approaches

Wilens et al. (1999) conducted a retrospective chart review of 26 adults with ADHD to assess the effectiveness of a modified individual CBT approach (e.g., McDermott, 2000) that was introduced after medication stabilization to control for medication effects. Results indicated that adults with ADHD responded well to CBT and that this positive response was over and above the positive response obtained from medication stabilization alone. Although medication stabilization alone was associated with many clinical improvements, the subsequent addition of CBT was associated with further improvements on measures of ADHD symptom severity, ADHD symptoms, depression, anxiety, and global functioning ratings.

Safren, Otto, et al. (2005) conducted a randomized control study of a modular CBT approach for adults with ADHD on stabilized medication regimens but who experienced ongoing residual symptoms. Safren, Perlman, et al.'s (2005) CBT approach is composed of three core modules, with sessions dedicated to organizational and planning skills, reducing distractibility, and cognitive modification with additional optional modules. When compared with control participants receiving ongoing medication management only ($n = 15$), participants completing CBT with concurrent medication management ($n = 16$) exhibited larger improvements on self-ratings of ADHD symptoms, blind examiner ratings of ADHD, self-ratings of depression and anxiety, clinician ratings of depression and anxiety, and ratings of global functioning.

Rostain and Ramsay (2006c) conducted an open clinical study of an individual CBT approach for adult ADHD (Ramsay & Rostain, 2003, 2008a) combined with pharmacotherapy for 43 adult patients. Over 80% of the participants had at least one current comorbid disorder. Outcome assessment was performed at the 16th session of CBT, which represented about 6 months of treatment. Participants completing combined treatment reported statistically significant improvements on measures of ADHD symptoms; self-report ratings of depression, anxiety, and hopelessness; clinician ratings of depression and anxiety, and clinician ratings of ADHD severity and overall functional status. However, because CBT and medications were administered concurrently, it is impossible to disentangle the contribution of separate treatments to overall improvement.

The Rostain and Ramsay (2006c) study was originally designed to be an open study comparison of individuals seeking combined treatment, pharmacotherapy only, and CBT only; however, the vast majority of individuals chose combined treatment, rendering the other groups too small for comparative analyses. However, subsequent analysis of the CBT-only group yielded interesting preliminary findings, although one cannot draw strong conclusions from so small a sample (*n* = 5; Ramsay & Rostain, 2007a). Of interest was the fact that individuals with generally mild symptoms (although fulfilling diagnostic criteria), mild and circumscribed areas of impairment, no or minimal comorbidity, average to above-average intelligence, stable life circumstances, good social support, and who decline pharmacotherapy may benefit from CBT alone for ADHD. Significant improvements on measures of activation, ADHD symptoms, depression, and clinician ratings of overall functioning and ADHD symptoms were obtained at the end of treatment as well as trends toward significance on most other outcome measures. It is interesting that there was greater ethnic–racial diversity among individuals seeking psychosocial treatment alone than was seen in those who completed combined treatment.

Finally, a nine-session manualized problem-focused therapy (PFT) approach was used in a randomized study comparing Paxil (paroxetine) and Dexedrine (dextroamphetamine) or their combination for adults with ADHD (M. Weiss, Hechtman, & The Adult ADHD Research Group, 2006). Psychological treatment was included in the study to increase retention of participants and to justify the use of a placebo group. PFT sessions were coordinated with study medication visits and were focused on psychoeducation and using effective coping strategies with a modular approach. Although concurrent medications and PFT were associated with a significantly higher number of treatment responders, participants receiving PFT and placebo demonstrated benefits on measures of overall improvement, mood and anxiety symptoms, and ADHD symptoms.

Group Treatment Approaches

Wiggins, Singh, Getz, and Hutchins (1999) examined the effectiveness of a four-session psychoeducational group provided to nine adults with ADHD. Each session targeted a different problem area commonly associated with ADHD, such as difficulties related to setting realistic goals, organizing and managing time, completing tasks, and managing their environments. The theoretical approach of the group focused on the reciprocal relationships of thoughts, feelings, and actions and how these connections affect efforts to change behaviors. Results indicated that statistically significant decreases on measures of three problem areas of interest—disorganization, inattention, and unexpectedly, self-esteem—for those completing treatment when compared with control participants and baseline scores. The finding of decreased self-esteem among treatment completers was counterintuitive, although it was interpreted as a grief reaction in the process of coming to terms with the effects of long-standing ADHD on their functioning.

Looper et al. (2001; as cited in M. D. Weiss et al., 2008) developed a 12-week, modular group treatment program with sessions devoted to specific themes, such as ADHD symptoms, organization, anger management, and education about medication treatment. Participants completing the group reported improvements on ADHD symptom scales, comorbid psychiatric symptoms, organization, and self-esteem.

Mandelbaum et al. (2002; as cited in M. D. Weiss et al., 2008) conducted a follow-up study of Looper et al. (2001) in which group participants with ADHD were not on medication and the treatment group was compared with a support group control. Although participants in the treatment group reported improvements on measures of organization, self-esteem, family life, and anger management (the control group reported only improvement on a measure of occupational functioning), the results were relatively modest compared with findings from the previous study in which group participants received concurrent pharmacotherapy.

Hesslinger et al. (2002) examined a modular, skills-based training program for adult ADHD conducted in a 13-week group format, each session focusing on a different skill-based module (e.g., impulse control, relationships, self-respect). The modular treatment approach for adult ADHD was adapted from Linehan's (1993) dialectical behavior therapy designed for the treatment of borderline personality disorder. Hesslinger et al.'s treatment was associated with statistically significant improvements on ADHD symptom checklists, a depression measure, neuropsychological tests measuring selective and split attention, and participants' ratings of overall personal health status when compared with baseline measures.

Philipsen et al. (2007) conducted a multisite follow-up study of the Hesslinger et al. (2002) modular group treatment approach for adult ADHD. Seventy-two patients with adult ADHD were seen at four different centers. Completion of treatment was associated with statistically significant improvements on measures of ADHD, depression, and personal health status. No differences in treatment response were a function of either treatment site or medication status. Sessions topics of "behavioral analyses," "mindfulness," and "emotion regulation" were rated by participants as being most helpful.

Stevenson, Whitmont, Bornholt, Livesey, and Stevenson (2002) studied a CRP for adults with ADHD. The CRP targeted problems associated with ADHD by modifying the physical environment, retraining cognitive functions, and teaching internal and external compensatory strategies. The

22 group members received in-session assistance from coaches. Group participants reported significant improvements when compared with wait-list control participants on measures of their ADHD symptoms, organization, self-esteem, state anger, and trait anger. Treatment gains were maintained at 2-month follow-up, and organizational and symptom improvements were maintained at 1-year follow-up.

Derksen and Ritmeijer (2007; as cited in Moyer, 2007b) conducted a study of a 10-week group CBT for 43 adults with ADHD receiving concurrent pharmacotherapy. The group emphasized psychoeducation about structuring day-to-day life, developing and implementing adaptive coping skills, and boosting self-esteem. Outcome measures were gathered at baseline and at 9- and 18-month follow-up. Group participants reported significant improvements after completion of the group that were maintained at follow-up, including improvements on measures of ADHD symptoms and psychological distress at 18-month follow-up.

Solanto, Marks, Mitchell, Wasserstein, and Kofman (2008) described their manualized group CBT approach as "metacognitive therapy" (see Wasserstein & Lynn, 2001) insofar as it targets interference with implementing effective executive skills, such as planning, organization, and time management. Their open study was composed of 30 adults who completed either an 8- or 12-week versions of a weekly, 2-hour CBT group program. The majority of treatment completers met diagnostic criteria for ADHD, Predominantly Inattentive Type. Depression and anxiety were the most common coexisting psychiatric diagnoses.

Solanto et al.'s (2008) results indicated that treatment completers exhibited significant improvements on a measure of inattentive symptoms, the Brown Attention Deficit Disorder Scale (Brown, 1996) total score, and a researcher-developed functional measure of various executive function skills. There was no statistically significant improvement on a measure of hyperactivity-impulsivity, although this result may be an artifact of the overrepresentation of participants with the predominantly inattentive type of ADHD.

Virta et al. (2008) reported the outcomes of 29 adults who completed a CBT-oriented group rehabilitation program composed of 10 or 11 weekly 1.5- to 2-hour sessions administered to four groups of 6 to 8 participants each. The interventions were aimed at reducing symptoms and impairments associated with ADHD and other manifestations of executive dysfunction. Outcome measures included self- and observer ratings and were gathered at initial assessment, at the start of the first group meeting, and at the end of the final group meeting.

There was no difference in participants' self-reports during the 3 months between assessment and start of treatment, which allowed participants to serve as their own controls. After completing treatment, however, there were significant improvements on measures of activation, attention, and affect regulation. It is interesting that observer ratings of participants using the same measures yielded a significant improvement in activation, attention, and effort between assessment and the start of treatment but only improved activation at the completion of treatment. However, only 29% of observers lived with participants. When analyzed separately, cohabiting observers rated only "effort" as improved during the pretreatment phase.

Bramham et al. (2009) tested a CBT group program for adults with ADHD (e.g., S. Young & Bramham, 2007) that targeted issues related to anxiety and depression, low self-esteem, and self-efficacy. Sixty-one adults (40 men, 21 women) attended the CBT group, although 20 participants dropped out before the end of the program. A group of 37 adults with ADHD (21 men, 16 women) who received medication only from the same center served as the control group. The first and last sessions focused on psychoeducation about living with ADHD. The middle four sessions addressed anger and frustration, emotions, relationship skills, and time management and problem solving.

Compared with the control group, participants completing the CBT group reported significantly improved knowledge about ADHD. Both CBT and control groups reported improvements on measures of anxiety and depression, although there were no between-group differences. The CBT group reported significantly improved self-efficacy and self-esteem when compared with the control group. Participants rated sharing of personal experiences of living with ADHD as the most valued aspect of group CBT, although it was not rated significantly higher than other aspects of the group.

Finally, Galina et al. (unpublished; as cited in Kolar et al., 2008) described an ongoing study of a 12-session, weekly, modular group CBT treatment for adult ADHD. In addition to individual sessions devoted to common coping topics (e.g., organization, time management, cognitive reframing), the group program also integrates therapists acting as coaches who contact participants twice each week to encourage between-sessions use of coping strategies. Monthly booster sessions continue for 3 months after the completion of the group program. No data have been reported yet on this promising group program.

Self-Directed Treatment

Stevenson, Stevenson, and Whitmont (2003) conducted a randomized control study of an 8-week self-directed version (e.g., minimal therapist contact) of their aforementioned CRP. Group participants (n = 17) were again paired with coaches, whose role was to provide reminders about self-help therapeutic assignments and to monitor compliance. All outcome measures (ADHD symptoms, organizational skills, self-esteem, and both state and trait anger) improved significantly for participants completing treatment when compared with wait-list control participants and with baseline scores. At

2-month follow-up, treatment gains were maintained for ADHD symptoms, organizational skills, and trait anger. Analysis of treatment compliance revealed a significant, positive correlation with outcome.

ADHD Coaching

There have been three preliminary studies of ADHD coaching provided to college students with ADHD and one involving high school students. Considering their specialized focus on learning strategies and dealing with the unique academic demands of college, these studies are reviewed in chapter 3 of this volume, which focuses on a review of academic accommodations and interventions for postsecondary students with ADHD. A group coaching component (i.e., psychoeducation and training in organizational skills for daily life) was also included as part of an intervention program for adults with ADHD with substance use disorders, but outcome data for the field trial were not reported (Goossensen et al., 2006).

Kubik (2007, 2009) conducted an open study of the effects of a 6-week coaching workshop on 45 adults with ADHD, the sole adult ADHD coaching outcome study. Participants rated 22 areas of concern (AOC) both before and after receiving coaching support. The AOC assessment is a 5-point Likert scale self-rating of the frequency problems, such as angry outbursts and mental restlessness. Factor analysis of AOC revealed five factor domains: cognitive, distractibility, social outcomes, inattentive concerns, and behavioral outcomes. Coaching sessions focused on developing an awareness of the functional impact of ADHD on daily life, formulating personalized coping strategies to improve productivity, and using planners to manage projects.

Follow-up data were gathered between 1 and 4 years after completion of the workshop. Results indicate that participation in the coaching workshop was associated with statistically significant improvements in most AOC. Coaching alone was also found to outperform combination approaches including psychotherapy and medication, although information about other treatments was not provided (e.g., whether they were delivered concurrently with coaching, how long treatments lasted). Notable limitations in the study include that immediate postcoaching outcome data were apparently not collected. Thus, it cannot be determined whether effects measured 1 to 4 years later truly reflect outcomes associated with the intervention; however, the rationale for the delayed outcome measurement was to allow adequate time for participants to sufficiently integrate new coping strategies in their daily lives (J. A. Kubik, personal communication, July 28, 2008). Moreover, information on the diagnostic procedures used to establish the ADHD diagnosis and measures of symptom severity and functional impairments were not reported. Thus, many questions about the efficacy of coaching for adults with ADHD remain unanswered.

CONCLUSION

To date, the aforementioned researchers have laid an initial empirical foundation for the benefit of psychosocial treatments for adult ADHD. Most of these studies made an effort to stabilize medication treatment before introducing therapy to assess the distinct contribution of psychosocial interventions to clinical and functional improvements. In the few cases in which participants were not taking ADHD medications at the time they received treatment, there were no significant differences in their outcomes when compared with participants concurrently taking ADHD medications (see Table 2.1).

CBT-oriented treatments (combined with medications) focused on addressing functional impairments in both individual and group formats emerged as the predominant psychosocial model for adults with ADHD, although there are diverse approaches within this framework. These findings could be, in part, the result of the inherent emphasis placed on session structure, collaborative problem solving, and cognitive and behavioral modification in the CBT model, and the obvious fact that it was the only model studied. CBT might also be helpful because it is an effective treatment for the common comorbid disorders seen in cases of adult ADHD. Predominantly unstructured or free associative interventions do not appear to be suited for treating ADHD, and no current evidence supports their use with this clinical population, although these and other psychotherapies for adult ADHD have not yet been studied.

Many problems with the extant psychosocial outcome studies limit the generalizability of their findings. First, the sample sizes were generally small, which greatly reduces the power of the statistical analyses. Second, only a few of the studies used random assignment or control groups for comparison. Only Safren, Otto, et al. (2005) used blind raters for outcome measures to control for experimenter rater bias and another active treatment group (e.g., medication management) as a control for comparison. Third, the great variability in diagnostic assessment and in the definition and measurement of therapeutic change across different studies limits cross-study comparisons, although the assessment procedures used were appropriate. Fourth, considering the chronic negative effects of the symptoms of ADHD on functioning, it will be important to include follow-up assessments of the longer term maintenance of treatment gains and to assess the association of treatment compliance and outcome, as was done in a handful of studies. Currently there is very little evidence regarding the maintenance of gains after the completion of active psychosocial treatment for adult ADHD. Fifth, adequate assessment and ongoing psychosocial treatment for adult ADHD can be costly, particularly if individuals do not have adequate insurance coverage. Moreover, it is unclear whether clinicians in the community are trained in, or effectively administer, these sorts of treatments. Even with competent treatment, it can be difficult for adults with ADHD to

TABLE 2.1

Summary of Psychosocial Treatments for Adult Attention-Deficit/Hyperactivity Disorder (ADHD)

Psychosocial treatment	Strengths	Limitations	Current status and future directions
Individual treatments	Good assessment protocols used in studies Variety of modalities and research methodologies Improvements in symptoms and impairments Treatment is well tolerated and acceptable Targets impairments related to ADHD	Participants may not be representative of adult ADHD population at large Diverse treatment protocols must be replicated Requires adherence Cost and availability	Psychosocial treatments are the most widely studied nonmedication treatment for adult ADHD Need for more randomized studies with active treatment controls Need for studies of participants who are not taking medications Need for greater diversity in study samples Cognitive–behavioral therapy–oriented approaches seem to be most effective
Group treatments	Good assessment protocols used in studies Specific skill modules improve symptoms and functional impairments Interactions with other group members Replication study of one group program	Participants may not be representative of adult ADHD population at large May not adequately address complex comorbidities Requires adherence Availability	Groups are growing in popularity Potential for different ADHD-related group themes (e.g., relationships) Need randomized controlled studies Group programs generally follow a cognitive–behavioral therapy format

Self-directed treatment	Modular treatment protocol Convenient, cost-effective Periodic phone check-ins	Participants may not be representative of adult ADHD population at large May not adequately address complex comorbidities Less monitoring of adherence Based on single study	May be attractive for people who do not want to enter formalized treatment Session modules could potentially be made available over computers Between-sessions contact to monitor progress could be an intervention to increase treatment adherence in all psychosocial treatments
ADHD coaching	Personalized intervention Focused on use of coping skills Flexibility in arranging follow-up with coach	Does not address complex comorbidities No insurance coverage Variable training and credentials of ADHD coaches Outcomes based on a single study	More outcome studies are needed Potentially helpful for individuals not requiring formalized treatment Field still developing credentialing and ethics

follow through with the necessary coping exercises, and some patients may drop out of treatment out of frustration. Thus cost, variable quality, and potential frustration must be considered as potential negative side effects of psychosocial treatments (see Ramsay, in press).

A final limitation of the studies reviewed is that most participants were Caucasian, employed, and had completed high school. Thus, there remains virtually no data on the effects of treatment for ADHD patients who are not White or whose symptoms create significant functional impairments (Ramsay & Rostain, 2008b). Because most psychosocial outcome research has been conducted in unfunded, clinic-based studies, participants represent those individuals who are able to find and afford (by means of self-pay or having jobs providing good insurance coverage) assessment and treatment for adult ADHD. Seeing as only 11% of adults with ADHD receive specialized treatment (Kessler et al., 2006), it seems likely that this group represents the better functioning individuals who have participated in the published outcome studies. It will be important for future studies to include samples representing greater diversity in terms of racial–ethnic backgrounds and income groups.

Although the field is not ready to propose definitive psychosocial treatment parameters, clinically useful guidelines can be drawn from the studies reported and from previous reviews of clinical outcome studies of psychosocial treatments for adult ADHD (Knouse et al., 2008; Kolar et al., 2008; Ramsay, 2007, in press; Ramsay & Rostain, 2005a, 2007b; Safren, 2006; M. D. Weiss et al., 2008). All psychosocial treatments for adult ADHD that have been studied include psychoeducation about ADHD and its impact on daily life. Consequently, treatments target specific functional difficulties experienced by ADHD adults, either through the use of skill-based modules or individualized problem-management approaches. Although most participants reported symptom improvement, it seems more likely that these positive results reflect improved functioning rather than reduced core symptomatology. Although not discussed explicitly in the clinical literature, helping patients identify and use personal strengths, aptitudes, and available resources goes hand in hand with addressing coping problems.

Despite the promising results offered by these initial studies, much more research is required to improve psychosocial treatments for adult ADHD and to determine the specific mechanisms of change that are most helpful. However, there is emerging evidence from the studies cited in this chapter regarding useful aspects of psychosocial treatment for adults with ADHD, making it a nonmedication treatment option with a good research foundation and a promising future.

3

ACADEMIC SUPPORT AND ACCOMMODATIONS FOR POSTSECONDARY STUDENTS WITH ADHD

A major reason that attention-deficit/hyperactivity disorder (ADHD) has been increasingly prominent in modern society has to do with the advent of compulsory public education. The traditional classroom, with a teacher charged with educating a group of children seated together in a room, placed newfound academic and behavioral demands on children and an emphasis on rule-governed conduct. Consequently, many parents of children with ADHD first seek assessment and treatment as a result of their children's difficulties adjusting to the structure and demands of elementary school.

ADHD is a developmental disorder, and symptoms often first appear during childhood. Children who are diagnosed and receive treatment represent more severe cases of ADHD insofar as their impairment is obvious at an early age. Other individuals exhibiting symptoms of ADHD, however, may experience less pronounced, if any, impairments in childhood but notice a slow, steady upsurge of various problems in their academic performance as they grow up that are not due to lack of effort or intelligence. Thus, many individuals with ADHD might not experience impairment until later adolescence or young adulthood. Consequently, college may be the first setting in which many young adults with ADHD experience significant impairment (e.g., Rostain & Ramsay, 2006b), although these problems might emerge during other academic pursuits, such as graduate school, professional licensing examinations, or required trainings at work.

This chapter reviews the unique challenges faced by postsecondary students with ADHD and the commonly prescribed academic accommodations and other support services. Although focused on college students, this chapter discusses issues that also have relevance for various levels of adult education. Outcome research on the benefit of accommodations and support services is sparse, although there are some promising findings from studies of academic coaching approaches for college students with ADHD.

RESEARCH ON COLLEGE STUDENTS WITH ADHD

For most young adults, going to college represents the initial step toward assuming the role of an adult, including, in most cases, leaving home to attend school. In addition to adjusting to new learning demands, college students must cope with the loss of the emotional and organizational support of parents and caregivers. They must independently establish effective organizational "scaffolding" at the same time they have lost the "collateral" they have accumulated with peers and teachers during high school. College administrators, faculty, peers, and other individuals who interact with these students with ADHD might be less inclined to "cut them some slack" when they hand in assignments late or do not follow through on personal commitments.

College represents an opportunity for early detection and intervention for adult ADHD. After a rise from 2.2% to 8.8% between 1978 and 1991 (American Council on Education, 1995; as cited in Weyandt & DuPaul, 2006), the prevalence of college students reporting disabilities has leveled off at around 9% (Wolf, 2001). However, the number of college students with disabilities identified as learning disabled has steadily increased. Wolf (2001) estimated that of the 9% of 1st-year college students reporting a disability in 1998, 42% were learning disabled, including students with ADHD. This represented an increase of students with a learning disability from 25% and 32% in 1991 and 1994, respectively, although the actual number of students with ADHD is speculative because these students are not mandated to identify with the disability services office at their schools (Weyandt & DuPaul, 2006).

Individuals with ADHD are less likely to attend college than individuals without ADHD (Barkley, 2002a; Barkley, Murphy, & Fischer, 2008; K. R. Murphy, Barkley, & Bush, 2002; Wolf, 2001), and two thirds of students with learning or other disabilities (e.g., emotional disorders, ADHD) will drop out of college, compared with one third of students without disabilities (Wolf, 2001). College student counseling centers, student health centers, student learning centers, and offices of student disabilities are seeing a rise in the number of students requesting academic accommodations and seeking specialized academic support to help them manage their academic load. However, how colleges assess for learning disabilities and help students make use of the available support services varies greatly (Goad & Robertson, 2000).

For many adults with ADHD who were not diagnosed in childhood, college is the setting in which they first experience significant impairment associated with their symptoms. What is more, although children diagnosed with ADHD attend and complete college at lower rates than control participants without ADHD, effective treatment and academic services in primary and secondary school have probably helped many students with ADHD attend college who would not have been able to do so in past generations.

Various surveys of college populations (including a cross-national study) indicate that on average about 2% to 9% of college students fulfill diagnostic criteria for ADHD (DuPaul et al., 2001; Heiligenstein, Conyers, Berns, & Smith, 1998; B. H. Smith, Cole, Ingram, & Bogle, 2004; Weyandt, Linterman, & Rice, 1995). Heiligenstein et al. (1998) reported 4% prevalence in a sample of college students when using strict *DSM–IV* symptom criteria. When the criteria were modified to reflect students whose symptoms fell at least 1.5 standard deviations above the mean (e.g., 93rd percentile rank, which is a commonly used threshold for defining *clinical significance*), 11% of students were categorized with ADHD. B. H. Smith et al. (2004) reported an ADHD prevalence of 6.4% when using modified symptom cutoffs in a freshman sample.

Although college students with ADHD endorse significantly more symptoms of the disorder than do college student control groups without ADHD on self-report inventories, these college student control groups endorse more symptoms of ADHD than do their nonstudent, peer control participants (Barkley, 2002a; A. G. Harrison, 2004; Lewandowski, Lovett, Codding, & Gordon, 2008). This result reflects the demands that college makes on all students' capacities for attention, organization, and self-management. Rachal, Daigle, and Rachal (2007) surveyed a nonclinical sample of 485 undergraduate students about their academic difficulties. The majority of students reported multiple domains of learning problems, with the main areas classified as information processing (e.g., concentration, memory), reading and writing (e.g., slow reading, poor comprehension, difficulty organizing thoughts while writing), motivation (e.g., getting started on academic tasks), mathematics, and test taking. Consequently, some college students encountering academic difficulties for the first time may be misidentified with ADHD (Gordon, 2000). Moreover, some college students may exaggerate symptoms of ADHD in the effort to seek help for difficulties at college or as outright malingering for secondary gains of academic accommodations and possible misuse of prescription medication (A. G. Harrison, 2004, 2006). Thus, it is important that assessments for ADHD in college students include corroborative information regarding symptoms (e.g., parent reports) and impairment (e.g., grades) in addition to the standard assessment of symptoms and use of ADHD screening instruments to establish the diagnosis (Reilley, 2005).

Aside from the prevalence of symptoms, college students with ADHD are less likely to use effective coping skills to manage the academic and social transition to college; report higher levels of internal restlessness; experience more task-interfering, intrusive thoughts; report more depressive symptoms; and have lower grade point averages (GPAs) when compared with students without ADHD (Hines & Shaw, 1993; Rabiner, Anastopoulos, Costello, Hoyle, & Swartzwelder, 2008; G. Shaw & Giambra, 1993; Shaw-Zirt, Popali-Lehane, Chaplin, & Bergman, 2005; Turnock, Rosén, & Kaminski, 1998; Weyandt et al., 2003). Although clinical issues related to mood or anxiety symptoms, substance use, and self-esteem issues are commonly reported by students with ADHD (Dooling-Litfin & Rosén, 1997; Heiligenstein & Keeling, 1995; T. L. Richards, Rosen, & Ramirez, 1999; Shaw-Zirt et al., 2005; Weyandt, Rice, Linterman, Mitzlaff, & Emert, 1998), students with ADHD do not seem to be at greater risk of psychiatric diagnoses than their peers without ADHD (Heiligenstein, Guenther, Levy, Savino, & Fulwiler, 1999). However, students with ADHD seeking career advice had significantly lower mean GPAs and higher rates of academic probation than did students without ADHD (Heiligenstein et al., 1999).

Studies of neuropsychological functioning of college students with ADHD have generally indicated that their performance on intelligence tests is on par with their peers without ADHD, with mixed findings on studies of performance on various cognitive tasks (Reilley, 2005; Weyandt & DuPaul, 2006). Self-ratings of impulsivity were significantly and inversely correlated with grades in a nonclinical sample of college students, with higher scores on impulsivity associated with lower exam grades (Spinella & Miley, 2003). A study of divided attention (i.e., multitasking) on a computerized task found no differences between students with ADHD and students without ADHD, thus not supporting the notion that ADHD confers a heightened ability to simultaneously attend to multiple tasks (Linterman & Weyandt, 2001; Weyandt & DuPaul, 2006). Individuals with ADHD who attend college, particularly if they are not diagnosed until then, may represent a distinct subgroup with lower levels of impairment than individuals first diagnosed with ADHD in childhood (e.g., Barkley et al., 2008).

Recent research has focused on the specific academic strategies used by college students with ADHD. Reaser, Prevatt, Petscher, and Proctor (2007) compared the learning and study strategies of college students with ADHD, students with learning disorders (LD) without ADHD, and students without disorders as well as areas of strengths and weaknesses as measured by the Learning and Study Strategies Inventory (LASSI; C. E. Weinstein, Palmer,

& Schulte, 2002). Students with ADHD scored lower than both students with LD and students without disorders on measures of time management, concentration, selecting main ideas, and test strategies. The students with ADHD and the students with LD both scored lower than students without disorders on measures of motivation, anxiety, information processing, and self-testing, with the LASSI subscales of motivation and time management being the strongest predictors of college GPA (Rugsaken, Robertson, & Jones, 1998). Motivation and time management are particularly difficult issues for college students with ADHD. Within the ADHD group, analyses of strengths and weaknesses indicated that attitudes, information processing, and study aids emerged as areas of strength; test strategies, selecting main ideas, and concentration were areas of weakness.

Educational interventions are paramount for college students with ADHD. Although pharmacotherapy remains a cornerstone of treatment and there are models of psychosocial treatment for college students with ADHD (Ramsay & Rostain, 2006a; Schulenberg, Melton, & Foote, 2006; Wedlake, 2002), academic impairment is often the primary reason they seek help. Academic accommodations, including formal modifications of the standard teaching and testing approaches and informal environmental adjustments, the use of assistive technology, and specialized educational support, are the commonly prescribed educational interventions for college students with ADHD, all of which are reviewed in the following sections.

ACADEMIC ACCOMMODATIONS

The specific academic accommodations available to postsecondary students with ADHD vary across different institutions. The presumptive purpose of each accommodation is to counterbalance the effects of disabilities that put affected but otherwise qualified students at a disadvantage inasmuch as their disabilities interfere with the demonstration of their knowledge of a subject (Latham & Latham, 2007; Lewandowski, Lovett, Parolin, Gordon, & Codding, 2007).

Before reviewing some accommodations recommended for college students with ADHD, a few commonly misunderstood points should be clarified to provide an important context for this discussion. The first is that the presence of a disorder (e.g., ADHD or LD) itself is not sufficient to fulfill the legal requirements for establishing the presence of a *disability* as defined by the Americans With Disabilities Act ([ADA], 1990). The ADA requirements, which set the legal standard for obtaining services in school, specify that a disability is a physical or mental impairment that creates substantial functional limitations in at least one major life activity. That is, the disability results in a restriction of life activities with regard to the conditions, manner, or duration under which they can be carried out compared with most people.

Primary and secondary school students with ADHD and/or LD are protected under the Individuals With Disabilities Education Act (IDEA; 1990), the Individuals With Disabilities Education Improvement Act of 2004 (IDEA; 1990, 2004), and Section 504 of the Rehabilitation Act of 1973 (RA). ADHD is one of the conditions identified under these acts as potentially associated with disabilities in important psychological processes involved in learning. Although self-report and professional clinical documentation of impairment constituting a learning disability are required, once they are established, students are entitled to an Individualized Education Plan (IEP; Tudisco, 2007a) that makes provisions for special education services. Under RA, a specific accommodation plan (e.g., 504 Plan) is developed that includes strategies for helping students better manage their disabilities, such as reduced number of homework problems, limited distraction test-taking rooms, nurse administration of medications, and so on. The use of a 504 Plan does not necessitate classification of special education status, which might entail attending separate classes in some cases.

Public and private postsecondary institutions (except those that are controlled by religious organizations) are bound by ADA guidelines (1990), with institutions receiving federal funding subject to RA standards (Latham & Latham, 2007). Having had an IEP or 504 Plan prior to college is not sufficient evidence of disability to guarantee ongoing accommodations in college. Moreover, ADA and RA do not require institutions of higher education to provide individualized learning plans; rather, they are required to provide equal access to classrooms and educational materials, including modifications to courses and testing and access to auxiliary aids. Recent psychological testing (i.e., within the past 3 years) that identifies specific learning problems and recommends precise accommodations based on these learning problems is required for documentation.

Although there is the prerequisite of a significant functional limitation in a major life activity, what constitutes a "limitation" is difficult to quantify. The *average person standard* (Mapou, 2009) has emerged as a guiding principle for establishing impairment. That is, rather than defining *average* in terms of scores on tests, the average person standard focuses on the ability for individuals to perform tasks "in the way that most people do." Likewise, it is important to clearly specify the manner in which ADHD creates impairment in a "major life activity" and in the case of a learning impairment, the specific areas in which students experience difficulties for which accommodations may be indicated.

It is important for students with ADHD to self-report their disability to the office of disability services at their schools at the earliest opportunity.

Individuals may later decide not to use their accommodations, but it is usually desirable to go through the documentation process so that services are in place should they be needed. ADHD is a heterogeneous disorder. Therefore, two college students sharing the diagnosis may have very different symptom profiles that create different problems in academic settings, thus requiring different accommodation plans. (See Latham & Latham, 2007, and Tudisco, 2007a, for discussions of legal cases involving students with ADHD and the interpretation of what constitutes a disability.)

Standardized Testing Accommodations

Qualifying for accommodations on various high-stakes entrance exams is a different matter from pursuing typical academic accommodations (Mapou, 2009). The Educational Testing Service (ETS) administers the Scholastic Assessment Test (SAT) and Graduate Record Examination, the primary entrance exams for college and graduate school, respectively. Other high-stakes tests include the Medical College Admissions Test, Law School Admissions Test, and the Graduate Management Admission Test. Thus, ETS and various other testing and professional licensing agencies (e.g., law, medicine; see Ranseen, 1998) have strict guidelines regarding the documentation of any disability that qualifies an individual for standardized test-taking accommodations under ADA, with extended time the most common requested accommodation for the SAT, granted to about 2% of all SAT takers (Lindstrom & Gregg, 2007). For example, qualification for SAT accommodations requires proof that academic accommodations have been granted and used during high school and a comprehensive psychoeducational assessment confirming the presence of disability has been performed within the past 3 years. Most standardized exams for graduate school admission require proof that accommodations were granted and used during college as well as current documentation. It should be noted that although many testing agencies no longer flag test scores administered in a nonstandard manner (e.g., extended time), some continue to do so (Lindstrom & Gregg, 2007). As noted by Mapou (2009), the diverse guidelines and interpretations of ADA for postsecondary students with ADHD or LD may create scenarios in which individuals are identified as being "disabled" in some setting or for some tests and not for others.

Classroom Testing Accommodations

The ADA and RA mandate that colleges provide accommodations for their students with disabilities, including ADHD and LD (Latham & Latham, 2007; Mapou, 2009). Of course, the range of services available to students varies across different campuses (Weyandt & DuPaul, 2006). Some schools have a single staff person dedicated to working with students with disabilities; other schools have an entire office devoted to disability services, with various programs supporting the learning activities of students with disabilities, including ADHD; LD; and emotional, physical, and sensory disabilities. More and more colleges have programs and staff versed in the academic needs of students with ADHD or LD, and there are institutions identified as serving the educational needs of students with ADHD or LD.

Although the granting of accommodations and use of assistive technologies to mitigate the effects of ADHD seem eminently reasonable and logical, and many students describe them as being helpful, their effectiveness has simply not been well studied in samples of college students (Weyandt & DuPaul, 2006). For example, a study of the accommodation of extended time on a mathematics test revealed that there was no difference between middle-school-age students with and without ADHD with regard to gains made with extra time (Lewandowski et al., 2007). However, the performance of students with ADHD after extra time was equal to the performance of students without ADHD after standard time, similar to the findings obtained in a study of community college students taking an algebra test (Alster, 1997).

Extended time on tests to help remediate distractibility and slow processing speed is one of the more common accommodations granted to college students with ADHD. The common extension increments are 50% and 100% added to the scheduled length of a test. Although critics might contend that extended time would also improve the performance of individuals without ADHD or LD, available research does not support this contention. That is, additional time on tests administered in a classroom helped students with reading- or math-related disabilities, whereas it conferred no advantage on students without disabilities (Alster, 1997; Runyan, 1991). A review of SAT data comparing students with ADHD and/or LD who were granted extended time compared with control participants without ADHD or LD indicated that this accommodation did not alter the constructs measured by the Reasoning Test (Lindstrom & Gregg, 2007). On the other hand, testing situations involving a time component could be unfairly manipulated with increments of added time given that would eliminate group differences or otherwise change the nature of what is being tested (Lewandowski et al., 2007).

Traditional test taking can also be modified to take place in a small group or individual format to reduce distraction (i.e., distraction-reduced setting). Such environmental accommodations are designed to minimize the types of stimuli that most students screen out but that are very distracting to individuals with ADHD.

Individuals with ADHD may also benefit from being allowed to complete written exams on a laptop computer. This testing modification can be beneficial to individuals who experience difficulties related to slow, excessively effortful, or difficult-to-read handwriting, not to mention those students with a coexisting writing disorder. The use of a computerized document also helps to counteract cognitive-organizational difficulties experienced by individuals with ADHD as they organize and express their ideas in a written form. Students are still required to produce written content that adequately demonstrates their understanding and synthesis of course content. Disability offices often provide "clean" computers that do not have Internet access for such test taking to allay instructor concerns about academic integrity.

In some cases of slow processing speed, alternative examination formats can be administered to students. This sort of accommodation is less common in cases of students with ADHD, but use of oral examinations, take-home projects, or more frequent testing of smaller amounts of information are common alternative formats. There is a risk, however, that altering the format of a test too much may change the essential meaning of what is being tested (e.g., Latham & Latham, 2007; Lewandowski et al., 2007).

Test-taking accommodations represent only one subset of accommodations, although one that is viewed by skeptics as giving ADHD students an unfair advantage. It should be remembered that the purpose of granting accommodations is to help counteract the effects of a disability that unfairly impedes an individual's ability to demonstrate her or his academic performance. It does not change the academic content but rather focuses on various academic and learning processes that may place individuals with a learning (or other) disability at an unfair disadvantage.

Classroom, Housing, and Other Accommodations

Academic accommodations deal with the effects of ADHD not only in testing situations but also in the day-to-day classroom and studying environments. Classrooms, particularly large lecture halls, contain many distractions that make it difficult to attend to the lecture at hand. Sitting in the front rows of a class or securing guaranteed preferential front row seating in classes with assigned seating is a simple step to reduce distractibility for students with ADHD. Gaining permission to record lectures is another easy-to-implement strategy that allows students to review the lecture material and to clarify points that might have been unclear or missed altogether in a student's lecture notes, although it is time- and labor-intensive to review recordings.

Some students with ADHD find it difficult to take notes and listen to a lecture at the same time. Many colleges offer note-taking services, allowing students to concentrate on a lecture while still having access to adequate notes. However, students with ADHD are encouraged to take some notes, however incomplete, as a strategy to avoid having their focus drift away from the lecture topic, thereby defeating the very purpose of the note-taking service. The service is meant to provide a backup to reduce anxiety associated with inefficient note taking. Obtaining copies of an instructor's lecture notes or slides prior to class allows a student with ADHD to familiarize him- or herself with the content of the lecture beforehand and to have access to the information as it is being presented.

Many bureaucratic accommodations may affect academic performance for students with ADHD. Above all, identification and documentation of the fact that a student has ADHD with the campus office of student disabilities is required to secure the aforementioned official ADA and RA accommodations. Although many of the strategies discussed in this section can be implemented without the need for permission (e.g., sitting in the front row of class) or can be granted by instructors on an informal basis (e.g., access to instructor's lecture notes), official identification of disability status is necessary to secure support services offered by a college as well as ADA and RA protection.

Students with ADHD can be granted priority registration status to enroll in their preferred courses. ADHD might be a justification for exemption from, or course substitution for, required classes, such as foreign language or math courses, if these courses are not considered fundamental for a program (Latham & Latham, 2007). However, recent research has called into question the justification for granting students with ADHD exemption from foreign language requirements (Sparks, Javorsky, & Philips, 2005). A case review of 68 college students classified with ADHD by standards accepted by their school examined their performance in foreign language courses. Results indicated that students with ADHD obtained grades in foreign language courses that were generally above average and all students passed the foreign language requirement, although comparisons with grades from students without ADHD in similar courses were not performed. However, the study focused on students with ADHD (a) without a coexisting LD and (b) who were graduated within 5 years of starting college. Thus, it is unclear whether students with ADHD who encountered severe problems with the foreign language requirement might have chosen a major without this requirement, taken more than 5 years to graduate, or left school altogether and, thus, were not included in the analyses.

Permission to have a reduced course load during a semester is another potentially useful accommodation for otherwise qualified students for whom full course loads may prove overwhelming. Of course, the reduced-course-load strategy (and enrolling for summer classes) often results in a situation in which students with ADHD may require extended time to fulfill graduation requirements. Many students with ADHD require more than the traditional 4 years to complete their undergraduate education. In fact, Department of Education statistics indicate 5 years is roughly the median time required by students to complete college, with 58% of incoming 1st-year students in 1995–1996 having completed a bachelor's degree by 2001 (T. D. Snyder, Dillow, & Hoffman, 2007). Thus, the notion of the "4-year college" has become an oxymoron for most students. The extra semesters result in increased tuition and housing expenses, not to mention the possibility that status as a full-time student might be a requirement to obtain financial aid or to be covered under a parent's health insurance plan.

Attending a local community college is an option that increasing numbers of students are using, for both academic and financial reasons. Considering problems encountered by students with ADHD during the transition to college, attending community college may represent an intermediate step. Further, students with ADHD who experience difficulties at college necessitating a leave of absence—either those who entered college aware of their condition but soon faced problems or those who were identified after encountering unanticipated difficulties at college—might resume their academic journey by first taking courses at a community college.

Finally, regardless of the postsecondary academic institution attended, it is important for students with ADHD to appreciate the effects of their living and studying environments on their academic and personal well-being. That is, a diagnosis of ADHD is sufficient justification to petition for individual housing for individuals who may be distracted by living with a roommate. There may be limitations on this option with regard to the availability of housing at a particular institution. Even if individual housing is not available, there may be options for living on a dorm floor that is designated a "quiet study floor." Students with ADHD may have to seek out specific locations conducive to studying, such as remote sections of a library or empty classrooms. Students who live off campus might have to arrange to study in the library after classes or set up study areas in their residence. Even when such a study space is established, students with ADHD have to guard against excessive recreational use of the computer that may interfere with completing their work (Ko, Yen, Chen, Chen, & Yen, 2008). Although the housing accommodation is not necessary for most college students with ADHD, it is all too easy to underestimate the negative effects of a chaotic dorm environment on academic performance (see Ramsay & Rostain, 2005b, for a case example).

The aforementioned accommodations and coping strategies represent a menu of potentially helpful support services. There is no one-size-fits-all recommendation. In fact, some accommodations may be unhelpful for some students with ADHD, such as a distraction-reduced testing environment or single-student housing. Many formal and informal accommodations can be time consuming and require diligence to use, which can be particularly difficult for college students with ADHD. As with all services for ADHD, the potential risks and benefits of coping options should be analyzed.

Assistive Technology

A number of useful assistive technologies may be helpful for individuals with ADHD, particularly those with coexisting LD. These coping tools are often suggested as accommodations for specific learning problems, such as reading or writing disorders. These technologies include, but are not limited to, voice-activated software and textbooks on compact disc or digitized audio books that provide both audio and text presentations to address slow speed and poor comprehension while reading, to name but a few assistive technologies. Many standard gadgets of contemporary society, such as cell phones, personal digital assistants, and word processing software applications often have under-used features such as alarms, calendars, and highlighting features that students with ADHD may find helpful. A thorough review of assistive technologies is beyond the purview of this chapter (see Mapou, 2009; Tuckman, 2009).

Managing Extracurricular and Social Activities

Students with ADHD should be mindful of how commitments outside of the classroom might affect academic performance. The goal is not to elim-inate recreational and social activities but to strike the right balance between academics and other enriching activities. For example, the decision of whether to pledge a fraternity or sorority is an important one for many students. The Greek system is a central institution for social activities on many campuses. However, it often involves a significant time commitment during the pledge semester. Subsequently, once involved in a fraternity, there may be mandatory activities that interfere with schoolwork. The group living situation in a fra-ternity house might create significant distractions for students with ADHD, including risk factors for alcohol and substance abuse. That said, there also have been anecdotal accounts of students with ADHD benefiting from the scaffolding and organization provided by a fraternity, such as seeing fraternity brothers leaving for class being a reminder to attend class, and receiving infor-mal tutoring and support for difficult class material and assignments from other members of the fraternity (Rosenfield, Ramsay, & Rostain, 2008).

Participation in other groups or activities, such as the campus news-paper, a theater program, intramural sports, or a regular study group, is an important source of structure and support for students and provides opportu-nities to develop interests and abilities. On the other hand, although social and extracurricular activities are a vital component of a fulfilling college experience, students with ADHD who experience learning problems may be inclined to avoid feelings of frustration with their schoolwork by spending time with friends or participating in extracurricular activities, often at the expense of attending classes. Inordinate social activity by students with

ADHD often reflects an avoidant pattern in response to academic stress. More often, however, students with ADHD misjudge the commitment of time and effort required of school and campus activities, running the risk of overcommitting themselves and quickly becoming overwhelmed by both academics and activities.

RESEARCH ON SPECIALIZED ACADEMIC SUPPORT SERVICES

Postsecondary institutions are increasingly providing academic support services that are designed to assist students with ADHD to navigate the demands of school. Many college learning centers provide services to the student body at large, such as sessions on effective study strategies, time management, and organization skills. Learning specialists are also available for individual students to help them handle difficult courses or projects, such as setting up a study schedule or developing an outline for a paper.

Students with ADHD might benefit from standing appointments throughout the semester to monitor and manage their course work. Further, academic support counselors may emphasize and monitor issues related to organization, time management, and procrastination insofar as they affect other domains of college life, such as keeping up with laundry; prioritizing schedules; and keeping abreast of important dates, such as registration for classes or housing that tangentially affect academic performance. In some ways, academic counselors for college students with ADHD may serve a role akin to being executive functioning coaches (Parker & Byron, 1998).

As was mentioned in the previous chapter, although ADHD coaching is an increasingly popular coping option for adults with ADHD that seems as though it would be beneficial (e.g., N. A. Ratey, 2008), its effectiveness has not been systematically studied. However, three preliminary studies have examined academic coaching approaches for college students with ADHD and one involved high school students with ADHD.

Zwart and Kallemeyn (2001) administered a peer-based coaching program for college students to 22 college students with ADHD and/or LD. A group of 20 students with ADHD and/or LD who did not participate in coaching served as the control group. Participant students were identified if the documentation submitted to the office overseeing student disabilities confirmed the presence of an LD (i.e., ADHD) and recommended some sort of coaching support. The coaching group averaged about five or six sessions each through the semester, although the exact number of meetings was personalized to individual needs. The coaching program was conducted by student peer coaches who received training in issues related to ADHD and LD and were supervised throughout the program. The coaching sessions emphasized self-advocacy, time management, study skills, organizational skills, and the use of a planner.

Results indicated important pretreatment differences between the coaching and control groups, with the coaching group having a higher number of individuals with the diagnosis of ADHD (either alone or with LD). The control group also scored higher on the motivation and time management subscales of the LASSI. The coaching group improved on all subscales of the LASSI and on a measure of self-efficacy. The coaching group had significant improvements when compared with the control group on self-efficacy and the LASSI subscales of attitude, motivation, use of time management principles, anxiety, selecting main ideas, and test preparation. In fact, the control group's outcome scores on self-efficacy, attitude, motivation, and time management got worse in the course of the semester. When reanalyzing data after removing participants with LD only from the control group, self-efficacy and attitude were no longer significant.

The study provides preliminary data indicating that a peer-based coaching program can be helpful for college students with ADHD. There were important pretreatment differences between groups, and thus the findings should be reviewed with caution. However, a personalized coaching program produced desired improvements on many academic domains important to students with ADHD. It remains unclear which specific interventions proved most helpful for this group, although the authors indicated that it may have been the promotion of motivation and time management skills.

A single case report of an 8-week coaching program provided to a female student with ADHD indicated that the semester-long intervention was helpful (Swartz, Prevatt, & Proctor, 2005). Pre- and postintervention responses on the LASSI and The Coaching Topics Survey, a self-assessment of the amount of work required in various domains of personal and academic life, were gathered from the student. Over the course of the semester, the student reported improvements on eight out of nine Coaching Topics goals, and on four of seven goals measured by the LASSI. She met or exceeded her weekly goals for time spent studying 4 out of 7 weeks. Although useful in introducing and pilot testing a promising intervention, single case studies do not provide adequate evidence to establish the effectiveness of interventions.

Finally, Allsopp, Minskoff, and Bolt (2005) examined the effectiveness of a course-specific strategy instruction approach matched to the circumstances of each student in a larger study of college students with ADHD and other LDs. Students identified with ADHD and/or LD from three different colleges participated in the study, although there was interinstitutional variability in the assessment strategies used to document the presence of ADHD and/or LD. Nearly half of the 46 participants were on academic probation or suspension, indicating significant academic impairment.

Students in the study received individualized strategy instruction that was adapted to meet the identified learning needs of each student and to be relevant for the particular classes in which each student was enrolled. The researchers developed several measures of academic coaching goals and progress, including the Learning Needs Questionnaire to identify specific academic problems, Instructor and Participant Evaluation Forms to rate the effectiveness of coaching sessions, and Session Logs in which instructors summarized each session. Strategy instruction sessions introduced various learning strategies designed to improve participants' academic skills in problematic domains and kept learning strategies relevant to the content of the students' respective classes.

Results obtained by Allsopp et al. (2005) indicated that participants who completed a semester of instruction demonstrated significant improvements on overall GPA when compared with overall GPA before treatment. Similarly, there were significant improvements when comparing the GPA of the semester immediately preceding instruction with the GPA of the semester during which participants received instruction. Participants maintained these gains for at least one semester after instruction. Subsequent analyses of participants deriving the most benefit from academic coaching indicated that students who implemented the academic strategies taught to them significantly improved their GPAs, whereas participants who did not use the academic strategies taught to them, not surprisingly, did not improve their GPAs. Thus, factors significantly related to academic improvement associated with academic coaching for college students with ADHD were (a) the independent use of learning strategies and (b) a supportive relationship with the instructor (as assessed by instructors).

Allsopp et al.'s (2005) study findings are limited because a matched control group of students with similar academic problems who did not receive academic coaching was not used for comparison. Although it appears that the learning instruction contributed to the academic improvements, it is not clear whether students who encountered academic difficulties who did not receive specialized services would have reported improved GPAs the following semester as a result of regression to the mean, self-directed changes in study approaches, or some other factors. It would also be interesting to tease apart whether the mechanism of change in the coaching intervention is the introduction of new learning strategies or whether the agent of change is the interpersonal support and regular accountability provided by the tutor that helps students implement the learning strategies with which they were already familiar.

More recently, Merriman and Codding (2008) studied a coaching approach administered to three high school students with ADHD who were identified as having low grades in mathematics because of problems with homework completion. An initial coaching session involved goal setting. That is, students were encouraged to set long-term goals for homework completion and accuracy, with a commensurate short-term objective. Barriers to achieving these objectives as well as available resources and coping tools also were identified.

Each student met with a coach for 10 to 15 minutes each school day. Progress toward short-term objectives was assessed and monitored, and daily plans and short-term objectives were addressed and modified, as needed. Two of the students were able to make sufficient progress to reduce frequency of coaching sessions to every other day, then weekly, and finally termination when sustaining their long-term performance goals. The completion and accuracy of mathematics homework improved for all three students compared with their performance at baseline, although the third student's performance was variable throughout the intervention, and this student did not meet the original long-term goal set during the initial session. Although not involving postsecondary students, this study is reviewed because of the paucity of ADHD coaching studies as well as to illustrate the potential benefit of academic coaching to help students with ADHD follow through on the regular homework tasks that affect learning and academic performance. Follow-up measures were not available to determine whether students would have been able to sustain improved performance without coaching support. Further, the precise coaching interventions that proved helpful to students were not explained in detail.

Taken together, these four studies of academic coaching approaches for college (and high school) students with ADHD provide preliminary evidence that academic coaching has the potential to be a helpful intervention. However, more research is needed on this promising intervention.

CONCLUSION

Young adults with ADHD who are first diagnosed in adulthood often encounter their first significant coping difficulties in college. Thus, college counseling centers and student health clinics may represent the front lines of early intervention for adult ADHD. Although the use of academic accommodations is an accepted form of academic support, they have not been well studied in college students. However, preliminary positive results for academic coaching and strategy instruction approaches warrant further research that may provide these students with the coping support necessary to help them make the most of their educational abilities and opportunities (see Table 3.1).

TABLE 3.1
Summary of Academic Support and Accommodations for Postsecondary
Students With Attention-Deficit/Hyperactivity Disorder (ADHD)

Academic interventions	Strengths	Limitations	Current status and future directions
Academic accommodations	Designed to address the effects of disability Personalized support Administered at point of performance	No research support for recommendations Disclosure and documentation required for legal protection	Legally protected, accepted modifications Accommodations make pragmatic sense but there is no outcome research on their efficacy Further research is needed to further guide accommodation selection
Academic support or coaching	Promising pilot research Personalized support for managing executive functioning deficits Direct relevance for academic impairments Targets important skills	No formal protocols outlining interventions Based on preliminary research Requires adherence Limited availability	Encouraging preliminary results Need randomized controlled studies Future studies needed to identify the essential elements of academic support and whether they outperform standard approaches

4

CAREER COUNSELING AND WORKPLACE SUPPORT

Individuals for whom high school marks the end of their formal education often view the workplace as a refuge from the classroom and a means for establishing one's adult identity. Individuals with attention-deficit/hyperactivity disorder (ADHD), in particular, seek jobs that allow them to put to good use their skills and aptitudes and that do not emphasize various academic skills that may represent areas of relative weakness for them. Young adults with ADHD who attend college and possibly pursue subsequent graduate or professional education do so with the goal of eventually establishing a professional niche. Regardless of one's particular occupational path, the ability to function in a work setting, including self-employment and stay-at-home parenting, is an inescapable feature of adult life that requires individuals to function relatively independently in terms of organization; time management; planning, prioritizing, and following through on tasks; and other skills related to self-management.

Although the academic demands of school can be very stressful for individuals with ADHD, the workplace presents similar challenges for adults with ADHD. Because adults in the workplace are expected to function independently with minimal supervision, ineffective self-management and organizational strategies create many problems with potentially serious consequences.

Students encountering academic difficulties may have access to support in the form of tutoring, or buffers, such as an interesting course, a positive connection with a teacher, or participation in extracurricular activities, each of which may promote a sense of confidence and competence. Even when facing extreme educational difficulties, students with ADHD may take heart from the knowledge that, should all else fail, if they can just stick it out, they will eventually reach the end of the semester or school year and be able to start over with a new teacher and a clean slate.

There is no end of the school year for workers with ADHD, and the consequences of impairment in the workplace can be particularly damaging. Although there is flexibility inasmuch as adults can choose to leave an unsatisfactory job for a better one, costs may be associated with starting over, such as loss of seniority, a cycle of being stuck in entry-level positions, and potential disruption in other aspects of life, such as loss of health care coverage and relocation costs. Whereas students have access to support services in school and (in most cases) do not have to simultaneously focus on managing a household, adult workers with ADHD do not have such support services available to them and have the added responsibility of organizing and managing personal affairs, including supporting their families. Thus, workplace impairments stemming from adult ADHD have significant ripple effects.

The twofold focus of this chapter is on interventions designed to help adults with ADHD with their (a) job choice and (b) job performance. Despite recent groundbreaking research outlining the degree of occupational underperformance of adults with ADHD when compared with control groups without ADHD (Barkley, Murphy, & Fischer, 2008), there is no empirical guidance regarding approaches for helping individuals choose occupations or interventions to improve work performance. However, some career counseling and workplace support approaches are being developed that are available for adults with ADHD looking for help specific to job-related issues. The next section provides an overview of the research on ADHD and workplace functioning. Subsequent sections review career counseling and workplace accommodations for adults with ADHD, respectively.

RESEARCH ON ADULTS WITH ADHD IN THE WORKPLACE

Along with college, the workplace is a setting in which many adults with ADHD first experience significant impairments for which they seek professional help. Research on adults with ADHD has consistently shown that they report higher rates of unemployment and lower rates of full-time employment than do workers without ADHD, as well as lower performance ratings (Barkley et al., 2008; Biederman et al., 2006; G. Weiss & Hechtman, 1993).

Recently published research has expanded understanding of the experience of adults with ADHD on the job.

On a societal economic level, a diagnosis of ADHD is associated with significantly greater health care costs, both for individual adults and families with at least one member with ADHD when compared with families without a member with ADHD (Birnbaum et al., 2005; Swensen et al., 2003). About one fourth of a sample of Swedish workers on long-term sick leave for emotional exhaustion syndrome on the job (i.e., burnout) fulfilled screening criteria for ADHD (Brattberg, 2006), and workers with ADHD reported significantly higher rates of sickness absence in a study of a manufacturing firm in the United States (Kessler, Lane, Stang, & Van Brunt, 2009).

Workers with ADHD earn significantly lower salaries than their coworkers without ADHD (Biederman et al., 2006), although this may be, in part, the result of lower educational attainment, which correlates with lower earning potential. However, low salaries might also result from work histories punctuated by being dismissed for poor performance, quitting from boredom, or escaping an overwhelming job by switching to a new one (Barkley et al., 2008). Upwards of 35% of a sample of adults with ADHD was self-employed by their 30s (Faraone & Biederman, 2005a). Although this might be a calculated and positive career choice arrived at by many individuals with ADHD, for others it is a default option after being unable to hold other jobs. Self-employment has its own unique challenges, such as scheduling and billing details that demand a high degree of discipline and organization, or at least the aid of a skilled assistant— very often a spouse without ADHD—to manage (Eakin et al., 2004).

In terms of individual productivity on the job, workers with ADHD report high rates of both absenteeism (i.e., not attending work) and "presenteeism" (i.e., attending work but being underproductive), which add up to over 3 weeks lost productivity each year when compared with workers without ADHD in both U.S. and international samples (de Graaf et al., 2008; Kessler, Adler, Ames, Barkley, et al., 2005; Kessler et al., 2009). The cumulative cost of workplace inefficiency associated with ADHD numbers in the tens of millions of dollars in salary-equivalent loss for the U.S. economy. The cost for individual households in which at least one worker has ADHD is around $10,000 per year per household in lost income. Workers with ADHD also have higher rates of on-the-job accidents and injuries than control groups (Kessler et al., 2009). Apart from the financial effects of ADHD on workplace productivity, likely untold costs are workplace stress, frustration, and job insecurity, not to mention the negative effects of these factors on one's future plans, including retirement planning (Barkley et al., 2008).

Using a simulated workplace environment to systematically compare adults with and without ADHD on a number of occupational skills, Biederman, Mick, et al. (2005) reported that unmedicated adults with ADHD had significantly greater difficulties performing a variety of work-related tasks as measured by a combination of task performance, self-reports, and blind rating scales. More specifically, adults with ADHD exhibited impaired reading comprehension and math fluency. Although there were no differences in performing logic problems, written tasks, or comprehending video presentations, individuals with ADHD exhibited more behavioral difficulties during these tasks (e.g., getting started on morning reading task) than did control participants without ADHD. Self-ratings of inattention and hyperactivity revealed that adults with ADHD reported significantly more restlessness and hyperactivity than control participants, although there was no difference in overall ratings of inattention. The lack of significant differences on observer and self-ratings of inattention might not indicate that participants with ADHD were necessarily attentive. That is, perhaps the attention difficulties experienced by adults with ADHD have been masked by procrastination behaviors that are more easily observed and contributed to their obvious difficulties completing tasks.

Pharmacotherapy can be very helpful for adult workers with ADHD by helping to improve their executive functioning. Similarly, many of the nonmedication treatment approaches for adult ADHD are geared to help patients increase their use of effective coping skills to manage various life situations, including in the workplace. Consequently, psychosocial treatment can be helpful for employees who experience stress and frustration related to difficulties keeping up the demands of work, although it is unclear how well the actual implementation of skills generalizes from the consulting room to the office. Just as college students with ADHD may require specialized educational interventions and accommodations, workers with ADHD may require specialized job counseling and occupational support.

Unfortunately, to date there have been no outcome studies of career counseling or workplace interventions or accommodations for adult ADHD. Of course, these are challenging research domains because it is difficult to quantify effectiveness outcomes in career counseling, and although workplace issues are often a focus of psychosocial treatment, it is difficult to measure the effectiveness of workplace accommodations and other workplace interventions. However, considering the occupational impairment associated with adult ADHD, the following sections provide a review of career counseling and workplace accommodation and coping strategy approaches.

CAREER COUNSELING

No jobs can be considered ADHD-specific. However, niche-selection theory (Scarr & McCartney, 1983) suggests that individuals with particular temperaments or personality features selectively seek relationships and environments compatible with these characterological tendencies. Along those lines, a national survey of workers in a variety of professions found that people in occupations without the constraints of a traditional office (e.g., carpenter, electrician, gardener, entertainer, elected official) are more likely to exhibit features of ADHD than people employed in an office, bank, or retail store as a clerk (Attention Deficit Disorder Association [ADDA], 2006a). However, a job or career choice is a personalized undertaking that involves a myriad of personal and pragmatic factors, not the least of which is the effects of ADHD.

Career counseling is a field devoted to helping individuals make informed choices about their occupational paths (e.g., Fellman, 2006). Career counseling sessions can be helpful for college students seeking guidance as they enter the workforce at the start of their careers or for individuals who have already worked in particular positions but who are exploring new career paths. Much of the counseling work involves finding an adequate match of an individual's personality and work skills and the demands of a particular job. High school guidance counselors often serve a similar role in helping graduating high school students identify potential occupational or educational paths consistent with their skills and temperaments (Schwiebert, Sealander, & Dennison, 2002).

Although it is hard enough for adults with ADHD to find a mental health professional familiar with the diagnosis and treatment of ADHD, it is even more difficult to find a career counselor trained in issues associated with ADHD and other learning disabilities. In many cases, mental health clinicians specializing in adult ADHD also serve as de facto career counselors for their patients (Nadeau, 2005).

Although career counseling for adults with ADHD has no empirical evidence with which to guide occupational recommendations (Schwiebert et al., 2002), Nadeau (2005) outlined some components of a career and workplace assessment. The bulk of the assessment involves conducting an accurate and comprehensive evaluation for adult ADHD, including neurocognitive testing to measure individuals' relative strengths and weaknesses on various cognitive skills. The diagnostic assessment and clinical interview is used to confirm the presence of impairment associated with symptoms of ADHD and to identify comorbid conditions. The features of the career and workplace assessment that might not be common to an adult ADHD evaluation are (a) personality testing to identify aspects of temperament that may affect job choice and (b) interest testing to determine goodness of fit between individuals' interests and potential job choices.

The results of personality and interest testing as well as a work history are reviewed to determine the long-standing tendencies of the individual and matching them to preferred work situations to fashion a good match of personality and job requirements (Crawford & Crawford, 2002; Fellman,

2006; National Resource Center on AD/HD [NRC], 2003c). Thus, an individual with an outgoing, extraverted personality who is not particularly detail oriented would probably not function well as an accountant working alone. In fact, many job problems are presumed to be the result of a poor fit between a worker's skills and sensitivities and the demands of a position (Crawford & Crawford, 2002).

Adults with ADHD often have more numerous and delicate sensitivities to various environmental stimuli than workers without ADHD. What is more, individuals with ADHD often experience confounding symptoms insofar as they undermine their strengths and the gratifying aspects of their work, such as an individual skilled with computers but who has difficulty reading through and comprehending the technical manuals for new software. Likewise, an individual who is an excellent consultant might have trouble producing brief summary reports for her clients. These individuals face obstacles related to ADHD despite holding jobs for which they are otherwise well suited.

Taking an extensive occupational history is an important aspect of an ADHD diagnostic evaluation, particularly when seeking career counseling or exploring job options as an aspect of psychosocial treatment. The workplace represents a context in which individuals with ADHD commonly experience impairment (Barkley et al., 2008). In the case of patients seeking treatment associated with work issues, reviewing examples of past workplace-related problems helps identify recurring patterns, including difficulties with specific tasks as well as interpersonal issues that may have arisen with supervisors or coworkers. For newly diagnosed adults, this sort of review helps to foster an understanding and acceptance of the influence of ADHD on work life as part of the psychoeducation component of treatment. In the context of career counseling, the occupational review helps inform a realistic approach to finding appropriate jobs for the prospective worker with ADHD.

In fact, unrealistic expectations regarding feasible job options, which can take the form of either overconfidence in one's ability to cope or excessively low expectations, is a common problem encountered in career counseling with adults with ADHD (Crawford & Crawford, 2002). Thus, counseling sessions focus on a thorough appraisal of an individual's relative strengths and weaknesses, including the possible effects of ADHD in different work settings. Individual factors, such as dependency, perfectionism, insecurity, or a lack of trial-and-error learning experiences in life might also affect adults with ADHD seeking work (Crawford & Crawford, 2002; Nadeau, 2005). It is important to help adults with ADHD understand and appreciate their job-related strengths and resilience factors that can be assets on the job (Nadeau, 2005). Bolstering self-esteem and promoting individuals' sense of efficacy and control, motivation, creative problem solving, and normalizing the need for persistence are important ways career counselors target factors that will increase the likelihood of a successful vocational match (Carroll & Ponterotto, 1998; Crawford & Crawford, 2002; Nadeau, 2005).

Although the issue of job and career choice is important for individuals with ADHD, nuanced difficulties related to the actual workplace environment and specific job duties also cause difficulties for workers with ADHD. For example, research on procrastination has indicated that blue-collar workers are less susceptible to putting off work than are white-collar workers, presumably because there are more immediate and salient environmental contingencies in manual labor (Hammer & Ferrari, 2002). These findings are consistent with a survey of adult ADHD workers that suggested the time-sensitive nature of a job (i.e., jobs requiring immediate response, such as law enforcement or construction) might moderate a tendency to procrastinate (ADDA, 2006a).

The assessment of goodness of fit goes beyond the congruence of worker strengths and weaknesses and ADHD symptom profile with specific job requirements. Day-to-day issues related to individuals' stress tolerance, personal values and temperaments, working pace, interests, commute, family considerations (e.g., child care), and so on, are standard components of career counseling (Nadeau, 2005). Workers with ADHD might have to consider issues related to the flexibility of a work schedule, such as arrival time at the office or length of the work day, with regard to one's ability to wake up in the morning and timing of medications. Some individuals experience sensory sensitivities that could affect performance in various occupational settings, such as finding the typical sounds of an office distracting, being bothered by fluorescent lighting, or lacking a quiet work space (Nadeau, 2005). Review of the safety of specific jobs is also useful, as recent research has indicated that college students with the inattentive type of ADHD tend to attribute less importance to workplace safety factors than do college students without ADHD or those with ADHD, combined type (Canu, 2007). Symptoms of inattention are commonly observed by supervisors and may contribute to functional difficulties on the job (Barkley et al., 2008). Workers without ADHD may view these items as minor details; however, it is important to review them with ADHD workers and to consider their potential impact on work performance.

In summary, it is important for adults with ADHD to use self-knowledge of their symptom profiles and their personality styles to pursue job opportunities that offer a good fit and a high likelihood of success and satisfaction. There are no "ADHD jobs," just as there are no "perfect" jobs. Once situated in a job, however, people turn their focus to job performance. Consequently, making use of coping strategies and accommodations to the workplace environment may be helpful for effectively managing symptoms of ADHD at work.

WORKPLACE ACCOMMODATIONS AND COPING STRATEGIES

The field of ADHD coaching that was discussed in chapter 2 developed as an offshoot of the life and executive coaching fields. ADHD coaching has a specific emphasis on helping adults with ADHD to better manage chronic difficulties with planning, organizing, and following through on various projects, particularly in the workplace. As was mentioned earlier, there is one published study of the efficacy of ADHD coaching (Kubik, 2009). It would seem logical, though, that having access to coping support, timely feedback, and accountability closer to the point of performance in the office or other work settings would be helpful for adults with ADHD.

Although not stated explicitly, the presumption is that ADHD coaching specializes in helping employees with office-based jobs that require many of the same skills as a classroom (e.g., planning, organizing). Many individuals work in jobs that make it difficult to take full advantage of the timely support and accountability afforded by coaching. It is unclear how coaching would be used to support individuals at the point of performance in, say, blue-collar jobs, retail settings, or restaurant work. Although these hands-on jobs might be somewhat immune to procrastination because they are performed in group settings and involve immediate task demands, disorganization and poor time management could negatively affect work performance on some important tasks, such as paperwork and scheduling.

Moreover, not everyone has access to ADHD coaching. Pharmacotherapy, again, represents the most effective and convenient intervention for symptoms that interfere with workplace functioning. Dosing patterns can be individualized to meet the job demands on workers with ADHD, such as prescribing long-acting medications for adequate treatment coverage during work hours, with augmentation with short-acting medications, depending on the length of the work day (Barkley et al., 2008).

That being said, making changes to the work environment, implementing accommodations, and using coping strategies to better manage interference from symptoms can be very helpful, as medications do not necessarily result in improved coping skills. Seeking specialized assistance from individuals well versed in vocational rehabilitation and accommodations (e.g., Americans With Disabilities Act [ADA], 1990) is indicated in cases of significant occupational impairment.

Requesting reasonable accommodations in the workplace is trickier than doing so in college. The ADA and the Rehabilitation Act of 1973 (RA) are the two laws designed to protect workers with disabilities, including ADHD (see Latham & Latham, 2002, 2007; Tudisco, 2007b). The RA is a statute that applies to federal agencies, federal contractors, or institutions that accept federal funding to ensure that individuals with physical or mental disabilities are not discriminated against. The ADA has the same purpose and definition of disability as the RA, although it is not limited to workplaces receiving federal funding. The ADA applies to all private employers with more than 15 employees as well as state and local governments and licensing agencies.

The requirement to demonstrate and document the specific negative effects of ADHD such that it constitutes a disability is the same as it is for college—the diagnosis of ADHD alone is not sufficient. There must be documentation that ADHD substantially limits an individual's functioning in a major life activity compared with the manner in which the "average person" in the population performs it. It is easier to document the specific negative effects of ADHD on learning issues in a school setting than it is to document how these same problems affect workplace functioning. Moreover, people with conditions that are remedied or well managed by treatment, surgery, or coping strategies (e.g., ADHD effectively treated with medications) may not have been considered disabled under ADA or RA law (Latham & Latham, 2002), although recent amendments to ADA have established that adequate treatment or remediation does not diminish one's status as being disabled (Long, 2008). Finally, individuals claiming disability from ADHD must be "otherwise qualified" for the job, school, or license for which they are applying.

Whereas colleges often have student disability offices and are equipped to grant most accommodations with little difficulty, many job sites or human resource departments might not be equipped to provide various accommodation requests or could claim that instituting proposed modifications would represent an undue hardship. Furthermore, in addition to documentation of disability, employees with ADHD must meet the minimum requirements of the job. Whereas admission to a college fulfills minimum requirements of being a student, and grades, although imperfect, provide a measure of academic progress, the definition of "minimum requirements" and assessment of work performance vary across jobs and are difficult to quantify. Finally, the effects of ADHD could be considered to interfere with a worker's ability to meet the minimum requirements of some jobs.

The ADA Amendments Act of 2008 was recently signed into law and is meant to address the results of court cases that have led to a restrictive definition of "disabilities" that seemed in conflict with the original spirit of the ADA (Long, 2008). In general, the 2008 amendments to ADA expand the definition of what constitutes a disability. Relevant to adults with ADHD, the determination of a disability that severely limits a major life activity can now be made without regard to mitigating treatment or coping (e.g., medications, compensations). Moreover, the 2008 amendments explicitly enumerate learning, reading, concentrating, and thinking among major life activities that can be considered impaired and limited by a disability. Although the definition of "reasonable accommodations" remains murky, the aforementioned revisions to ADA address some areas of controversy that had limited protections for disabled workers.

Not all employers are motivated or legally obligated to accommodate workers with ADHD. Recall that ADA requirements apply only to private businesses with 15 or more employees. Smaller, private businesses are not obligated to provide accommodations. What is more, even if disabilities are demonstrated and documented, particular accommodations, although potentially helpful for a worker with ADHD, might not be "reasonable" insofar as they cause an undue financial hardship for the employer; however, most accommodations cost less than $500 (Fellman, 2006).

There is no clear guideline for determining whether workers should disclose their diagnosis of ADHD to employers (Fellman, 2006; Tudisco, 2007b). It is truly a decision that must be made on a case-by-case basis. Individuals are not legally obligated to disclose their ADHD to their employers unless they are requesting formal workplace accommodations, a circumstance in which it is preferable to disclose as early as possible. Some individuals express concern that they will be treated differently than coworkers and that the information may put them in a negative light, a concern that has some support from recent research. Individuals rated vignettes describing people with ADHD more negatively than they rated vignettes of people with medical problems or vague difficulties (e.g., perfectionism; Canu, Newman, Morrow, & Pope, 2008). However, a different study also using ratings of vignettes found that preventative disclosure was associated with less socially rejecting attitudes by raters (Jastrowski, Berlin, Sato, & Davies, 2007).

In fact, some workers report that their disclosure has enabled them to receive informal accommodations from their bosses and, in some cases, to discover that supervisors or coworkers have experienced ADHD, either personally or through family members. However, these disclosures usually occurred after the workers with ADHD had established themselves in their positions, demonstrated a degree of proficiency, and consequently possessed some leverage when making their informal requests. Individuals who disclose during the interview process in an attempt to be forthright about their condition run the risk of being rejected for a job ostensibly for other reasons (although it should also be noted that employers might hire a different applicant for legitimate reasons, such as previous experience, specific training, etc.).

Workers with ADHD who choose to not disclose their diagnosis or who work in a job not covered by ADA law can implement personal coping strategies or informal accommodations. A common personal accommodation made by workers with ADHD is to spend extra hours at the office to complete work. Ironically, although the extra time is made necessary by inefficient work habits earlier in the day, staying late may result in the perception that the worker is particularly dedicated. However, when employees are paid hourly and are entitled to overtime pay, the extra hours are likely to be met with resistance from employers. Moreover, these extra hours at work can have negative effects on the personal lives of the workers with ADHD.

In cases in which an employee with ADHD is more productive during specific hours of the day than others, or simply has difficulties getting to work on time in the morning, flexible work hours could be informally negotiated with a supervisor. Flex time provides employees latitude with which to fulfill their requisite weekly hours at work. Similar accommodations are often granted to employees who have conflicts during work hours because of child care arrangements, regular medical appointments, and various other legitimate reasons. Individuals who have difficulty arriving on time or getting work done in the morning may contract to arrive, for example, at 11 a.m. and work until 7 p.m. The specifics of what works for an individual should be negotiated with a supervisor, including the potential benefit for the employer of granting the accommodation (e.g., "Let's monitor my productivity over the next 3 months to see if it makes a difference").

Having an individual office rather than a shared office or open cubicle space helps reduce the effects of environmental distractions. Some offices have open-door policies requiring that a worker is accessible to others at all times. A reasonable accommodation is to have certain times dedicated to completing work-related tasks during which the employee with ADHD is allowed to close the door, silence the phone, and so on, to create a minimal-distraction environment.

Computers are ubiquitous in most work settings, and it can be helpful for workers with ADHD to have access to adequate software for assistance with reading, writing (including voice-activated word processing), and scheduling systems, similar to the assistive technologies beneficial for college students with learning difficulties. Dictation services might also be available in certain settings, and ADHD workers should take advantage of such services when available. Compatible technologies, such as personal digital assistants or cell phones with scheduling systems that can be synchronized with the personal computer at work can be important tools with which to improve planning, time management, and organization.

Much of business is done interpersonally in the form of meetings or receiving verbal instructions from a supervisor. The coping skill of repeating and summarizing a job assignment, getting confirmation from the supervisor, and writing down detailed instructions necessary to complete the assignment are good coping skills. Obtaining follow-up written confirmation (paper or e-mail) of expectations and instructions is a useful backup for spotty memory (although it is a good practice for any worker). Written summaries of group meetings (akin to a note-taking service for college students) are useful for workers with ADHD. This sort of accommodation allows the worker to focus attention on the content of the meeting and later to have a concise summary of the main points.

If possible, a weekly performance meeting with a supervisor offers a useful way to track progress on work assignments and to provide reminders or clarification of expectations. Regularly scheduled meetings regarding specific, large tasks can also help the worker with ADHD to break down large projects into smaller units with discrete deadlines for each unit instead of working under a looming final deadline for the entire project. Furthermore, this approach offers more regular feedback, both encouragement and corrective problem solving, to hopefully avoid last-minute surprises that could jeopardize a project and, in turn, an ADHD employee's performance review.

Some jobs involve significant reading to keep up with new developments in the field or for required continuing education. When available, books on compact disc are an alternative for individuals who are slow readers or have comprehension difficulties. In the case of various trainings that might be required for a job, either for purposes of professional certification or simply to learn new office procedures (e.g., new software or voice mail system), individuals with ADHD may require additional one-on-one support and hands-on practice to fully comprehend and implement the new skill.

Most of these coping suggestions can be implemented informally without necessarily disclosing one's diagnosis of ADHD. In fact, many individuals without ADHD find these coping strategies helpful, such as someone who is not technically proficient asking the "computer person" in the office to guide them through the use of new software or requesting periodic check-in meetings with a supervisor on a large project. In some cases, however, more significant modifications of job responsibilities or a position change might be necessary to moderate the negative effects of ADHD.

Outwardly positive changes in job status and responsibilities can prove overwhelming for some workers with ADHD. For example, a worker might be promoted to a supervisory or project coordinator role that calls for stellar time management, organization, and prioritization skills and requiring her or him not only to manage personal work performance but also to facilitate the productivity of other workers. Such a role could easily prove to be a poor fit for the worker with ADHD. To address the problem, the worker could be returned to the previous position or an alternate work role could be found if the demands of the new position prove unmanageable. In cases in which a specific job task is inordinately difficult for a worker with ADHD to complete in an otherwise appropriate position, job requirements could be modified to shift the problematic task to another worker and the worker with ADHD could take on an equivalent task that is more conducive with his or her skills.

On the other hand, a promotion to a supervisory level can be beneficial for someone with ADHD if the new role carries with it the added benefits of greater administrative support, such as an assistant whose job it is to orchestrate and monitor various organizational and scheduling details. Similar to career counseling approaches for adults with ADHD discussed earlier, dealing with workplace issues for adults with ADHD involves the ongoing assessment of the goodness of fit of specific job assignments and an individual's skills and weaknesses and attempting to find ways to effectively manage the demands of the environment.

The workplace accommodations mentioned above represent a wide range of possibilities, from those that are relatively common in office settings (e.g., a person assigned to keep the minutes of a meeting) to those that represent special services that would require the cooperation and funding of an employer (e.g., hiring a personal administrative assistant or a job coach). The assumption underlying these coping options is that the worker with ADHD has demonstrated an ability to meet the basic demands of the job but that impairment associated with symptoms interferes with some aspects of job performance. Most of the accommodations represent coping strategies that do not require documentation of disability to implement on an informal basis (for other accommodations and coping strategies, see Fellman, 2006; Grossberg, 2005; Latham & Latham, 2007; Mapou, 2009; and NRC, 2003c).

In sum, it is important for workers with ADHD to have an understanding of precisely how their symptoms affect their functioning in the workplace. From this self-understanding, individualized coping strategies can be developed to set up a plan for success, consulting with an ADHD coach, therapist, vocational counselor, or others who can provide direction and encouragement.

CONCLUSION

Regardless of when individuals are diagnosed with ADHD, they will eventually have to address how their symptoms affect workplace functioning. Although some individuals experience mild symptoms or work in settings that represent good fits for them, many others will encounter difficulties on the job that will require taking active steps to manage. The workplace is considered a domain of life in which ADHD has profound negative effects on workers; it is also an area in which there has been no outcome research on the potential benefits of nonmedication interventions on occupational functioning. However, it is a domain of study and for intervention that could be fruitful, particularly for most adults with ADHD (see Table 4.1).

TABLE 4.1
Summary of Career Counseling and Workplace Support
for Adults With Attention-Deficit/Hyperactivity Disorder (ADHD)

Workplace interventions	Strengths	Limitations	Current status and future directions
Career counseling	Systematic approach for exploring aptitudes, interests, and job options Available at most postsecondary schools	No research Hard to quantify outcomes Cost for adults seeking private career counseling Hard to find counselors with ADHD expertise	Useful service Research might identify areas of concern in occupational settings that are particularly relevant for adults with ADHD Studies might also assess if career counseling outperforms standard job or career search behaviors
Workplace accommodations	Personalized support Designed to address specific work impairments Administered at point of performance Many useful informal accommodations	Hard to secure legally mandated work accommodations Unclear whether workplace approaches are effectively instituted without medications No outcome research	Workplace coping strategies are pragmatic and acceptable Target an important area of impairment Systematic research of accommodations and related interventions (e.g., ADHD coaching) is needed

5

RELATIONSHIPS AND
SOCIAL FUNCTIONING

Freud is said to have described the two elements of a fulfilled life as "to love and to work" (Erikson, 1963, p. 265). Although it may represent an all-too-neat dichotomization, most people derive a sense of overall well-being from striking the right balance between, on the one hand, developing a sense of efficacy in the ability to accomplish goals (i.e., "to work") and, on the other hand, having relationships that are sufficient in number and quality to provide a sense of connection (i.e., "to love"). Although copious literature exists on the negative effects of attention-deficit/hyperactivity disorder (ADHD) on the areas of life from which individuals derive a sense of autonomy and efficacy, namely school and work, there is less research documentation of the negative effects of adult ADHD on social functioning. However, there is a growing appreciation of the interpersonal costs of adult ADHD (e.g., Halverstadt, 1998; National Resource Center on AD/HD [NRC], 2003b; Novotni & Petersen, 1999; Pera, 2008).

Drawing on social support from trusted friends, mentors, or support meetings is a common feature of the psychoeducational and coping suggestions for managing adult ADHD. Many individuals with ADHD, however, harbor feelings of shame and embarrassment related to their circumstances and life stories. Adults with ADHD often struggle with some form of isolation or a sense of not fitting in, either having lost social connections as a downstream consequence of dropping out of school, repeated job changes, or having difficulty maintaining relationships.

The purpose of this chapter is to review the various ways in which adult ADHD affects interpersonal functioning. Even mild symptoms of ADHD can cause difficulties in circumscribed relationships or may create global skill deficits across most social interactions. Research on the negative effects of ADHD on social functioning as well as the clinical intervention literature is reviewed. More specifically, family therapy, marital therapy, and social skills training for adults with ADHD are discussed. For consistency and clarity, the phrase "marital therapy" is used throughout the chapter to refer to treatment for couples in any sort of committed relationship in which improving their partnership is a central goal of therapy and is not limited to people in traditional marriages.

REVIEW OF RELATIONSHIP AND SOCIAL FUNCTIONING PROBLEMS

Although the negative effects of adult ADHD on educational and occupational pursuits have been well documented, the past few years have seen a rise in the study of the interpersonal effects of the disorder. The following sections review the multiple domains of social functioning that are impacted by ADHD.

ADHD and Families

Families affected by ADHD experience diverse and significant stressors compared with community control families, reporting types and levels of dysfunction similar to clinic-referred families without members who have ADHD (Barkley, Murphy, & Fischer, 2008; Lange et al., 2005). Families with children or teens who have ADHD exhibit less warmth, less engagement, and use less effective communication strategies. Parents in these families rate themselves lower on measures of parenting efficacy; children report higher levels of rejection by their parents; and families report and exhibit higher levels of conflict than do families without members who have ADHD (Edwards, Barkley, Laneri, Fletcher, & Metevia, 2001; Johnston & Jassy, 2007; Johnston & Mash, 2001; Lange et al., 2005; Lifford, Harold, & Thapar, 2008; Minde et al., 2003; Pressman et al., 2006; Tripp, Schaughency, Langlands, & Mouat, 2007).

ADHD subtype and comorbidity profiles also differentiate families of ADHD children. Families of children with ADHD, combined type, experience greater adversity than families with children with inattentive type (Counts,

Nigg, Stawicki, Rappley, & von Eye, 2005). Families of children with ADHD and anxiety, although reporting similar levels of dysfunction as families of children with ADHD but without anxiety, have been found to be exceedingly insular, controlling, and less likely to promote child autonomy (Kepley & Ostrander, 2007). Moreover, trends observed in research indicate that families of children with ADHD and comorbid oppositional-defiant disorder or conduct disorder fare worse than families of ADHD without these comorbidities, suggesting that behavioral conflicts make a unique contribution to family stress (Barkley, 2006a).

A small but growing research base suggests that sibling relationships of children with ADHD are characterized by higher levels of conflict when compared with children without ADHD. Sibling relationships are further strained when the sibling with ADHD also exhibits significant externalizing behaviors, which are associated with lower ratings of warmth and closeness (Greene et al., 2001; Kendall, 1999; Mikami & Pfiffner, 2008; A. J. Smith, Brown, Bunke, Blount, & Christopherson, 2002).

Whereas positive sibling relationships play an important and adaptive role in child development and family functioning, strained sibling relationships, particularly when paired with the perception of differential treatment by parents, can be associated with problems (Brody, 2004). For example, Kendall's (1999) qualitative study found that siblings without ADHD reported that ADHD in the household resulted in disruption and chaos. Siblings without ADHD described feeling victimized by the aggressive behaviors of their siblings with ADHD, resented being placed in a caretaking role by their parents, and conveyed feelings of sorrow and loss. The siblings without ADHD managed these issues through a combination of retaliation, avoidance, and accommodation. Siblings with ADHD in this study described "other people" as their biggest problem.

Adult ADHD and Marriage

Elevated ratings of marital discord are cited in the research literature in studies of families both with children with ADHD (Whalen & Henker, 1999) and with adults with ADHD (Barkley et al., 2008; Eakin et al., 2004; Minde et al., 2003; K. R. Murphy & Barkley, 1996a; Robin & Payson, 2002). However, it is unclear whether rates of separation or divorce among married couples in which at least one spouse has ADHD are higher (e.g., Barkley et al., 2008; Biederman et al., 2006). Partners with ADHD, in fact, tend to provide higher ratings of relationship discord or negativity than do their partners without ADHD (Eakin et al., 2004; Robin & Payson, 2002), although Barkley et al. (2008) noted that spouses of adults with ADHD report being less satisfied in their marriages than do control participants.

Robin and Payson (2002) conducted a survey of 80 heterosexual married couples in which one spouse was identified with ADHD and the other spouse did not have ADHD (in 45% of the marriages, the husband had ADHD; in 55% of the marriages, the wife had ADHD). The first striking result was the agreement of spouses' ratings of behaviors that make the spouse without ADHD feel unloved, unimportant, or ignored. When examining the top 10 items rated by people with ADHD and their partners without ADHD, there was agreement on 5 task-completion items, 2 communication items, and 1 item related to self-regulation of affect. However, the overall correlation of spousal ratings was moderate.

There were significant differences between people with ADHD and their spouses without ADHD on number of issues cited, ratings of how unlovable spouses without ADHD felt because of these issues, and ratings of their negative impact. In fact, spouses with ADHD reported significantly more issues affecting the marriage, rated these issues as making their spouses feel more unloved than their spouses without ADHD reported, and reported a more negative impact on the marriage than did their spouses without ADHD.

Finally, there were significant gender differences in ratings provided by spouses without ADHD. Husbands without ADHD reported more ADHD-related behaviors and rated these behaviors as having a greater negative impact on their marriage when reporting on their wives with ADHD than did wives without ADHD when reporting on their husbands with ADHD. That is, it appears that there is greater marital disruption when a wife has ADHD than when a husband has ADHD. As Robin and Payson (2002) noted, it may be that ADHD interferes with women's abilities to fulfill societal gender-role expectations more than it does for men. Husbands without ADHD also may express their frustration more directly than wives without ADHD.

Parental ADHD

Considering the heritability of ADHD, an all-too-overlooked subgroup of families is that in which at least one parent has ADHD (Biederman, Faraone, & Monuteaux, 2002; Harvey, Danforth, McKee, Ulaszek, & Friedman, 2003; M. Weiss, Hechtman, & Weiss, 2000). Although parental ADHD does not appear to add to the risk of the diagnosis of ADHD or dysfunction in offspring beyond the risk already conferred by genetics and the nature of the disorder, offspring without ADHD of parents with ADHD experience increased problems (Biederman et al., 2002). Thus, detection and effective treatment of adult ADHD in such families would seem to set the stage for improved parenting behavior and/or relationship functioning with a spouse.

Studies have started to look at the effects of parental ADHD on family functioning, such as preliminary support for the similarity-fit hypothesis. That is, mothers with high levels of ADHD implemented higher levels of positive and affectionate parenting strategies (although they did not use lower levels of negative parenting strategies) when responding to their children with high levels of ADHD than when responding to their children with lower levels of ADHD (Psychogiou, Daley, Thompson, & Sonuga-Barke, 2008).

In a separate study, fathers' self-reports of inattention and impulsivity were strongly associated with a lax parenting style and impulsivity associated with a tendency to argue with their children during an audio-recorded interaction; mothers' self-reports of inattention were moderately associated with lax parenting (Harvey et al., 2003). Thus, screening for parental ADHD may become a standard component of evaluations for childhood ADHD, considering the unique effects of the disorder on family functioning (Biederman, Faraone, & Monuteaux, 2002).

Adult ADHD and Social Relationships

For individuals with ADHD, social difficulties extend outside the home. Children with ADHD, compared with control participants, tend to be rated by peers as lower on social preference, are less well liked, are more often rejected, and are less likely to have friends (de Boo & Prins, 2007; Henker & Whalen, 1999; Hoza et al., 2005). Girls with ADHD who experience peer rejection are at increased risk of lower academic achievement and eating pathology as teenagers, and they experience more difficulties in childhood than girls without ADHD (Greene et al., 2001; Mikami & Hinshaw, 2006). Likewise, boys with ADHD who have significant social problems have worse outcomes than boys with ADHD without social problems in terms of mood and anxiety problems, disruptive behaviors, and substance use (Greene, Biederman, Faraone, Sienna, & Garcia-Jetton, 1997).

Adults with ADHD face social functioning difficulties outside the family, either as a continuation of difficulties encountered in childhood, such as those noted earlier, or as newfound problems dealing with the wide-ranging and complex relationships in adulthood (Able, Johnston, Adler, & Swindle, 2006; Barkley et al., 2008; Canu & Carlson, 2004). Children with ADHD who have been tracked into adulthood are found to have higher rates of substance abuse, increased interactions with the criminal justice system, and a higher prevalence of antisocial personality disorder than do control groups (Barkley et al., 2008; Mannuzza, Klein, Bessler, Malloy, & LaPadula, 1998; Rasmussen & Gillberg, 2000; G. Weiss & Hechtman, 1993).

In a preliminary study, college-age individuals with the inattentive type of ADHD were found to exhibit a pattern of passivity and social inexperience that was rated somewhat negatively by female confederates (naive to participants' group membership), whereas individuals with the ADHD, combined type, reported increased sexual drive and started dating at an earlier age (Canu & Carlson, 2003). Studies of similar college populations indicate that although young adults with ADHD were no more sensitive to rejection than were control participants without ADHD, low rejection sensitivity (i.e., less social inhibition) predicted positive social outcomes for individuals with the inattentive type; it is interesting to note that high rejection sensitivity (i.e., more social inhibition) for the ADHD, combined type, group was associated with positive social adjustment. However, young adults with ADHD score lower on ratings of self-esteem than do control groups without ADHD and report a greater number of lifetime romantic partners (Canu & Carlson, 2007).

Adults with ADHD report being aware of their social functioning difficulties but are particularly less attuned to emotional information than are control participants without ADHD (Friedman et al., 2003). Individuals with ADHD report attempting to be vigilant about breaching social norms but end up doing so anyway because of poor self-regulation. Because of receptive problems (e.g., not reading subtle emotional or nonverbal cues), an adult with ADHD might not recognize that she or he has committed a social faux pas.

Social appraisal research indicates that adults with ADHD tend to be rated negatively by observers. For example, college students read accounts of young adults with a "weakness" (i.e., ADHD, medical condition, or ambiguous weakness [perfectionism]) and completed social appraisal questionnaires. Accounts of individuals with ADHD were rated more negatively than those of individuals without ADHD, with men with ADHD judged more negatively than were women with ADHD (Canu, Newman, Morrow, & Pope, 2008). Because the accounts differed only by use of a label (e.g., "ADHD" or "perfectionism") without specific behavioral differences, the results suggest a stigma is associated with the term ADHD used with adults. Raters were less likely to want to associate with adults with ADHD in academic or work group settings. Adults with ADHD also received lower ratings by peers and supervisors in the workplace, even though raters were not aware of workers' ADHD diagnostic status (Barkley et al., 2008).

The negative effects of ADHD on social functioning can be pervasive and chronic. However, positive social support is an important emotional buffer and source of encouragement for individuals with ADHD. Thus, dealing with the social aspects of adult ADHD is an important part of treatment, particularly in the form of family therapy, couples therapy, or social skills training. The next section describes each of the available treatment options.

DESCRIPTION OF TREATMENTS

Research has shown that effective treatment, most often combining medications with parenting and teacher training in behavior management, results in improved functioning in children and teens with ADHD (Barkley, 2002b; Pelham, Wheeler, & Chronis, 1998; Root & Resnick, 2003). Treatment approaches designed specifically to help families handle the difficult-to-manage behaviors of ADHD children and teens at home are helpful in many ways but have achieved mixed results (e.g., Barkley, Edwards, Laneri, Fletcher, & Metevia, 2001; Barkley, Guevremont, Anastopoulos, & Fletcher, 1992; Robin, 2006). Thus, rather than ineffective parents causing ADHD, ADHD can make standard parenting strategies appear to be ineffective. What is more, the behavior of children with ADHD is particularly susceptible to inconsistent or suboptimal parenting strategies, creating a self-perpetuating, complementary process (Bernier & Siegel, 1994; Johnston & Jassy, 2007; Johnston & Mash, 2001).

Beyond the positive effects of medication, individual psychosocial treatment can help adults with ADHD address potential negative or unrealistic expectations about parenting, marriage, and personal relationships (Phelan, 2002). Improving parenting and relationship enhancement skills, in fact, may be an explicit component of psychosocial treatment for some adults with ADHD.

Many adults with ADHD experience social skills deficits directly related to their core symptoms (Novotni & Petersen, 1999). That is, adults with ADHD make social errors of *omission* by missing out on important information, such as not hearing something said, not picking up on subtle social cues (which are often nonverbal), or simply forgetting to follow common social niceties such as saying "thank you" or "goodbye." Adults with ADHD also make social errors of *commission* by saying the wrong thing at the wrong time, interrupting because of impulsivity, forgetting to follow through on a promise, or appearing rude because of impatience and restlessness. Finally, some individuals with ADHD report that seemingly odd social behaviors, such as minimizing eye contact, are strategies to reduce distractions that may interfere with their ability to process information.

Although the negative effects of ADHD on social skills cut across all types of relationships, two prominent areas where such effects are particularly taxing are in family households and in marriages or other committed relationships. The following sections review some frameworks used in the treatment of adult ADHD insofar as it affects family and relationship functioning.

It is important to note that the discussion of the effects of ADHD on relationships is not meant to assign blame to individuals with ADHD or to imply that all difficulties stem from ADHD. The goal of these treatments is to identify and modify maladaptive patterns and to promote mutual understanding, empathy, and cooperation to improve relationship functioning.

Family Therapy

Traditional models of family therapy provide frameworks within which to understand the family system as a whole—how its context, structure, and rules, as well as the beliefs, behaviors, and roles of its individual members affect the functioning of the family unit (Everett & Everett, 1999; Labauve, 2003; Ziegler & Holden, 1988). Contemporary views of family therapy emphasize the transactional and contextual nature of families' difficulties, including biobehavioral models of the influence of ADHD on functioning (Diamond & Josephson, 2005; Orr, Miller, & Polson, 2005; Robin, 2006). Changing entrenched relationship patterns is difficult because individuals working together as a unit or system generally settle into a comfortable equilibrium or homeostasis that might not be satisfactory but is familiar and therefore resistant to change. Interventions strive to help families break out of maladaptive patterns and improve the family atmosphere.

ADHD introduces another layer of complexity to families that already may be struggling. Whether a family has a child with ADHD, a parent or caregiver with adult ADHD, or both, ADHD in a household, even in subthreshold form, makes coping with the typical demands of family life more difficult. There may be greater levels of household conflict, anxiety, noise, and disorganization in a family affected by ADHD (Phelan, 2002). In fact, the presence of ADHD in a household magnifies many commonplace family issues, such as money management, parenting, school-related issues (e.g., homework, academic or behavior problems), sibling rivalries, and so on. Individual family members diagnosed with ADHD often struggle with comorbid psychiatric problems, substance abuse, and learning and workplace difficulties, which further affect the household.

As noted by Phelan (2002), ADHD affects coordinated, goal-directed activities of families, such as getting out of the house in the morning for work and school. In such cases, there is a need for planning and organization, and the expectation that each family member will be able to perform developmentally appropriate tasks and roles (e.g., children getting dressed for school, teenagers organizing backpacks, parents assuming supervisory roles and all departing the house on time). ADHD also affects unstructured family activities, such as free time in the evenings or on weekends. In such case, there is an unspoken expectation that individual family members will be able to prioritize their activities, monitor and manage their time, transition between tasks, respect the needs of other family members, negotiate and resolve conflicts with each other, and follow household rules. Many of the characteristics of adaptive family functioning represent areas of difficulty for many children, adolescents, and adults with ADHD.

Subgroups within each family have different experiences with ADHD. For instance, managing ADHD in a marriage is more difficult than it is during dating because of the increased demands of a long-term, committed relationship and the added stress of coparenting. Similar to modifying family functioning, changing relationship patterns in a marriage requires an adjustment in expectations regarding how things should be and in interaction styles. Solo parents with ADHD face particular difficulties managing a household and coordinating additional support. (Marital issues are addressed in the next section.)

Parents and siblings without ADHD have distinctive experiences in an ADHD household (Biederman, Faraone, & Monuteaux, 2002; Everett & Everett, 1999; Kendall, 1999; Phelan, 2002). Family members without ADHD may express feelings of neglect with regard to the attention family members with ADHD receive and embarrassment in response to social missteps made by siblings or spouses with ADHD. In some cases, family members experience emotional or physical abuse when ADHD is manifested in the form of angry outbursts and verbal or physical acting out.

Family interventions for ADHD generally focus on instilling hope that family relationships and functioning can be improved by identifying and modifying ineffective patterns (Everett & Everett, 1999; Phelan, 2002; Robin, 2006). Managing the effects of ADHD has been described as akin to "battling an octopus" (Phelan, 2002). As with other nonmedication treatments for ADHD, family treatment starts with psychoeducation. In addition to standard information about the symptoms and effects of ADHD, family-specific education includes an analysis of the manner in which ADHD affects household functioning. Conceptualizing the family patterns and frustrations provides a blueprint for change, both for treating clinicians and for family members.

However, as with erecting a building from a blueprint, the difficult clinical work involves implementing the plans. It is helpful for families to start small and be encouraged to work on simple behavioral changes that are relatively easy to execute (Phelan, 2002; Ramsay & Rostain, 2008a). That is, identifying small, discrete steps congruent with a family's goals, such as setting up a household calendar or pointing out positive behaviors performed by others, represents a few user-friendly assignments that introduce important foundational skills for changing family patterns.

Phelan (2002) offered some useful interventions that target common sources of family discord, such as noise, conflict, disorganization, and stress. Many suggestions are akin to environmental engineering; that is, families are encouraged to set up the home environment, as much as is possible, to promote positive coping skills and to reduce distractions. Managing the amount and level of incoming noise can be accomplished by reducing unnecessary sounds, setting up certain noise-free areas, or making use of portable media players. Likewise, separating from the family at large to engage in solitary activities or having one-on-one interactions with a spouse or child helps reduce distractions and improve communication. These sorts of coping suggestions may lead to discussion and modification of unspoken family beliefs, such as "families should want to spend their free time together as a group" or "we should not have to put this much thought into how we set up our house and plan our schedule."

Family treatment for ADHD often includes specific topics affecting family functioning, such as behavior management and constructive communication (Robin, 2006). Parents of children with ADHD might benefit from parent training regarding principles of behavior modification and positive parenting strategies, such as catching their children doing things well and providing praise. Although this is an important principle for all parents to remember, it is even more important when interacting with children with ADHD, as it is too easy to respond to the problematic behaviors and ignore adaptive behaviors. Likewise, parents with ADHD can be reminded of the personal relevance of this principle, such as by giving themselves credit for positive behaviors or noting the use of effective parenting skills by a coparent.

Another useful reminder for families affected by ADHD is the notion of nonjudgmental acceptance and times devoted to simply being with other family members (e.g., Greco & Eifer, 2004). That is, although living with ADHD requires attention to teaching moments and consistent follow-through on behavioral plans, it is equally important to have times in which family members can simply foster positive bonds (Labauve, 2003). Unfortunately, with the diverse demands on individual family members and on a family unit, it is often these sorts of activities that are sacrificed to keep up with various tasks related to work, school, and household projects. Although it sounds cliché, it is beneficial to make appointments for family time, be it as a family unit or as various subgroups, to maintain these positive connections.

Dealing with school and homework is an important part of life for families with school-age children. Parents often need extra support when dealing with academic issues, particularly because school and learning are difficult for children with ADHD and may lead to parent–child conflict. In fact, dealing with homework is an important issue in family therapy for ADHD (Robin, 2006) and provides the orienting framework for some parent training programs designed for families with school-age children with ADHD (e.g., Power, Karustis, & Habboushe, 2001).

Family treatments for ADHD have often been anchored in their focus on children and teens with ADHD. Although there is a higher than average likelihood that at least one biological parent of an ADHD child will have

ADHD, little explicit attention has been paid to the unique effects of ADHD on caregivers in family treatment or parent training approaches. It seems logical, however, that parents with ADHD would have problems implementing therapeutic recommendations.

A domain of family functioning that can be negatively affected by ADHD is the marital (or coparenting) relationship. The next section reviews treatment strategies used with couples affected by ADHD.

Marital Therapy

Although many of the principles of family treatment are relevant in marital therapy, the effects of ADHD on marriage warrant special attention. Relatively little research has examined the effects of ADHD on marriage (or committed relationships) other than documenting the high ratings of relationship discord.

Kilcarr (2002) summed up the characteristics of successful relationships as high self-esteem and self-worth, toleration of each other's idiosyncrasies and foibles, the ability to communicate about difficult issues, good humor, expression of affection, minimal displays of negative affect, and acceptance and normalization of the ebbs and flows of life. These qualities are similar to those cited in research on successful marriages (Gottman, 1998). Furthermore, couples often present for treatment only after there has been significant erosion of coping skills and problems related to angry communication, emotionality and hostility, and reduced ability to maintain perspective and realistic attributions about the actions (or inaction) of a partner.

Marital therapy for ADHD starts with eliciting highly specific examples of difficulties encountered by the couple on a regular basis (Kilcarr, 2002; Rosenfield, Ramsay, & Rostain, 2008). Reverse-engineering problematic situations allows a couple to delineate the unfolding of conflict, including each partner's explanation and personal interpretation of events. This sort of discussion, or *prolongation,* to use the language of executive functions (Barkley, 1997a), slows down what has become an automatic and speedy process for the couple. Rather than reflexively skipping from a triggering event to a negative attribution and culminating in a maladaptive reaction, the couple reexamines and reconsiders the connection between events and their respective reactions. Said differently, the methodical review allows the couple to reprocess events, understand the experiences of the partner, directly express personal experiences, and develop a spirit of collaboration and mutual respect in relationship problem management (Everett & Everett, 1999; Halverstadt, 1998; Kilcarr, 2002; Rosenfield et al., 2008).

Creating a safe, collaborative environment provides couples with much-needed feelings of hope and a sense that their relationship can be changed for the better. This context supports the implementation of specific coping and relationship-enhancing behaviors. Although suggestions that it is important for individuals to increase the frequency of positive behaviors in the relationship might seem to be common sense, it is easy for couples to slip out of this pattern and into destructive communication patterns (Gottman, 1998). A guided review of past positive behaviors, enjoyable experiences, and fond memories often provides clues for how a couple can modify behaviors, with each partner agreeing to make a concerted effort to implement a new behavior (Kilcarr, 2002).

However, partners without ADHD often state that they have already made inordinate concessions and accommodations for the good of the relationship without reciprocity (Pera, 2008). Consequently, spouses without ADHD might be reticent to invest yet again in the hope that things will be different. However, their partners with ADHD are most often acutely aware of how their symptoms create tension in the marriage and may be equally self-critical of their mistakes and defensive in response to feeling blamed for marital problems (e.g., Robin & Payson, 2002). Identifying patterns that affect the relationship is an important step in moving forward in marital therapy for ADHD. Working on modifying attitudes that interfere with relationship enhancement and generating motivation for following through on specific behavioral change recommendations increases the likelihood of treatment success. Allowing partners to share their concerns and to express commitment to the relationship may enhance trust (or at least suspend mistrust) and allow them to develop effective quid pro quo behavioral trade-offs.

Many of the features of successful marital therapy, such as correcting misattributions and reducing "mind reading," developing accepting attitudes toward personal foibles, and so on, hold true whether or not ADHD is an issue for a relationship. However, ADHD in a marriage adds layers of complexity to the aforementioned issues (Pera, 2008). The partner with ADHD faces the challenge of coming to terms with her or his symptoms and learning to manage them. Many adults with ADHD share their struggles with their partners and rely on them to assume many household responsibilities, such as managing the bills or serving as a de facto personal coach. Consequently, partners with ADHD might feel shame that they are unduly burdening their partners and are accumulating debt in the relationship, which may result in a combination of subjugation and resentment on their part.

Increased attention is being paid to the experience of partners without ADHD who are in committed relationships with adults with ADHD (Pera, 2008). Anecdotal accounts of the frustrations experienced within the relationship, particularly before diagnosis and treatment of a partner's ADHD, are quite moving. Although choosing a particularly organized spouse might be a way that some adults with ADHD compensate for their symptoms, many partners without ADHD struggle with the effects of ADHD on their marriage. Spouses without ADHD often conclude that their spouse with ADHD does not care about them or the relationship.

Many of these relationship complaints are common to those voiced in most struggling marriages. However, in cases of relationships involving a partner with ADHD, addressing these issues must include awareness and acknowledgment of the role ADHD symptoms play in relationship patterns. The partner with ADHD must be willing to take steps to implement coping strategies to enhance rapport and affection, to follow through on reasonable behavioral changes, and to demonstrate that he or she is making a good faith effort to improve the relationship. The partner without ADHD, on the other hand, must come to terms with the fact that ADHD is a condition that can cause significant impairment in many domains of life. This acceptance includes recognition that many of the difficulties experienced by the partner with ADHD that affect the relationship are not intentional or evidence of disregard for the relationship or partner.

Changing relationship patterns involves a combination of behavior change and cognitive change. Considering the influence of ADHD on relationship issues, accurate assessment of adult ADHD and psychoeducation are important first steps for both partners (Kilcarr, 2002; Pera, 2008). Reinterpreting chronic relationship frustrations through the lens of ADHD helps increase understanding of some sources of the partners' difficulties and to externalize the problem, thereby allowing the couple to work together to address it. There is evidence that couples who maintain an attitude of acceptance of others' foibles, express mutual respect and affection, and avoid destructive communication patterns are more likely to stay married than couples without these qualities (Gottman, 1998).

In addition to marital therapy, adults with ADHD may benefit from peer support groups dealing with issues related to the diagnosis, such as managing relationships (including groups for partners without ADHD; e.g., Pera, 2008). Individual medication, psychosocial treatment, or both might also help the partner with ADHD develop coping skills. In some cases, explicit social skills training might be needed to improve relationship functioning. The next section reviews social skills training for adults with ADHD.

Social Skills Training

The notion behind social skills training for adults with ADHD is that, similar to children with ADHD, individuals might be missing some basic strategies for managing interpersonal situations and relationships (Aberson, Shure, & Goldstein, 2007; Monastra, 2008; Novotni & Petersen, 1999). Consequently, therapeutic support for identifying problematic interpersonal situations and promoting the use of social skills, such as eye contact, active listening, and basic courtesies can be helpful. However, many adults with ADHD possess sufficient knowledge of, and proficiency in, social skills but experience difficulties from the inconsistent or ineffective application of them at the point of performance.

Whether the source of an individual's social functioning difficulties is the acquisition of social skills or their implementation at the point of performance, the core deficits of ADHD are the main culprits. Executive dysfunction interferes with the social learning that occurs in the course of childhood development. Consequently, children with ADHD have a harder time deciphering and encoding social rules and behaviors. These rules are generally unspoken and are learned through observation and trial-and-error learning. However, ADHD interferes with rule-governed behavior. Thus, even when there are explicit rules for social behavior (e.g., "whisper in the library"; "do not tease other students"), children with ADHD have difficulty following the rules despite being able to recite them. Thus, children with ADHD may withdraw from social situations because of feeling rejected or being unable to grasp social norms, and struggle with chronic loneliness. What is more, some children with ADHD are subjected to outright teasing or being labeled as "weird" or "bad kids," experiences and messages that many carry with them into adulthood.

Although more research has been conducted on children with ADHD than on adults with ADHD, these adults also experience difficulties in their social and interpersonal lives. Some adults with ADHD experience inflexibility in their thoughts and behaviors, are impulsive, or have difficulties with memory and distractibility. Moreover, similar to children with ADHD, adults with ADHD describe recurring frustrations with not being able to effectively recognize or follow the social rules of adulthood, despite knowing the rules (e.g., "do not interrupt someone else"; "do not joke during the meeting"). Each of these problems, or any permutation of them, can create interpersonal difficulties with coworkers, friends, acquaintances, or romantic partners and may mask an adult with ADHD's personal strengths and positive characteristics.

Whereas children with ADHD might participate in social skills training groups focused on school-related scenarios, adults face a wider array of social situations in which they have difficulties. Thus, a one-size-fits-all, skills training treatment approach is too broad to be much help for most adults with ADHD. Moreover, as was mentioned earlier, the main problem faced by adults with ADHD is the ability to implement the skills they possess when needed. Very good informational resources exist in which social skills details and coping strategies are outlined for adults with ADHD (e.g., Novotni & Petersen, 1999; NRC, 2003b). However, modifying social behaviors probably requires a more personalized approach.

Although improvements in executive functioning provided by medications can generalize to improve social functioning, social skills training explicitly targets impaired performance of these skills. Because many important social situations occur with a relative low frequency but are highly significant (e.g., job interview), role-play and rehearsal in session are useful to gain in vivo practice with the use of various skills and strategies. Other social skills that are fundamental in interactions, such as eye contact and active listening, can be practiced in day-to-day situations, such as when dealing with store clerks or engaging in small talk with coworkers. Because the therapeutic objective is to increase the implementation of social skills, personalized reminders for target behaviors are helpful, such as catchphrases (e.g., "three-sentence rule" to counteract monologues; Rosenfield et al., 2008) or functionally incompatible physical reminders to monitor one's presentation (e.g., holding a coffee cup during a meeting as a reminder not to tap fingers on a table). Likewise, developing externalized reminders, such as cards with a checklist of reminders, can be helpful (e.g., three behavioral goals for a meeting at work).

Some adults with ADHD experience troubles related to overcompensation. That is, adults with ADHD may attempt to make up for functional difficulties, such as chronic lateness or procrastination at work, by putting emphasis on strengthening connections with others. Although strengthening and building up collateral in relationships is adaptive, some adults with ADHD may come on too strong in their interactions as a means to neutralize mistakes, such as forgetfulness. Although individuals dealing with these adults with ADHD cannot point to any obvious social "mistakes," they may observe that the person is "trying too hard" or exhibiting other examples of subtle social dyspraxia. Social skills interventions may focus on cognitive modification, such as decatastrophizing the effects of mistakes or the use of coping skills ("it is okay to ask someone you've just met to repeat his name if you've forgotten it"), developing coping skills to minimize future mistakes, and maintaining appropriate interpersonal boundaries.

Evidence and Current Status

Unfortunately, despite the increased interest in relationship issues affecting adults with ADHD, there are currently no outcome studies from which to recommend relationship-oriented treatments designed exclusively for this clinical population. Although not geared specifically for adults with ADHD, family treatment programs for children and teens with ADHD emphasizing behavior management training (BMT), family problem solving and communication training, stress and anger management, and school advocacy may be helpful for parents with ADHD who are dealing with children with ADHD (e.g., Chronis, Chacko, Fabiano, Wymbs, & Pelham, 2004).

Barkley et al. (1992) compared problem-solving communication training (PSCT) and BMT with traditional structural family therapy administered to families with ADHD teenagers. Although all treatments were associated with improvements, only a minority of families demonstrated reliable change. In a follow-up study, Barkley et al. (2001) compared PSCT with a sequential combination of BMT followed by PSCT administered to families with teenagers with ADHD and oppositional-defiant disorder. The treatments produced significant improvements in ratings of parent–teen conflict at midpoint (i.e., after BMT and before PSCT) and at the end of treatment. There was no significant difference between the two treatments, although more individuals dropped out of the PSCT-alone condition. Although once again only a minority of families demonstrated reliable changes associated with treatment, 42% to 80% of families were considered normalized by the end of treatment, depending on the rater.

A variety of other studies suggest that family treatment for ADHD in the form of some sort of parent training results in benefits above those provided by community care alone, with particular benefits for mothers, who are most often the primary caregivers (Treacy, Tripp, & Baird, 2005; van den Hoofdakker et al., 2007). Parent involvement in treatment may have greater effects on children's internalizing problems and academic functioning than on core symptoms of ADHD and externalizing behaviors (Corcoran & Dattalo, 2006). Although family-based treatments do not outperform medications alone for ADHD, they can help reduce treatment dropout rates (which are higher for families with children with more disturbed behavior) by giving parents hope and helpful coping strategies (Friars & Mellor, 2007). Mothers of children with ADHD, a group at elevated risk of depression (and ADHD), can benefit from specialized treatment for depression and parenting strategies in combination with specialized treatment for their children (e.g., Chronis, Gamble, Roberts, & Pelham, 2006; Chronis et al., 2007).

None of the family-based treatments mentioned in this section, however, specifically identified parental ADHD. Biederman et al. (2002) suggested that assessments for ADHD in children should include parental screening for ADHD as standard practice. Parental ADHD seems to be a potential moderator of treatment outcome in parent management training that warrants specialized clinical attention. To this end, the University of Pennsylvania's (PENN) Adult ADHD Treatment and Research Program and the Children's Hospital of Philadelphia's (CHOP) Center for the Management of ADHD have entered into a unique collaboration to develop and study a family-based treatment program for families with at least one parent and one child diagnosed with ADHD. The treatment program targets a number of interactions that are important for family well-being, including the parents' marriage, coparenting relationship, or both; parent–child relations; interaction with the child's school; and issues related to adult ADHD within a family. A pilot study of the CHOP–PENN program is underway.

A feature of the CHOP–PENN collaboration relevant to adult ADHD is a focus on the marital relationship. Marital relationships are consistently linked with parenting (Cunningham, 2007). However, parental ADHD as a factor in family or couple's treatment outcomes has not been studied, despite the topic gaining attention in the clinical literature (Betchen, 2003; Halverstadt, 1998; Kilcarr, 2002; C. A. Robbins, 2005; Rosenfield et al., 2008).

There have been no studies of targeted social skills interventions for adults with ADHD. Studies of social skills training in children with ADHD have produced equivocal results and are not a recommended treatment (American Academy of Child and Adolescent Psychiatry, 2007; Antshel & Remer, 2003). As was mentioned earlier, the primary difficulty for adults with ADHD seems to be the effective implementation of social skills. A preliminary study of psychoeducation and social problem-solving therapy provided to adults diagnosed with personality disorders compared with control participants indicated that treatment was associated with reduced anger expression, better problem-solving skills, and higher overall social functioning (Huband, McMurran, Evans, & Duggan, 2007). Although not having the same characteristics as a personality disorder, ADHD's associated chronic course and pervasive impairment overlap somewhat with personality features, and adults with ADHD may benefit from social problem-solving approaches that address barriers to the appropriate implementation of socials skills (e.g., de Boo & Prins, 2007).

CONCLUSION

In many ways, the status of marital and family therapies and social skills training for adult ADHD is similar to the state of affairs for psychosocial treatments for adult ADHD about 15 years ago. That is, therapeutic approaches have been adapted from existing treatment models and encouraging anecdotal accounts of their effectiveness are appearing in the popular and clinical literatures, although they have not yet been subjected to research. Family therapy, marital therapy, and to a lesser extent, social skills training modified for use with adults with ADHD will be fruitful lines of study in the coming decade, and there will likely be increased referrals for clinical services in these areas. However, in the absence of evidence-supported approaches, it is important that consumers seek out clinicians well versed in how adult ADHD issues affect these treatment modalities. (See Table 5.1.)

TABLE 5.1

Summary of Relationships and Social Functioning Interventions for Adults With Attention-Deficit/Hyperactivity Disorder (ADHD)

Relationship treatments	Strengths	Limitations	Current status and future directions
Family therapy	Targets area of impairment, particularly considering heritability of ADHD Personalized treatment Accepted treatment approach	Existing treatments focus on children and teens with ADHD Difficult to quantify outcomes Limited availability of family therapists versed in adult ADHD	Family treatments are acceptable and address a common source of stress Existing family treatments can be modified to address parental ADHD Future outcome studies might consider parental ADHD as a moderator variable and as a focus of intervention
Marital therapy	ADHD is a common source of marital stress Personalized treatment Accepted treatment	No outcome research Difficult to quantify outcomes Limited availability of marital specialists versed in adult ADHD	Marital therapy is viewed as acceptable Preliminary clinical outcome research is needed for marital therapy for couples with at least one partner diagnosed with ADHD
Social skills training	Targets of impairment relevant for many areas of life Personalized treatment Accepted treatment	No outcome research No formalized, stand-alone intervention approach Problems may result from ineffective use of skills rather than skills deficit	Social skills training is viewed as an acceptable approach, although it is unclear whether adults with ADHD seek it as a stand-alone treatment Preliminary research of the efficacy of social skills training for adult ADHD is needed Social skills training modules might be integrated with existing psychosocial approaches

6

NEUROFEEDBACK AND NEUROCOGNITIVE TRAINING

The purpose of this chapter is to review the status of neurofeedback and neurocognitive training approaches for the treatment of attention-deficit/hyperactivity disorder (ADHD). Note that the term *neurocognitive training* is used to describe a group of computer-based attention and working memory training approaches to avoid confusion with *cognitive training*, a term often used to describe interventions designed to improve self-control by using adaptive self-talk. Although there are important differences between these treatment approaches, their shared guiding principle is the notion that ADHD is characterized by differences in aspects of brain functioning, which is consistent with the current scientific conceptualization of ADHD. Hence, neurofeedback and neurocognitive training protocols aim to alter brain functioning to reduce core symptoms and to improve overall functioning.

Pharmacotherapy for ADHD is currently the only empirically validated treatment that directly treats the underlying symptoms of ADHD. Other non-medication treatments heretofore reviewed target the functional impairments experienced by individuals with ADHD. Although studies of psychosocial treatments, for example, have reported improvements in symptom ratings (probably reflecting reduced impairment rather than reduced symptoms), the effects of these interventions on underlying neurobiological functioning have not been measured, although Hesslinger et al. (2002) reported that their modular group treatment was associated with posttreatment improvements on some neuropsychological tests.

The use of neurofeedback in the assessment and treatment of ADHD has been a lightning rod for controversy for many years (National Resource Center on AD/HD [NRC], 2008a, 2008b). Thus, before delving into a review of the literature and potential clinical applications of neurofeedback and neurocognitive training for adults with ADHD, the first section of this chapter briefly reviews the heated debates about neurofeedback (and, by extension, neurocognitive training) to provide a context for subsequent discussions of research and clinical issues.

THE NEUROFEEDBACK DEBATE

Computerized neurocognitive training exercises, primarily those targeting working memory, are lumped in with neurofeedback approaches for the purpose of this discussion, although they are somewhat different approaches. However, the controversies about these treatments are connected with the history of the use of neurofeedback in the treatment of ADHD. More specifically, the evolution of neurofeedback and its introduction as a clinical intervention for ADHD have likely contributed to the strong opinions that are still held about neurocognitive training approaches. (See Johnson, 2004, and J. Robbins, 2000, for reviews of the history of neurofeedback.)

Biofeedback (of which neurofeedback is one type) involves gathering information about automatic physiological processes that usually occur outside of conscious awareness (Demos, 2005). These processes are translated into observable, analogue representations, such as tones or lights representing muscle tension, heart rate, stress level, or some other physiological process. For example, electromyography (EMG; or surface electromyography) involves obtaining measurements of electrical activity associated with muscle contractions in the body. Therapeutic applications of EMG include stress and pain management. Likewise, measures of the physiological activity of the skin (including sweat glands), such as galvanic skin response, electrodermal response, or skin conductance level, have been used in research on stress and emotion and have been used in stress management, relaxation training, and systematic desensitization.

At a basic level, taking one's body temperature with a common household glass or digital thermometer (or even a palm placed on a forehead) provides thermal biofeedback. Different types of sensors can be used to gather specific temperature information, such as readings taken from the extremities that provide a measure of sympathetic nervous system arousal and consequent constricted blood flow to the fingertips and toes. Again, such data are useful in stress and pain management training for a number of stress-related disorders. Individuals can be trained to use relaxation techniques to produce desired physiological changes, such as lowered pulse rate, decreased muscle tension, increased temperature in fingertips, and thereby to reduce their stress. Thus, individuals are empowered by a greater awareness of their bodies' functioning and the ability to influence their physical experience.

Similar to other forms of biofeedback, *electroencephalographic (EEG) biofeedback,* otherwise known as *neurofeedback,* is biofeedback targeting brain functioning. More specifically, neurofeedback targets central nervous system functioning. Neurofeedback involves gathering information about a patient's brain through readings of electrical activity occurring therein. (See Demos, 2005, and Monastra, 2008, for discussions of standard neurofeedback procedures.)

Other forms of neurocognitive training directly targeting problems with inattention, working memory, and behavioral control have been developed and studied (see Klingberg, 2006; Monastra, 2008; and Riccio & French, 2004). For the most part, these neurocognitive training protocols emphasize the identification and isolation of an underdeveloped or weakened cognitive skill (e.g., attention, working memory). Specific, specialized computerized exercises requiring repeated practice are used to improve and strengthen the targeted cognitive skill, akin to strengthening a muscle through repeated exercise.

Although the use of neurofeedback training (NFT) to achieve mentally relaxed states was noted in the 1960s and 1970s, the controversy related to NFT and ADHD dates back to the mid-1980s, when some independent practitioners started using NFT in the treatment of some brain-based disorders, including ADHD. The proliferation of personal computers in society and continued advances in computer technology have paralleled improvements in neuroimaging technology, thus making NFT technology more portable and the use of technology in assessment and treatment more acceptable to consumers. Anecdotal reports of positive therapeutic results led to wider use of NFT and the establishment of treatments centers offering NFT services and training. Subsequent media attention created increased public awareness of, and interest in, NFT (see J. Robbins, 2000).

Disputes about neurofeedback in the ADHD community resulted from the nature of the claims made about the therapeutic benefits of NFT. NFT was not introduced as an experimental, potentially beneficial, adjunctive treatment option but rather was promoted as an equally effective and safer alternative to pharmacotherapy for ADHD. A combination of miracle claims, testimonials, concerns about the use of medications, and accounts in various magazine and television stories led to the slow and steady growth of the NFT movement for ADHD.

Moreover, the scientific community voiced significant concerns about the lack of research supporting the use of NFT for ADHD and, in particular, unsupported claims that it was equally as effective as medications and was without negative side effects. Early outcome studies conducted with children were composed mainly of case reports, did not randomize participants, and used suspect assessment strategies to diagnose ADHD. Additional concerns were that the most visible NFT advocates had significant financial investments tied with a positive view of their treatments, which could influence statements made. The same concerns exist when researchers receive funding for research or consultation fees from pharmaceutical companies or other organizations for which there is the appearance of a potential conflict of interest. Consequently, NFT remains a point of contention in the ADHD community, among both professionals and lay individuals who otherwise agree on various aspects of the disorder.

Research on NFT, including a handful of studies of adults with ADHD in the past decade, has occurred in the long shadow of these early debates and controversies. Although many improvements have been made in neurofeedback basic research and there is growing interest in having effective, nonmedication treatment options for ADHD, some important questions remain to be answered: Are NFT and other forms of neurocognitive training effective interventions? Is the active ingredient of treatment, in fact, modified brain wave patterns or improved working memory on a neural level (as opposed to the development of cognitive coping strategies, i.e., Barkley, 2006c; Loo, 2003)? Does this result in improved daily functioning? On the one hand, some zealous supporters of NFT continue to offer it as an equally effective (if not superior) treatment option to pharmacotherapy for ADHD; on the other hand, ardent detractors dismiss NFT on the basis of its reputation. Although the debate about working memory exercises has not been as heated as that about NFT, in part because working memory training for ADHD was introduced from the outset through peer-reviewed research, the same issues of effectiveness and mechanisms of action will need to be addressed (see Barkley, 2006c; Klingberg, 2006).

As is often the case in debates in which opinions and emotions run passionate, residents of the middle ground express optimistic skepticism. That is, the theories underlying NFT and working memory training make sense on the basis of extant neurobiological models of ADHD, but strong empirical support is necessary to consider these sorts of interventions as standard components of a multimodal treatment plan.

The current middle-ground view of neurofeedback and ADHD is illustrated in a survey of leaders in the research and practice of psychological treatments conducted to establish an expert consensus on a collection of treatments with uncertain credibility (Norcross, Koocher, & Garofalo, 2006). Expert ratings were compiled to establish a continuum of psychological treatments from the category of "unlikely discredited" (i.e., behavior therapy for sex offenders) to "certainly discredited" (i.e., "angel" therapy). "Neurofeedback for ADHD" fell in the upper range of the "possibly discredited" category, that is, much closer to being "unlikely discredited" than to being "certainly discredited." It should be noted, however, that over 30% of experts surveyed did not supply a rating for the credibility of NFT, citing insufficient familiarity with its research or clinical use. (For completeness, it should be noted that "psychosocial [nonbehavioral] therapies for ADHD" fell in the "unlikely discredited" category, i.e., the category for interventions with greatest expert support for their use; "office-based cognitive task assessments for ADHD" fell in the "unlikely discredited" category among expert ratings of mental health tests.) The upshot of the expert survey is that NFT has spurred professional interest but it is left to solid, replicated research to determine its ultimate place in the ranks of ADHD treatments.

Having provided a cursory background of the strong opinions associated with neurofeedback for ADHD, the purpose of the rest of this chapter is to provide an overview of the basic NFT and neurocognitive training protocols that are prominent in the current clinical and research literatures. As with other chapters, an overview of the treatment procedures is presented, followed by a discussion of the available empirical literature. Considering the somewhat different approaches of NFT and neurocognitive training, these topics are treated separately.

NEUROFEEDBACK

Practitioners who use neurofeedback in their practices do so as a component of the initial assessment, as an intervention tool, or both. The next sections discuss each of these clinical applications of neurofeedback followed by a review of available research on their usefulness.

EEG Assessment Strategies

EEG measures the electrical functioning and processing of the brain through the relationship of intercranial electrical currents and subsequent voltage readings obtained on the scalp (Loo & Barkley, 2005). EEGs connected to computers gather readings of electrical currents from synaptic firing obtained through sensors placed on the scalp.

Acquired EEG readings are used to create topographical maps of the brain and isolate specific regions of the cerebral cortex that may not be functioning within normal limits (Demos, 2005). That is, as the brain goes through different states, such as focusing on a cognitive task, worrying, or relaxing peacefully, it generates different electrical currents related to the amount and type of energy that is required for a task. EEG data help identify atypical patterns associated with problematic symptoms of ADHD.

Most EEG data are gathered by the placement of one or two sensors moved around to different scalp locations. More recently, the use of quantitative electroencephalography (QEEG) data has increased. As with EEG, QEEG involves gathering information about the electrical functioning of the brain from sensors placed on the scalp. QEEG differs from EEG, however, in that it uses multiple sensors contained in a specialized cap, allowing information to be gathered simultaneously from multiple scalp sites.

When gathering EEG data, two sensors (made from silver, gold, or tin) are attached to the scalp and a third grounded sensor is attached to an earlobe of the patient (i.e., bipolar referential montage). The scalp sensors are active, with one serving as a reference and the other providing comparative data. The sensor cups are filled with conductive gel or paste to increase electrical conductivity. Cords affixed to each sensor are connected to an amplifier that enhances and transforms the electrical signals obtained from the scalp into raw data about brain waves. Computer programs transform raw EEG data into distinct brain wave patterns. QEEG data are gathered in a similar manner, except a cap containing multiple sensors gathers readings from the scalp. (See Demos, 2005, for a thorough review of EEG procedures.)

To ensure uniform placement of the sensors, neurotherapists use the International 10-20 System, a standardized series of letters and numbers used to identify the 19 scalp positions associated with specific brain locations (Demos, 2005; Monastra, 2008). This system is akin to the use of longitude and latitude to provide geographic coordinates. The assessor monitors data during assessment or training sessions to ensure that sensors are suitably attached and readings are not distorted by muscle movements. A device called an *impedance meter* also ensures the quality of the sensor connections.

Electronic filters break down raw EEG data into distinct brain wave frequencies. Each frequency can be measured in terms of hertz and microvolts. A *hertz* (Hz) is a measure of the rhythm of the wave. The term refers to the number of wave cycles per second. Thus, 1 Hz is equal to one cycle per second. *Slow waves* are characterized by frequencies below 10 Hz, and *fast waves* are characterized by frequencies above 13 Hz.

Microvolts (μV) are a measure of the amplitude or height of a brain wave, which is the difference between the highest and lowest peaks. Amplitude measurements range from just over 0 to 100 μV. As a general guideline, slower frequencies have higher amplitudes than faster frequencies. A preponderance of slow brain wave frequencies indicates that a brain is resting or contemplating action; fast brain wave frequencies indicate that a brain is actively engaged in tasks. NFT aims to change the brain wave amplitudes within targeted frequency bandwidths.

Different brain states have been associated with different brain wave frequency bandwidths. *Delta waves* (1–4 Hz) are associated with sleep or complex problem solving. *Theta waves* (4–8 Hz) are associated with creativity, insight, and "deep states." *Alpha waves* (8–12 Hz) are characterized by alert, peaceful states of mind, such as in meditation. *Sensorimotor rhythm waves* (SMR; 12–15 Hz) are associated with mental alertness and physical relaxation. *Beta waves* (13–21 Hz) are evident during tasks requiring sustained and focused attention and active thought. *High beta waves* (20–32 Hz) are most evident during anxiety and states of hyperalertness or intensity. Finally, *gamma waves* (38–42 Hz) are prominent during cognitive processing and learning.

EEG assessment data provide baseline brain wave profiles that can be used to develop an NFT plan. Training plans usually involve some combination of uptraining and downtraining of particular brain wave frequencies (Demos, 2005; Monastra, 2008). *Uptraining* refers to increasing the amplitude of targeted desired brain wave frequencies, or *reward frequencies*; conversely, *downtraining* refers to decreasing the amplitude of targeted undesired brain wave frequencies, or *inhibit frequencies*. There has been recent interest in EEG training of deficiencies in slow cortical potentials, which belong to the family of event-related brain potentials that represent reactions to internal or external events (Strehl et al., 2006). Children with ADHD have been found to exhibit poor self-regulation of negative slow cortical potentials.

Excessively slow EEG frequencies (i.e., theta waves), reflecting slow cortical activity, are associated with inattention or being unfocused and are the most common EEG profile in ADHD patients (Demos, 2005; Monastra, 2008). The theta-to-beta ratio is used as an indication of ADHD. Common theta-to-beta ratios in children are 2.5:1 and about 2:1 in adults; ratios exceeding 3:1 indicate a *slow-wave disorder*, or cortical hypoarousal. ADHD characterized by cortical hypoarousal is often treated by downtraining theta to inhibit slow waves.

Alpha waves also are thought to play a role in ADHD insofar as some adults (and children) may have difficulty adequately suppressing these slower waves during tasks requiring focus, leaving them feeling "foggy." Likewise, some individuals with ADHD demonstrate excessive SMR waves (reflecting an excessive internal orientation) and disproportionately high beta waves. The profile of high SMR and high beta waves indicates cortical overarousal that may not respond to treatment with stimulant medications (Demos, 2005; Monastra, 2008), although this is a relatively uncommon EEG profile among individuals with ADHD (5%–15%). Downtraining these frequency bandwidths is indicated for ADHD cases with this profile.

Neurofeedback Training Strategies

The main focus of NFT is to modify targeted brain wave patterns associated with the symptoms of ADHD. Neurotherapists vary widely in their use of NFT in their clinical practices. Some neurotherapists' practices are composed exclusively of patients seeking NFT, although they may collaborate with other treating professionals. Other neurotherapists, however, report using NFT as one of many treatment modalities, which may include pharmacotherapy, psychosocial treatment, and other standard components of a multimodal treatment approach (Monastra, 2008; Nash, 2005). Furthermore, different NFT protocols are tailored to different EEG profiles.

The physical setup of the EEG training is the same as it is for the assessment, with sensors attached to the scalp that are connected to an amplifier and computer. The training is administered by means of some sort of computer game or task through which neurofeedback, that is, reinforcement, is provided. Performance on the computer game reflects a trainee's ability to stay within targeted brain wave frequencies.

NFT is based on a nonconscious, operant conditioning paradigm, the use of contingent reinforcement to shape behavior (Monastra, 2004, 2008). The particular training task allows a neurotherapist to set thresholds for targeted brain wave frequencies. Performance on the training task (e.g., computer game) requires active focus and engagement of the areas of the brain associated with the targeted brain waves. Exceeding training thresholds for identified brain wave frequencies is positively reinforced by pairing the behavior (i.e., brain wave frequency) with a reinforcer (e.g., image of a bicyclist pedaling faster, accumulating points, pleasant tone) that increases the likelihood of the behavior. The trainer might also provide positive verbal reinforcement and encouragement. When the trainee's brain wave frequencies do not fall within predetermined thresholds, there is no reward.

Individual training sessions last about 45 to 60 minutes, on par with standard psychotherapy sessions, although introductory sessions may be shorter to allow individuals to become accustomed to NFT (Demos, 2005; Monastra, 2008). Each session consists of gathering baseline data and configuring that day's training thresholds accordingly. Within individual sessions, there are multiple short training sessions adjusted to a trainee's endurance. Training frequency varies according to the complexity of problems being treated, ranging from several times a week to biweekly. The range of 30 to 60 sessions is often given as a guidepost for length of treatment, with some significant improvements in ADHD symptoms in children reported in as few as 15 to 20 sessions. Monastra, Monastra, and George (2002) reported that 43 sessions, on average, were required to achieve QEEG normalization for three consecutive 45-minute training sessions.

Neurofeedback Research

Findings from various studies of brain functioning have resulted in ADHD being characterized as a slow-wave disorder, although a minority of ADHD individuals exhibit excessive fast-wave activity (Demos, 2005; Monastra, 2008). Relevant to adult ADHD, some bandwidth frequencies normalize during the course of development, such as beta waves (with activity increasing into adulthood) and theta waves (with activity decreasing into adulthood), with a subsequent decrease in theta-to-beta ratios. Nonetheless, adults with ADHD tend to exhibit higher levels of theta activity and higher theta-to-beta ratios than do adults without ADHD. Loo and Barkley (2005) provided a cogent reminder, however, that the brain functions as a dynamic whole and data on a single bandwidth cannot explain the functioning of the entire brain.

There are two clinical domains in which EEG is relevant in a discussion of the treatment of adult ADHD. The first is as an assessment tool with which to diagnosis ADHD. The second is NFT to treat the symptoms of ADHD. Although this book focuses on nonmedication treatments for adult ADHD, considering that some neurotherapists use EEG to make the diagnosis and set training thresholds, the next section reviews research on its use as an assessment tool. The subsequent section reviews NFT outcome research.

EEG as an Assessment Tool

EEGs have been studied as a diagnostic assessment tool for ADHD. Drawing primarily from samples of children (although some studies have included older adolescents and young adults), several studies have examined the ability of EEG to differentiate between clinical and control samples. Monastra et al. (1999) conducted a study of QEEG as an assessment tool in which they reported impressive rates of diagnostic *sensitivity* (i.e., percentage of ADHD probands who have abnormal EEGs) and *specificity* (i.e., percentage of control probands without ADHD who have normal EEGs).

Although various assessment protocols have been studied in ADHD samples, until recently none had exhibited sufficient predictive diagnostic use to be considered a reliable diagnostic indicator, or at least not to warrant being a stand-alone diagnostic test outside the context of a comprehensive assessment (Loo, 2003; Loo & Barkley, 2005). That is, from a clinical standpoint, a measure must demonstrate *positive predictive power* (i.e., the ability to predict that an individual with an abnormal EEG will receive a clinical diagnosis of ADHD) and *negative predictive power* (i.e., the ability to predict that an individual with a normal EEG will not receive a clinical diagnosis of ADHD; Loo & Barkley, 2005). Whereas an abnormal EEG is associated with a high degree of diagnostic accuracy for identifying children with ADHD

(Monastra, Lubar, & Linden, 2001), it is much less effective for identifying ADHD in children who do not have an abnormal EEG profile (Loo & Barkley, 2005).

However, recent studies of EEG as an assessment tool for ADHD, including a masked, prospective study, provide new and encouraging data on the diagnostic sensitivity and specificity (Quintana, Snyder, Purnell, Aponte, & Sita, 2007; S. M. Snyder et al., 2008). In samples of individuals seeking an assessment for ADHD, ranging in age from childhood to young adulthood, a diagnosis was obtained using semistructured psychiatric interviews, providing a diagnostic standard against which to compare other assessment approaches. A little more than 60% of the participants in the two studies received a diagnosis of ADHD, whereas the rest had other diagnoses. EEG data were collected in a masked protocol, and other diagnostic data were gathered from rating scales commonly used in the assessment of ADHD. EEG, namely the theta-to-beta ratio, produced higher levels of both sensitivity and specificity than rating scales when compared with the assessment results from the semistructured interviews. EEG did not identify comorbidity patterns or alternative diagnoses in those individuals without ADHD, but these studies provide evidence of its potential usefulness in the differential diagnosis of ADHD.

The variability in the clinical presentations of individuals with ADHD is a common problem facing diagnosticians. Thus, even if future research replicates the usefulness of EEG as an assessment tool for ADHD, it would likely serve as a complement to a standard clinical evaluation. The current standard for establishing the diagnosis of adult ADHD remains the clinical interview focusing on the assessment of symptoms causing impairment, particularly considering the high rates of comorbidity (K. R. Murphy & Gordon, 2006).

NFT for Adult ADHD

Riccio and French's (2004) comprehensive review of treatments for attention has categorized NFT as a "tentatively supported treatment" for adults and children with ADHD, with its supporting research characterized by case studies, inconsistent results, methodological flaws, or some combination thereof. However, only a few studies have included adults with ADHD in their samples; these studies are reviewed in this section.

Rossiter and La Vaque (1995) studied 46 patients (8–21 years old) drawn from a larger pool of patients seeking services at two outpatient clinics. Two treatment groups of 23 participants each were formed, with one group receiving NFT and a second group receiving medication treatment only (i.e., psychostimulants). The medication group was selected to match the NFT group by age, although precise selection criteria for this group were not described. Participants were not randomly assigned, as treatment regimens were chosen in consultation with treating clinicians and based on insurance coverage, previous medication response, and so on. The study used a mixture of different outcome measures, including a continuous performance task (CPT), intelligence testing (IQ), behavior rating scale, and age-appropriate personality inventories.

The NFT protocol was personalized for each patient but was generally focused on downtraining theta activity and uptraining beta activity for older adolescents and adults. NFT required three to five 30-minute sessions per week (part of a longer treatment session), for 20 sessions administered over 4 to 7 weeks. Participants received concurrent individual or family therapy during the study and were provided additional interventions (including medications, in some cases) as needed.

Results indicated that individuals receiving NFT exhibited significant improvements on the CPT and parent ratings of children's behaviors and internalizing symptoms. There were no differences between improvements reported by the medication group. It should be noted that pre- and post-EEG data were not reported; thus, it could not be determined whether NFT was associated with hypothesized improvements in bandwidth amplitudes (Loo & Barkley, 2005). Likewise, the unsystematic combination of concurrent treatments makes it difficult to tease apart the contribution of individual approaches to reported improvements.

Kaiser and Othmer (1997) used pre- and posttreatment CPT performance to measure the effect of SMR–beta neurofeedback on a sample of 530 individuals (122 adults, defined as 17–67 years old with a mean age of 37.2 years) who were characterized as having "attentional problems." Participants were patients of a clinic with multiple sites that specializes in NFT. Although ADHD was described as the most common presenting diagnosis, there was a wide range of symptom severity and numerous comorbidities. Diagnostic assessment procedures were not described, assessment data were not reported, and there was no control group.

NFT involved uptraining SMR–beta frequencies (12–18 Hz) and downtraining low and high frequency ranges. Training sessions included 30 minutes of visual and auditory feedback within a 45-minute contact session. Outcome measures were obtained before NFT and after about 20 training sessions, with 62 individuals who required further NFT undergoing testing again after 40 sessions (mean of 24.1 sessions, with the range of 18–61 training sessions). Participants were not on medication while performing the CPT. No group differences were associated with medication status, gender, or age. Comparison of pre- and posttreatment CPT performance indicated that NFT was associated with statistically significant improvements on measures of inattention, impulsivity, and variability of response time. Although CPT scores improved, additional measures of ADHD symptoms and/or functional status were not used. Again, pre- and posttreatment EEG data were not reported, and thus it is unclear whether NFT produced changes in brain wave amplitudes.

Kaiser (1997) conducted a study of NFT on 142 adults with ADHD (ages 19–79 years, with a mean age of 40.8 years). Recruitment, NFT protocol, and outcome measures were the same as described in Kaiser and Othmer (1997). Comparison of pre- and posttreatment CPT performance indicated that NFT was associated with statistically significant improvements on measures of inattention, impulsivity, and variability of response time. Although the positive results obtained were the same as those reported by Kaiser and Othmer (1997), so too were the limitations: unclear diagnostic procedures, no control group, no functional outcome measures, and no reported EEG data.

L. Thompson and Thompson (1998) conducted a chart review of 111 students with ADHD (including 7 young adults, ages 17–18 years, and 6 adults, 28–63 years). ADHD diagnosis was established using clinical interview and standard symptom questionnaires. Participants received forty 50-minute sessions of NFT. Pre- and posttreatment data were culled from clinical records, although there was a high rate of incomplete data. The NFT protocol focused on decreasing slow-wave activity (theta) and increasing fast-wave activity (beta). Metacognitive coping strategies necessary for educational tasks also were highlighted throughout NFT and included time management, efficient reading strategies, and math skills for adult students.

Results indicated that 11 of the 13 adult students demonstrated statistically significant improvements on the CPT Variability and Inattention subscales and on a measure of arithmetic ability. Nine adults exhibited significant improvements on verbal, performance, and full IQ scores. Finally, while demonstrating improvements in theta-to-beta ratios, EEG changes were not statistically significant for the 8 adults completing NFT, although there was a trend toward significance. Regarding treatment of adult ADHD, the study has low numbers of adult participants and variability of available outcome measures. Also, the fact that metacognitive coping strategy training was conducted during NFT in the absence of controlled comparison groups makes it difficult to disentangle the contribution of each treatment. There was no report of psychiatric comorbidities, and it is unclear whether the diagnostic assessment included a screening for them.

Monastra et al. (2002) studied 100 individuals (ages 6–19 years) diagnosed with ADHD, none of whom had received prior treatment for ADHD. Participant screening included a physician evaluation to rule out medical conditions that could mimic ADHD symptoms and a comprehensive evaluation conducted by a psychologist experienced with ADHD that included parent and teacher behavior ratings. QEEG assessments were conducted to confirm that all participants exhibited the typical ADHD profile of excessive slow-wave activity relative to fast-wave activity (i.e., high theta-to-beta ratio). NFT was provided to 51 participants in addition to the standard, 1-year multimodal treatment program that included medication (i.e., methylphenidate), parent counseling, and academic support at school. Follow-up measures were gathered while participants were both on and off of their prescribed medications and included an assessment of parenting style.

There were no pretreatment group differences. All study participants started with methylphenidate on a systematic titration schedule. Dosage was stabilized if side effects were well tolerated and when subsequent CPT results fell in the normalized range (i.e., within one standard deviation of the mean). Parent counseling involved a 10-session parent group and individual parent consultation as needed thereafter, with families averaging a meeting every other week. School consultations were conducted to help coordinate and support the implementation of academic accommodations. Study participants averaged three in-school consultations.

NFT involved weekly training sessions, lasting about 30 to 40 minutes. The visual and auditory feedback provided as part of the NFT system was augmented by a point system for positive training response that could be redeemed for cash rewards when certain milestones were met. NFT continued until the trainee demonstrated normalized cortical slowing on the QEEG scan (i.e., within one standard deviation of age peer norms; Monastra et al., 1999) for three consecutive 40-minute sessions. The average number of sessions required to achieve this criterion was 43, with a range of 34 to 50 sessions.

Results after 1 year of treatment indicated that the group receiving NFT exhibited significant improvements on outcome measures (including both parent and teacher ratings) when compared with the standard treatment group, including improved theta-to-beta ratios as measured by QEEG. The NFT group exhibited sustained improvement both on and off medication. Moreover, there was no significant effect of parenting style on results for standard treatment, but consistent parenting (i.e., consistent use of effective reinforcement strategies at home) was associated with significant improvements within the treatment group receiving NFT. When all participants were retested 1 year after starting treatment and after a medication washout, the treatment group that received NFT demonstrated normalized cortical slowing on the basis of QEEG assessment, while the standard treatment group continued to demonstrate levels of cortical slowing that approached clinical elevation.

The finding of QEEG differences between treatment groups, however, could be associated with the fact that the criterion for discontinuing NFT was normalization of theta-to-beta ratios. Likewise, only participants exhibiting ADHD characterized by high theta-to-beta ratios were included in the study. It is interesting to note that a review of the results indicates that the standard treatment group that did not receive NFT did not demonstrate much change at all associated with treatment, including an unusual nonresponse to medications. Consequently, some reviewers wondered whether the standard treatment group without NFT received a "degraded version" of treatment or were simply nonresponders to treatment (Loo & Barkley, 2005). Of course, lack of random assignment to treatment conditions and the fact that individuals receiving NFT by definition had more therapeutic contacts than the standard treatment group are significant limitations of the study.

It should also be noted that a nonsystematic parenting style was associated with no significant improvements on measures of parent ratings of behavior regardless of whether NFT was included in the treatment package. On the other hand, teacher ratings of behavior were unaffected by parenting style, although this finding could be associated with the school consultation component of the treatment program (Monastra et al., 2002). Likewise, it is difficult to disentangle the effects of individual treatments on specific outcomes, although medications and NFT were the only modalities in the study specifically targeting neuropsychological functioning.

Finally, although conducted on a sample of children, a recent randomized controlled trial of NFT for ADHD was published (Gevensleben et al., 2009). Participants (102 children, ages 8–12 years) were randomized to either 36 sessions of NFT or a computerized attention-skills-training task, with sessions conducted several times a week at the treatment centers and the protocol completed in about a month. Parents were not informed of the treatment group assignment of their children. The diagnosis of ADHD was made using a semistructured interview and a diagnostic checklist administered by a mental health professional. Participants with comorbid disorders other than conduct disorder were excluded from the study. None of the participants received treatment (medication or psychotherapy) in the 6 weeks prior to treatment, with most children having never taken medications for ADHD.

NFT involved downtraining theta activity and uptraining beta activity as well as a component targeting slow cognitive potentials. The results indicated that NFT was associated with improvements on parent and teacher ratings of ADHD symptoms as well as on ratings of oppositional behavior, home behavior, homework behavior, and social behavior, with a medium effect size of .60. Parental attitudes about treatment did not differ between groups. A little over half of the NFT participants were considered responders compared with 29% of the attention-skills-training control group. Is it encouraging that positive results with NFT are being obtained with stronger study designs and controls. Ongoing research is needed to assess the maintenance and generalization of improvements in children and adults with ADHD, particularly those with comorbid diagnoses.

Summary

The Monastra et al. (2002) and Gevensleben et al. (2009) studies as well as the recent EEG assessment studies (Quintana et al., 2007; S. M. Snyder et al., 2008) represent significant steps forward in research on neurofeedback for adults with ADHD. However, more examples of these sorts of quality studies are required to establish neurofeedback as a conventional treatment and assessment option for adult ADHD. In particular, rigorous assessment criteria for ADHD and comorbidities and the use of functional outcome measures relevant to daily functioning are needed. Randomized trials that control for number and length of therapeutic contacts will be important to account for nontherapeutic factors that might affect outcomes, particularly among populations that might be particularly motivated to participate in NFT.

Patients may seek out NFT for ADHD because of poor response to medications or a desire to pursue alternative treatments (Hirshberg, 2007). Support for the use of NFT for adult ADHD is tentative and not conclusive, and the precise mechanisms of change remain unclear, although a recent neuroimaging study indicated that NFT resulted in increased activation of brain regions associated with selective attention and response inhibition in a sample of children with ADHD (Beauregard & Lévesque, 2006). However, it is important that clinicians and consumers stay aware of the developing research on NFT to make informed decisions about its potential usefulness.

NEUROCOGNITIVE TRAINING

Neurocognitive training approaches differ from NFT to the extent that rather than modifying brain wave patterns, these training approaches emphasize the isolation and exercise of inefficient cognitive skills common to ADHD, such as inattention and working memory problems. These approaches are often delivered in the form of computerized exercises, with the notion being that various cognitive skills can be uptrained.

Although some attention treatments yield positive results for children with ADHD, only NFT has produced enough positive results to be classified as a tentatively supported program for adults with ADHD, with no computerized attention training program achieving that status for adults with ADHD (Riccio & French, 2004). More recently, however, published studies of positive preliminary results obtained from working memory training for children with ADHD have been adapted for use with adults with ADHD. Hence, working memory training is reviewed next.

WORKING MEMORY TRAINING

In the past several years, promising research has been conducted on a computerized working memory training (WMT) program (Klingberg, Forssberg, & Westerberg, 2002; Olesen, Westerberg, & Klingberg, 2004). Working memory is one of the executive functions that have been implicated in the symptoms and impairment associated with ADHD (Barkley, 1997a; Brown, 2005). Working memory problems also play a role in many learning disabilities and can be an aftereffect of traumatic brain injuries or strokes. Similar to other executive functions, working memory is primarily associated with the functioning of the prefrontal cortex and basal ganglia as well as the availability of adequate dopamine (Conway, Kane, & Engle, 2003; McNab & Klingberg, 2008) and is responsive to treatment with medications.

Working memory is an important function that is involved in many complex tasks, and differences in working memory capacity explain one third to one half of the variance of interindividual differences in general intelligence (Conway et al., 2003). Working memory plays a role in daily life insofar at it involves the ability to sort through information and hold it in mind (i.e., "online") to assess and manipulate it. Therefore, it is an important skill for planning, problem solving, mathematical calculations, and decision making as well as screening out distracting information, among other processes.

WMT, developed by Klingberg (2006) and colleagues, and commercially available as Cogmed Working Memory Training, involves a specific set of tasks presented on a computer that are designed to improve working memory (Cogmed America Inc., 2008). Separate WMT software programs have been designed for children and adults, the latter introduced in 2007. After an initial screening session and start-up sessions (presumably to familiarize trainees with the training procedures), the WMT computer program guides trainees through rotating tasks that train both verbal and visuospatial working memory. The difficulty level is adjusted throughout a training session to match the current performance level of the trainee using specific algorithms. Daily training sessions last 30 to 40 minutes and involve a set number of trials in each session. Training sessions occur 5 days a week for 5 weeks.

In addition to the computer-based exercises, WMT is supervised by a qualified "coach" (Cogmed America Inc., 2008). The coach is considered a necessary component of the training program to monitor progress and compliance with the training protocol and to provide direction and encouragement to the trainee. The coach provides support to the trainee (including by phone or Internet) and in cases of children receiving WMT, helps parents set up a reward system. After completion of the WMT protocol, there are weekly follow-up contacts from the coach, a wrap-up session, written summary report, and a 6-month follow-up session. A booster program also is available after 6 months that includes a start-up session and 3 weeks of training and coaching. The completion of the WMT protocol is purported to improve working memory capacity.

Working Memory Training Research

To date, studies of WMT for ADHD have been conducted exclusively with children, although there have been studies of WMT for adults without ADHD and there are reportedly adult ADHD trials underway. The first study of WMT for children (ages 7–15 years) used a double-blind, placebo-controlled design (Klingberg et al., 2002). Fourteen children who had been diagnosed with ADHD by a pediatrician using *Diagnostic and Statistical Manual of Mental Disorders* (4th ed.; American Psychiatric Association, 1994) criteria composed the study sample. One group of 7 children received the WMT protocol in which the difficulty level was adjusted to match trainees' current performance level. A comparison control group of 7 children performed the same WMT tasks but at a much lower level of difficulty. Results indicated that the WMT group significantly improved not only on measures of targeted areas of working memory but also on nontrained measures of visuospatial working memory and complex reasoning. Trainees receiving WMT also exhibited fewer head movements during the tasks, which was used as an indicator of improved motor control.

A second experiment was reported in the Klingberg et al. (2002) study in which 4 healthy adults (without ADHD) in their 20s participated in WMT. The adult participants demonstrated significant improvements on both trained and untrained visuospatial working memory, complex reasoning, and completion time on a directed attention task when compared with their pretraining scores on these measures and when compared with the control group used in the study of children with ADHD.

Klingberg et al. (2005) conducted a multicenter, randomized, controlled, double-blind follow-up study of WMT for children with ADHD. Fifty-three children (ages 7–12 years) diagnosed with ADHD and who were not medicated were assigned to either the WMT group or a comparison control group identical to those described in Klingberg et al. (2002). The ADHD diagnosis, in most cases made prior to study screening, was confirmed by a study physician using teacher and parent ratings of ADHD (i.e., Conners Rating Scales; Conners, 2001) and clinical impression. Outcome measures were obtained before intervention, immediately after intervention, and at 3-month follow-up.

Three participants dropped out of the study, and 6 more did not achieve sufficient training compliance, leaving 44 children who completed the program. Results indicated that participants completing WMT exhibited significant improvements on measures of nontrained visuospatial and verbal working memory tasks, response inhibition, and complex reasoning. Most of these positive effects were maintained at 3-month follow-up. Parents' ratings (but not teachers' ratings) of ADHD symptoms were improved at both postintervention and follow-up assessments.

More recently, Gibson, Seroczynski, Gondoli, Braungart-Reiker, and Grundy (2007) conducted a study of 12 adolescents with ADHD (ages 12–14 years) who completed WMT while on prescribed medication for ADHD. The study tested the hypothesis that WMT improves symptoms of inattention by improving executive aspects of fluid IQ. *Fluid IQ* can be understood as the ability to deal with novel situations and problems that are encountered for which there are not straightforward solutions. Such situations require cognitive flexibility and adaptability.

Results replicated improvements on measures of visuospatial and verbal working memory and complex reasoning skills (i.e., fluid IQ) found in previous studies of WMT. Moreover, the main treatment effects of WMT for ADHD replicated those reported by Klingberg et al. (2005) in that there were improvements on measures of inattention beyond those provided by medications. It is interesting to note that the researchers explored the relationship of fluid IQ, visuospatial working memory, and inattention, hypothesizing that improvements in visuospatial working memory mediate improvements in fluid IQ, thereby resulting in reduction in inattentive symptoms of ADHD. Said differently, improved visuospatial working memory might be the mechanism of action for clinical improvements obtained through WMT. Although this direct connection model did not achieve statistical significance, there is preliminary evidence of a moderate, indirect association that warrants further study.

WMT has not yet been studied in samples of adults with ADHD, although there have been studies involving adult trainees. Westerberg and Klingberg (2007) studied WMT for 3 healthy, young adult men who were compared with a control group that did not receive WMT. Results indicated that WMT training was associated with improvements on targeted working memory tasks, nontrained working memory tasks, and complex reasoning, findings similar to previous studies of WMT. Functional magnetic resonance imaging conducted during performance of a working memory task and a baseline task for each participant showed increased brain activity in the middle and inferior frontal gyrus regions after WMT. The imaging results were interpreted as similar to those obtained in comparative research of skill learning.

WMT was administered to a sample of working-age adults (mean age of 54 years) with cognitive functioning difficulties related to acquired brain injury, that is, 1 to 3 years poststroke (Westerberg, Jacobaeus, et al., 2007). Eighteen participants were randomly assigned to a WMT group or to a passive control group (no WMT). Compared with the control group, the WMT group reported significant improvements on measures of both trained and untrained working memory tasks as well as attention. There were no differences between groups on measures of complex reasoning, interference control, or declarative memory. The treatment group also reported significantly greater improvements on a measure of cognitive functioning in daily life than did the control group.

More recently, WMT was studied in a sample of 45 seniors (mean age of 63.7 years) to determine its effects on age-related decline in working memory (Westerberg, Brehemer, D'Hondt, Söderlund, & Bäckman, 2007). Participants were randomly assigned to either a WMT group or a control group (low difficulty WMT). To compare age-related differences, 55 young adults (mean age of 26.3 years) were randomized to either a WMT group or a control group. Results indicated that the senior WMT group exhibited improvements on targeted working memory tasks, although the young adult WMT group showed greater improvements. Both age groups receiving WMT had comparable improvements on nontargeted working memory tasks and on measures of attention and cognitive functioning in daily life, and gains were generally maintained at 3-month follow-up. However, there were no improvements on measures of complex reasoning, interference control, or episodic memory.

Finally, a neuroimaging study conducted on 13 healthy men provided some evidence of the possible mechanisms of action of WMT (McNab et al., 2009). Participants received 35 minutes of WMT each day for 5 weeks. The training resulted in the expected improvements in working memory functioning. Functional magnetic resonance imaging (fMRI) was used to identify brain regions involved during working memory tasks. The binding potential (receptor density) of dopamine receptors for these regions was measured before and after treatment using positron emission tomography. Improvements in working memory after WMT were associated with changes in cortical (but not subcortical) dopamine receptors in the prefrontal and parietal regions. Thus, these preliminary data suggest that WMT may operate by inducing changes in dopamine receptor density.

Summary

The positive findings reported in studies of WMT for children with ADHD and initial studies of adults without ADHD are encouraging. It seems that a study of WMT administered to a sample of adults with ADHD is destined to be published in the not-too-distant future.

Because WMT has been introduced to the ADHD community by means of well-designed, progressive research, it has likely avoided much of the controversy associated with NFT. However, some of the concerns expressed about NFT are relevant in reviews of WMT. Some of the leading researchers and developers of WMT have vested business interests in commercial versions of WMT. These interests do not negate the research findings but simply must be disclosed and considered in the review of the evidence for these and other treatments. There is a concern that WMT was made commercially available too quickly after only limited, although promising, initial findings (Barkley, 2006c). Moreover, as the clinical use of WMT undergoes further research, it will be important to examine its effectiveness in ADHD samples (child, adolescent, and adult) with various patterns of comorbidity and learning issues that reflect the realities of clinical practice. In a related line of study, it will be important to continue to include functional outcome measures as dependent variables to assess the degree to which WMT is associated with generalized improvements in daily functioning.

CONCLUSION

The review of the current research evidence for NFT and WMT indicates that there remain important issues to be addressed (see Table 6.1). Despite improved research and promising findings, there are unanswered questions about the efficacy of these treatments, particularly in cases of complex psychiatric comorbidity, learning problems, and significant functional impairment in adults with ADHD. Is it the proposed changes in brain functioning that produce improvements, or are there nonspecific factors, such as the therapeutic role of trainers or coaches, that are associated with the results? What are the limits of brain training, and to what degree can it generalize and produce functional improvements in daily life? Despite the limitations with existing research, one is left with the notion that there might be "something" to NFT approaches, WMT approaches, or both, but one is not exactly sure yet what that "something" is.

The clinical reality is that some adults with ADHD who do not respond to medications or other treatments might seek out NFT or WMT, as might others seeking symptom relief through nonpharmacologic means. Growing interest in issues of neuroplasticity, brain exercise (i.e., "use it or lose it"), and the use of technology in treatment ensures that these interventions will be part of the ongoing dialogue about ADHD treatments. However, the research on NFT and WMT for adults with ADHD remains at a preliminary stage. I hope that randomized clinical trials of NFT and WMT for adults with ADHD will be performed in the coming years to answer some important questions. Thus, it will be important for clinicians to keep abreast of this interesting, although controversial, area ADHD treatment.

TABLE 6.1

Summary of Neurofeedback and Neurocognitive Training for Adult Attention-Deficit/Hyperactivity Disorder (ADHD)

Neurocognitive treatment	Strengths	Limitations	Current status and future directions
Neurofeedback training (NFT)	Tentative positive results for adults with ADHD Anecdotal support Preliminary support for its usefulness as a possible component of assessment	Few studies of adults with ADHD Significant flaws in most studies Unclear whether NFT outperforms standard assessments and treatments	Randomized control designs with adults with ADHD are needed Future studies must contro for therapeutic time and support Measurements of functional outcomes are needed to determine whether treatment improves daily functioning It will be necessary to clarify mechanisms of action—How exactly does it work?
Working memory training (WMT)	Various computerized neurocognitive training approaches have tentative support Positive results in studies of WMT for children and teens with ADHD Strong research designs Generalized gains in other areas of working memory	No studies of adults with ADHD receiving WMT Unclear whether positive outcomes also result in improved daily functioning	Randomized control designs with adults with ADHD are needed Measurement of functional cutcomes is needed to determine whether treatment improves daily functioning It will be necessary to clarify mechanisms of action—How exactly does it work?

7

COMPLEMENTARY AND ALTERNATIVE TREATMENTS

Most treatments reviewed in this chapter, similar to neurofeedback and neurocognitive training, claim to target core symptoms of attention-deficit/hyperactivity disorder (ADHD). Moreover, the interventions discussed here fall outside what are considered mainstream treatments for adult ADHD, hence they are known collectively as *complementary and alternative medicine (CAM)* approaches.

These CAM treatments are not considered conventional interventions for adult ADHD and, in most cases, are deemed ineffective in the treatment of ADHD. However, many adults with ADHD may pursue them to augment standard treatments, because standard treatments have not been effective for them, because they have heard anecdotal claims of their effectiveness, or because of concern about conventional treatments (i.e., medications) stemming from negative stories in the media. Although most clinicians are rightly skeptical of these treatments, it is understandable that many people seek hope in the form of additional CAM treatments that promise to provide relief from the wide-ranging effects of ADHD. However, the problem is that pursuit of these treatments might interfere with engaging in treatments with documented efficacy.

The prevalence of the use of CAM in the general population is quite surprising. A recently published Swiss longitudinal study indicated that CAM use in the year prior to interview increased from 21.9% in 1993 to 29.5% in 1999, with individuals experiencing physical or emotional problems twice as likely to use them compared with individuals without such difficulties, probably reflecting a desire to seek additional relief from distress (Rössler et al., 2006). In fact, the majority of CAM use is done in concert with conventional treatments. In the United States, it is estimated that 73% of adults use a minimum of one supplement annually, running the gamut from taking a daily multivitamin to ingesting an assortment of herbal and other alternative remedies, despite few evidence-based standards guiding their use (D. Hurley, 2007). Although there are no studies of adults with ADHD, parents often seek out CAM treatments for their children with ADHD, with rates of use ranging from 28% to 67% (Chan, 2002; Chan, Rappaport, & Kemper, 2003; Gross-Tsur, 2003; Rojas & Chan, 2005; Sinha & Efron, 2005; Stubberfield & Parry, 1999). Thus, despite the professional skepticism about most CAM approaches and products, the market for them seems to be growing.

Arnold (2006) made an important distinction between *complementary* and *alternative*. The former term refers to treatments used in tandem with standard treatment approaches, attempting to obtain some additional symptom relief beyond that provided by orthodox interventions. The latter term suggests a treatment that could be used as a comparable substitute for standard treatments, the risk being that the initiation of potentially effective treatments could be delayed to pursue an unproven and likely ineffective course of treatment. Considering the impairments associated with ADHD, delays in receiving effective treatment may have dire consequences. Although the terms *complementary* and *alternative* are often used interchangeably, the treatments reviewed in this chapter should be considered only complementary.

It should be noted at the outset that not one of these CAM treatments has adequate research support to be considered a stand-alone treatment for ADHD (Reiff & Tippins, 2004; Rojas & Chan, 2005). A few CAM interventions are at the early stages of investigation and have yielded interesting pilot data that warrant follow-up study. The majority of treatments, though, have limited, if any, support, or a proposed treatment might represent an accepted "good health practice" but is not truly an intervention for ADHD. Eventually, researchers may find a few CAM approaches that provide slight benefits but do not outperform standard treatments or are helpful only for a small subset of people with ADHD.

Thus, to be complete in the review of nonmedication treatments for adults with ADHD, CAM treatments for which there is published research or that are frequently mentioned in the clinical literature are discussed. Approaches for which research has been conducted only with children with ADHD but that could be used with adults with ADHD are also included. The chapter sections on different CAM treatments are presented in roughly descending order of their potential benefit for adults with ADHD. Within each section, the specific treatments are similarly presented in descending order of their potential benefit on the basis of available research—studies either on treatments specific to ADHD populations or treatments considered to be useful for other conditions that have been adapted for use with ADHD. Nevertheless, as was noted previously, none of these treatments can be considered as a component of a standard treatment package for adult ADHD, and none can be considered to have adequate research support for its efficacy for this clinical population; thus, as the saying goes, "buyer beware."

REVIEW OF CAM TREATMENTS AND RESEARCH

Considering the severe and wide-ranging effects of ADHD on functioning, it is understandable that individuals with ADHD and their loved ones would seek out a range of treatments in attempt to ameliorate the symptoms of the disorder as much as possible. However, the desire for treatment alternatives may create a situation in which adults with ADHD seek out therapeutic approaches based on compelling anecdotal data but that have not been adequately studied. The following sections review a variety of methods that have been used in the treatment of ADHD, but none can be considered a well-established approach.

Therapeutic Interventions and Exercises

Similar to adapting traditional psychosocial treatments to the needs of adults with ADHD, several CAM approaches and exercises that address other psychological and medical issues have been adapted for use with adults with ADHD. The following sections review these adapted CAM approaches.

Mindfulness Meditation Training and Yoga

Mindfulness meditation has been increasingly integrated into many psychological treatments. In a nutshell, *mindfulness* involves paying attention to one's "in-the-moment" experience as a nonjudgmental observer. That is, thoughts, emotions, and physical states of being are noticed without taking steps to change them. Broadening one's awareness and acceptance of experience, thereby promoting follow-through on adaptive coping, is associated with many clinical benefits, such as stress reduction and pain management (Kabat-Zinn, 1994), emotional regulation (Linehan, 1993), and behavioral change (Hayes, Strosahl, & Wilson, 1999).

Mindfulness meditation training (MMT), then, is an experiential learning process in which individuals quietly devote purposeful attention to daily tasks that are typically performed automatically, such as walking or eating (Baijal & Gupta, 2008; Zylowska et al., 2008). Said differently, MMT teaches individuals to check in with themselves when physically, emotionally, or mentally distressed or distracted and to reorient by focusing on the act of breathing or other simple activities to develop a sense of peace.

More specific to its potential application to adult ADHD, there is evidence from basic research that MMT is associated with changes in attentional networks (Jha, Krompinger, & Baime, 2007) and on a cognitive allocation task (Slagter et al., 2007). Mindfulness training has also been included as a treatment module in a psychosocial treatment program for adult ADHD (Hesslinger et al., 2002; Philipsen et al., 2007). Zylowska et al. (2008) examined an 8-week MMT program administered to 24 adults and 8 adolescents with ADHD. Twenty-five participants, including 18 adults, completed the study. There were no differences between completers and noncompleters on ADHD subtype, symptom severity, or medication status. Adults practiced mindfulness for significantly more minutes per week than did adolescents. Participant ratings for the program were very high, averaging over 9 out of 10, with 10 being "most satisfied."

More than three fourths (78%) of completers reported reductions in total ADHD symptoms, with 30% achieving clinically significant symptom improvement. Regarding neurocognitive measures, significant improvements were made on conflict attention and set shifting but not on working memory. Although adults reported significant improvements on measures of anxiety and depression, there were no significant changes in depression or anxiety for adolescent participants. Thus, mindfulness meditation was associated with clinical and neurocognitive improvements for adults with ADHD and was well tolerated.

Z. B. Rosen et al. (2008) conducted a randomized study of the effects of an 8-week MMT course for adults with ADHD on neuropsychological functioning. Specifically, participants were asked to remember two faces or scenes over a brief delay and to indicate whether a probe image matched the face or scene. During the delay, two distractor images were presented that were either congruent or incongruent with the original images. There was no difference between the experimental and wait-list control group on performance on congruent trials. However, the results for performance on the incongruent trials indicated that adults with ADHD who completed the MMT course demonstrated improved performance when compared with the control group. These preliminary findings suggest that mindfulness meditation may improve working memory in adults with ADHD, although more research is needed, particularly seeing as working memory did not improve in the Zylowska et al. (2008) study.

A pilot study of yoga meditation (Sahaja Yoga Meditation, to be precise) was conducted with families with a child diagnosed with ADHD (L. J. Harrison,

Manocha, & Rubia, 2004). The program involved parents and their children attending twice-weekly, clinic-based yoga meditation sessions followed by at-home practice. Parent questionnaires and child interviews were used as pre- and posttreatment measures. Results indicated that parents rated their children as improved on measures of self-esteem, behavior, and relationship quality. Parents reported feeling happier, less stressed, and better able to manage their children's behavior. Children noticed improvements at home (e.g., less anxiety) and at school (e.g., better concentration). Another small study of boys with ADHD suggested there may be some circumscribed positive effects of yoga for boys already on stabilized medication regimens (Jensen & Kenny, 2004); however, it seems that yoga provides children (and their parents) with a healthy activity that may provide some short-term stress reduction.

Thus, MMT-related approaches have yielded preliminary positive results warranting further study, although these pilot findings must be interpreted cautiously. Ultimately, MMT's potential therapeutic benefit for adults with ADHD may be as a useful coping tool rather than improving cognitive functioning. It is unclear whether improvements from MMT result from improved cognitive functioning, decreased frustration when experiencing attention problems, or a combination thereof. That is, MMT may promote a mind-set of acceptance and normalization of attention difficulties, as well as serving as a distress management tool, thereby increasing the likelihood that adults with ADHD will implement effective coping strategies rather than giving up out of frustration. Moreover, the positive results in studies might result from nonspecific factors of a positive alliance with trainers and other group members with ADHD.

Light Therapy

Recent studies have indicated that many adults with ADHD experience sleep and circadian problems related to delayed sleep onset, less uninterrupted sleep, and in some cases, a greater need for sleep compared with control participants (Boonstra et al., 2007; Gau et al., 2007; Rybak, McNeely, Mackenzie, Jain, & Levitan, 2006, 2007). These sleep issues may be a reason why many adults with ADHD report an evening circadian preference (i.e., being an "evening person") and may magnify the effects of ADHD symptoms. Of course, ADHD can create sleep difficulties, as individuals describe "procrastinating on going to sleep," hyperfocusing on a computer or video game, or using evening hours to catch up on work not completed during the day (e.g., Tuckman, 2009).

An open trial of light therapy, a treatment for seasonal affective disorder (SAD), was administered to 29 adults (age range = 18–60 years) diagnosed with ADHD (Rybak et al., 2006). The ADHD diagnosis was established through previous assessment by a mental health professional or self-report of both childhood (e.g., Wender Utah Rating Scale; Ward, Wender, & Reimherr, 1993) and adulthood ADHD symptoms (Brown Attention Deficit

Disorder Scales [BADDS; Brown, 1996], Conners Adult ADHD Rating Scale [CAARS; Conners, Erhardt, & Sparrow, 1999]). Over half of the sample was treated with antidepressants, psychostimulants, or both, throughout the study.

Light therapy was self-administered according to a 3-week protocol. Each participant received a full spectrum fluorescent light box fitted with a screen that filtered out ultraviolet wavelengths. Participants sat in front of the light box for 30 minutes each morning, starting no later than 8:00 a.m. Daily treatment logs, phone inquiry, and face-to-face inquiry were used to monitor compliance. Light therapy was administered during fall and winter months, when seasonal depression is typically at its peak.

Of the original 37 individuals enrolled in the study, 4 dropped out and 4 others were deemed noncompliant with the protocol. Nineteen participants had either current or past major depression; 7 reported either SAD or significant seasonal worsening of chronic depression. Results indicated that the strongest correlation of improvement in ADHD self-ratings was a phase advance in circadian preference. That is, symptom improvement was associated with a shift away from being an evening person and toward "morningness," consistent with research on SAD. Light therapy was associated with moderate improvements on most subscales of the BADDS and CAARS. Categories of response for outcome measures were operationalized such that at least 25% improvement was deemed "partial response" and at least 50% improvement was considered "full response." For the BADDS total scores, 10% of participants had a full response and 17% had a partial response; only 10% of participants were partial responders as measured by the CAARS. The primary treatment effects of light therapy for adult ADHD seemed to occur within the domain of inattentive symptoms, corroborated by improvements on various neuropsychological measures of attention.

Previous research has indicated that individuals without ADHD but with depression and/or anxiety produce BADDS scores that fall in the clinically elevated range (Crisp, Brown, Sheets, & Reilley, 2005; Reilley, Charles, & Smith, 2004). Consequently, the better response rates to light therapy measured by the BADDS might reflect improved mood rather than reduction in ADHD symptoms. Moreover, the emphasis on getting out of bed and starting light therapy by 8:00 a.m. might have been an effective behavioral intervention that prompted participants to start their days earlier, which contributed to the circadian shift toward a morning orientation. An interesting controlled study would be a comparison of an adult ADHD group receiving the light therapy protocol with a comparison group encouraged to spend 30 minutes planning and prioritizing their activities for the day starting no later than 8:00 a.m. As it is, light therapy for ADHD is an experimental treatment requiring more study, although it may be helpful for individuals with comorbid seasonal mood problems.

Repetitive Transcranial Magnetic Stimulation

Transcranial magnetic stimulation (TMS) is a noninvasive brain stimulation approach (Hirshberg, Chiu, & Frazier, 2005; Sporn & Lisanby, 2006). TMS involves the administration of time-varying magnetic fields via small electromagnets to stimulate electrical current flow and neuronal depolarization in targeted areas of the cerebral cortex (Barker, Jalinous, & Freeston, 1985; as cited in Sporn & Lisanby, 2006). Repetitive TMS (rTMS) is a specific form of brain stimulation characterized by repeated magnetic pulses at frequencies ranging from 1 to 20 Hz, with low-frequency rTMS (≤ 1 Hz) associated with decreased neuronal excitability and high frequency (10–20 Hz) associated with increased neuronal excitability (Sporn & Lisanby, 2006). TMS has been the subject of increasing study for a variety of disorders, although its primary use has been in the treatment of depression (Morales, Henry, Nobler, Wassermann, & Lisanby, 2005). TMS is approved in Canada as a treatment for depression (Sporn & Lisanby, 2006) and was similarly approved by the U.S. Food and Drug Administration (FDA) in 2008 as a treatment for depression (after at least one failed trial on an antidepressant).

Because cortical hypoarousal has been implicated in ADHD, rTMS is being studied for use with individuals with ADHD. TMS (i.e., single and paired pulse) is associated with minimal risk. However, rTMS carries with it the risk of seizure when it is administered to adults who are at risk of seizure activity (e.g., epilepsy, cortical lesions), when rTMS is given at dosages exceeding safety guidelines, or when trains of rTMS are administered in rapid succession (Morales et al., 2005). In rare cases, on the basis of anecdotal reports, seizures have been reported in adults without the aforementioned risk factors. The common side effects of rTMS in adults include headache and scalp pain. The sonic artifact of rTMS could affect hearing; thus, it is recommended that ear plugs be worn during the procedure.

Forty children who were administered single-pulse TMS, equally divided among groups with ADHD and groups without ADHD, provided ratings of its acceptability (Garvey, Kaczynski, Becker, & Bartko, 2001). One child dropped out of TMS because of discomfort, and 5 other children said that they would not want to receive TMS again, although these 5 children said that they preferred it to a trip to the dentist. The remaining 34 children said they would be willing to repeat TMS.

Weaver et al. (2008) pilot tested the safety and efficacy of rTMS in a sample of 8 adolescents and young adults (ages 14–21 years) diagnosed with ADHD who were unmedicated during the study. The study used a double-blind, crossover design in which each participant received daily rTMS targeting the right dorsolateral prefrontal cortex for 2 weeks (10 sessions), a 1-week washout of no treatment, and 2 weeks (10 sessions) of sham treatment. Participants and raters were naive to the treatment condition.

Results indicated that rTMS was well tolerated, and there were no negative changes in neuropsychological or audiometry assessments. Treatment with rTMS was associated with significant improvements on clinical ratings of overall improvement, although changes on a measure of ADHD symptoms were not significant. Moreover, rTMS was associated with improvements on ratings of functioning just shy of 88% of the time; sham treatment was associated with improvements on functional ratings 50% of the time. More data are needed to establish the safety and efficacy of rTMS as a CAM approach for adult ADHD, particularly considering no significant change in ADHD symptoms was associated with treatment, but it may be found to be helpful in cases of comorbid depression (Morales et al., 2005). Thus, rTMS remains at the early stages of being an experimental treatment for ADHD.

Vestibular and Cerebellar Exercises

It has been suggested that ADHD symptoms result from vestibular problems associated with the inner ear system. The theory is that deficits in the inner ear system may cause motor coordination and behavior regulation difficulties seen in ADHD. Thus, sensorimotor and other training approaches have been used to target various motor deficits in children with ADHD (e.g., Banaschewski, Besmens, Zieger, & Rothenberger, 2001).

However, the theory appears to stretch beyond data insofar as the inner ear system has not been established as playing a role in the deficient impulse control, hyperactive behavior, or pervasive attention problems seen in ADHD. Thus, proposed treatments with antiemetic (e.g., anti–motion sickness) medications have not been found to be effective for ADHD. Vestibular interventions (e.g., spinning exercise) that have been pilot studied have been associated with mild improvements in some young children with ADHD (Arnold, 2006), although a recent randomized controlled trial produced no significant therapeutic benefits of vestibular stimulation in a sample of children with ADHD (Clark et al., 2008). Thus, vestibular stimulation is not effective for children with ADHD, nor would it seem that it would be effective for adults with ADHD.

Treatment programs have been developed around the notion that cerebellar functioning plays a role in ADHD and other learning problems. There is growing interest in the role of the cerebellum in higher order cognitive processes (Bower & Parsons, 2003; J. J. Ratey, 2008) and the finding that individuals with ADHD have smaller cerebellar volumes than control participants without ADHD (Castellanos et al., 2001; Krain & Castellanos, 2006; Pliszka, 2003). Thus, cerebellar underdevelopment is considered as a factor in some neuropsychological deficits observed in ADHD, such as poor motor control and inefficient procedural learning. In turn, interventions have been developed that are alleged to improve cerebellar functioning.

Dyslexia dyspraxia attention treatment (DDAT), commercially available as the Dore program, the most prominent exercise-based program for ADHD, uses unique, individually prescribed exercise programs to promote automaticity of performance (Dore, 2007). DDAT exercises are to be performed for 10 minutes twice a day for a period of 12 to 18 months. The program is touted as being effective for both children and adults with ADHD (as well as for other learning and developmental disorders; Hallowell & Ratey, 2005).

The results of a randomized controlled study of the DDAT program administered for 6 months to children with reading difficulties (including many with ADHD) indicated that children completing the program demonstrated improved cerebellar functioning (e.g., balance, dexterity, eye movement control) and better scores for reading fluency than did a control group (Reynolds, Nicolson, & Hambly, 2003). However, the study was roundly criticized on various methodological and statistical grounds. The specific DDAT interventions were poorly described, there were important pretreatment differences between the treatment and control groups, and concurrent literacy interventions were received by many participants, with the end result being that the conclusions drawn from findings are highly suspect and not considered adequate to recommend the use of DDAT (I. L. Richards et al., 2003; Snowling & Hulme, 2003; Stein, 2003; cf. Nicolson & Reynolds, 2003).

More recently, an abstract presented at an American Psychological Association convention (Rutherford, Nicolson, & Arnold, 2006) reported the results of the DDAT program administered to children and adults with ADHD in the United Kingdom. Of 895 consecutive clients seeking treatment at DDAT specialty clinics, 193 were over 16 years old (i.e., adults). Of the entire sample, 609 were identified as "ADHD positive" based on *Diagnostic and Statistical Manual of Mental Disorders* (4th ed.; American Psychiatric Association, 1994) criteria, although the precise diagnostic procedures were not explained. The average length of treatment was 13 months and involved twice-daily, customized exercises for 5 to 10 minutes as well as eight 90-minute follow-up clinic appointments.

Although adults reported slightly lower levels of pretreatment inattention, there were no differences either in pretreatment hyperactivity or impulsivity symptoms or in treatment response between adults and children with ADHD. Although not reporting adults' treatment response separately, the authors reported a significant reduction of both inattentive and hyperactive or impulsive symptoms for the entire sample and for the ADHD positive group, although ADHD subtypes were not reported. Furthermore, although presenting effect sizes, the study did not have a control group, and the statistical analyses performed and specific p values (i.e., statistical significance) were not reported. Instead, average number of symptoms endorsed, percentages of participants with ADHD positive status, and other descriptive statistics were presented.

The authors used the Multimodal Treatment Study of Children With ADHD (MTA Cooperative Group, 1999) as a control group for comparison of treatment effects after the fact, citing that the exercise-based program demonstrated higher effects. However, it seems that the DDAT study did not have a methodology or inclusion–exclusion criteria as rigorous as the MTA study. It would have been preferable to have had a control group drawn from the DDAT sample against which to compare outcomes and effect sizes. Thus, although critics of the aforementioned studies encourage the ongoing study of potential connections between cerebellar deficits and learning difficulties (Stein, 2003), the extant research on DDAT is sufficiently limited and flawed to render its positive results unconvincing.

What is more, the specifics of DDAT remain vague to readers of the research literature because of developers' concerns about disclosing commercially sensitive information. Limited accounts of DDAT exercises suggest that they include exercises to improve balance, coordination, eye movements, dual tasking, memorization, and so on (Hallowell & Ratey, 2005; Reynolds et al., 2003). It is yet unclear whether these exercises provide improvements above and beyond what can be obtained from the myriad benefits of regular exercise and athletics that promote balance and coordination (e.g., J. J. Ratey, 2008).

Massage

Massage was found to be beneficial in a preliminary study of adolescents with ADHD (Field, Quintino, Hernandez-Reif, & Koslovsky, 1998). Teens with ADHD who received daily massage therapy for 2 weeks reported feeling happier than peers who received relaxation training. Observers and teachers noted various improvements in the massage therapy group, such as less fidgetiness, more on-task behavior, and less hyperactive behavior.

Khilnani, Field, Hernandez-Reif, and Schanberg (2003) conducted a study of 30 child and adolescent students with ADHD who were randomly assigned either to receive massage therapy or a wait-list control group. Participants in the massage therapy group received 20-minute sessions twice a week for 1 month. Students with ADHD who received massage therapy exhibited significant improvements in self-ratings of mood and teacher ratings of classroom behavior. Students also received school-based support while participating in the study, but it is unclear whether students received other treatments (i.e., medications). Massage therapy is generally benign, barring some physical or emotional contraindication (e.g., past sexual abuse) for its use. Although it has not been studied in adults, it seems that adults with ADHD would experience similar benefits to those reported by teens with ADHD, although massage therapy seems to make a relatively short-lived contribution to stress reduction and overall well-being rather than specifically targeting and reducing ADHD symptoms.

Interactive Metronome

Interactive metronome (IM) training is a computerized version of a simple metronome, a device used by musicians to maintain a steady rhythm. The IM produces a rhythmic beat that trainees match by tapping either a hand or foot. The underlying theory is that IM training promotes the development of central nervous system processing capacities underlying motor regulation and timing abilities and thereby reduces symptoms implicated in ADHD (Shaffer et al., 2001).

As with most CAM, there are no studies of adult patients with ADHD. However, an initial randomized controlled study of 56 boys with uncomplicated ADHD (established by a diagnosis by a community clinician) indicated that individuals participating in IM training derived benefits on outcome measures of attention and motor regulation when compared with pretreatment scores and results obtained by individuals in control groups (Shaffer et al., 2001), although a video-game-playing control group also exhibited improvements on a number of outcome measures. More research is needed to replicate these preliminary findings, to determine whether IM is helpful for adults with ADHD, to explore whether IM is associated with functional improvements in daily life, and to replicate the limited positive findings in the childhood sample (Riccio & French, 2004). Moreover, if these positive results are replicated, it will be important to explore the possible mechanisms of change of IM training (including the role of nonspecific factors) for individuals with ADHD of all ages. However, there are no current data to support a recommendation of IM for adult ADHD.

Chiropractic Treatment

Chiropractic theory suggests that symptoms of ADHD result from spinal problems, and consequently, spinal adjustments or manipulations and additional somatosensory stimulation may produce symptom reduction. However, this theory is not consistent with current neurobiological models of ADHD (Barkley, 2006a; National Resource Center on AD/HD [NRC], 2008b). Nonetheless, a recent study of a chiropractic intervention reported a case series of 9 adults who received 2 months of network spinal analysis (NSA; Pauli, 2007). Of the 9 participants, 3 cited attention difficulties as their primary problem and the other 6 described these difficulties as "additional" problems for which they sought help.

The ADHD diagnosis was operationally defined as a pretreatment score on a continuous performance task (CPT) that fell below the average range, with most participants' scores falling significantly below average. Participants were seen twice a week for 2 months and were asked to make no changes in their medical or lifestyle routines (unless medically necessary). They received Level-1 NSA, which involves a series of gentle contacts designed to produce "entrainment of respiratory motion with spinal motion, release of tension from spinal stability subsystems, reduction of parameters of spinal cord tension" (Pauli, 2007, p. 2). A posttreatment analysis of the CPT performed after 2 months (i.e., 16 sessions) indicated significant improvements in attention with 8 of 9 participants scoring in the normal range (with the nonresponder later diagnosed with hypothyroidism). A posttreatment static paraspinal surface electromyography (sEMG) indicated improved neurospinal integrity among participants. However, there were no significant correlations of either pre- or posttreatment sEMG and CPT scores. There were no data on treatment effects on daily functioning status.

Although the 9 individuals consulted a chiropractor for "attention problems," a below-average CPT score as the sole marker of ADHD is an inadequate diagnostic assessment. There was no other reported evidence indicating that these adults had ADHD. This is not to say that these individuals did not experience attention problems. Indeed, their attention problems may have been a downstream consequence of physical discomfort. Perhaps NSA provided some relief from physical discomfort, thereby reducing a source of distraction, as was suggested by improved posttreatment sEMG. In the absence of better documentation of ADHD and an empirically persuasive chiropractic theory of ADHD, however, it goes beyond the data to say that chiropractic treatment (or any number of other CAMs) helps attention and the wide-ranging functional difficulties resulting from ADHD. Insufficient diagnostic procedures for ADHD are a common drawback of CAM studies, akin to operationally defining patients as having malaria if they present for treatment with a fever of 100°F or higher (which is one symptom of malaria) and then claiming that acetaminophen effectively treats a majority of cases of malaria. Thus, there is currently no scientifically compelling connection between neurobiological models of ADHD and chiropractic theory or interventions for ADHD.

Vision Therapy

Some optometrists and ophthalmologists view vision problems, such as poor convergence, focusing problems, and faulty eye movements, as contributing to ADHD. Although assessing for possible vision and auditory problems is good clinical practice to rule out factors that could better explain attention problems, these sorts of visual and auditory problems are considered differential medical diagnoses for circumscribed symptoms and do not account for the wide-ranging behavioral and cognitive impairments seen in the full ADHD syndrome. Said simply, no data support the use of optometric training, vision training, or "lens therapy" for ADHD in patients of any age (NRC, 2008b; Reiff & Tippins, 2004).

That said, a review of the connection between convergence insufficiency (CI) and ADHD in children revealed that there might be identifiable subgroups for which CI treatment is indicated (Granet, Gomi, Ventura, & Miller-Scholte, 2005). CI can be diagnosed in both children and adults and is characterized by the inability to converge the eyes (i.e., binocular convergence) toward a nearby visual target or maintain convergence without undue effort. Affected individuals have difficulty maintaining focus on reading, desk work, or other near tasks. Individuals may report having "tired eyes," double vision, or that words they are reading move or "swim."

Chart reviews were performed to identify children diagnosed with CI who also were diagnosed with ADHD; conversely, children diagnosed with ADHD in a medical database who subsequently underwent eye examinations also were identified (Granet et al., 2005). Of children diagnosed with CI, 9.8% were also diagnosed with ADHD. Among the sample of children with ADHD, 15.9% were identified with coexisting CI. These data indicate a threefold greater incidence of ADHD among CI patients than the incidence of ADHD seen in the general population; conversely, ADHD patients have a threefold greater incidence of CI than that of the general population.

To be clear, there is not sufficient evidence with which to draw a causal relationship between ADHD and CI. Considering the overlap of some symptoms and availability of effective treatments for both, a consultation with an ophthalmologist may be indicated if an individual reports symptoms of CI. Although CI treatment has been found to have a positive effect on CI symptoms, no research data indicate that vision exercises are effective treatments for ADHD in patients of any age. Similarly, it seems that effective treatment for ADHD would not treat CI symptoms. Moreover, the co-incidence of CI and ADHD has not yet been studied in adult samples.

Acupuncture

Acupuncture is a relatively popular CAM treatment. However, no studies have been published on its use with adults in the treatment of ADHD. Loo (1998; as cited in Arnold, 2001) conducted an unpublished pilot study in which young children with ADHD reportedly benefited from acupuncture, although children with the most severe symptoms did not cooperate with treatment. It seems that adults with ADHD would be better able to complete acupuncture, although there are neither extant data on its efficacy nor explanatory models of acupuncture's relevance or appropriateness for ADHD.

Mirror Feedback

Mirrors were used in a study of middle school students with hyperactivity, inattention, or both, who were compared with peers without these difficulties (Zentall, Hall, & Lee, 1998). Students performed partially solvable word puzzles either with or without the presence of a mirror. There were no performance differences between groups when the mirror was present; there were expected differences in the no-mirror condition, with the hyperactive or inattentive students scoring lower than did control participants on puzzle performance. Control children performed worse in the mirror condition than control children without the mirror, making it important to establish an accurate diagnosis before recommending this intervention (Arnold, 2001, 2006). Although drawing from data from one small pilot study of children, working at a desk in front of a mirror may help some adults with ADHD to reorient to task when distracted, although this trivial coping strategy should not be considered "treatment."

Supplementation and Nutrition

The CAM approaches heretofore reviewed in this chapter have concentrated on adapting various therapeutic strategies to treat the symptoms of ADHD. The treatments reviewed in this section, on the other hand, focus on the effects of various dietary supplements and nutritional approaches on attention and other features of ADHD.

Essential Fatty Acid Supplementation

In addition to various health benefits such as prevention of heart disease, specific polyunsaturated fatty acids play an important role in the myelination of the axons of neurons. Myelin is the fatty sheath that insulates the axons of some neurons and speeds up the transmission of electrical signals between cells. Polyunsaturated fatty acids, known as essential fatty acids (EFAs) or "fish oils," also form the membrane for receptors and other surface structures of neurons. In particular, phospholipids containing large amounts of omega-3 fatty acids (eicosapentaenoic acid, docosahexaenoic acid, and alpha-linolenic acid) and omega-6 fatty acids (arachidonic acid and linoleic acid) make up these neuronal membranes but cannot be manufactured by the body; hence, it is "essential" that these fatty acids be acquired through the diet (Arnold, 2001; Stevens, 2000; Stoll, 2001). Cold-water, fatty fish (e.g., salmon, fresh tuna), particular plant oils (e.g., flaxseed, linseed, canola, soybean), and some nuts (e.g., walnuts, almonds, pecans) are common dietary sources of EFAs.

Although the omega-3 and omega-6 series fatty acids provide a wide range of health benefits (Martinez & Marangell, 2004), they have been thought to play a special role in ADHD. Some studies have reported lower levels of EFAs in samples of children with ADHD compared with control groups without ADHD (Arnold, 2001; Mitchell, Aman, Turbott, & Manku, 1987; Mitchell, Lewis, & Cutler, 1983; Stevens et al., 1995). Regarding treatment effects, there is evidence that use of an omega-3 fatty acid reduced aggression in a nonclinical sample of young adults (Hamazaki et al., 1996), and combinations of omega-3 and -6 fatty acids were associated with improvements on ratings of ADHD-related behaviors in samples of children (Richardson & Montgomery, 2005; Stevens et al., 2003). However, other studies of EFA supplementation in samples of children with ADHD have been equivocal.

In general, studies with indiscriminate supplementation have not reported positive therapeutic effects. However, studies selecting children with ADHD with EFA deficiency (either assessed by symptoms of deficiency or by measuring plasma levels) and using a balanced combination supplementation of both omega-3 and omega-6 have reported limited positive results, although at least one study reported significant placebo effects in the control group (Arnold, 2001, 2007; Burgess & Stevens, 1998, cited in Arnold, 2001). A controlled study of adjunctive treatment administering omega-3 alone produced disappointing results (Martinez & Marangell, 2004; Voigt et al., 2001), although the trial may have been too brief, selected a questionable form of omega-3 fatty acid, or both (Richardson & Puri, 2002; Rojas & Chan, 2005). The benefits of EFA supplementation might be short-lived, akin to findings obtained in studies of amino acids, discussed in the next subsection. Moreover, many studies have been flawed by choice of placebo, poor diagnostic procedures, and so on.

Two preliminary studies reported reduced plasma levels of omega-3 EFAs in adults with ADHD when compared with control groups without ADHD (Antalis et al., 2006; G. S. Young, 2004). However, there are no studies of the effects of supplementation for adults with ADHD, although it seems that they would yield the same equivocal findings as obtained in samples of children with ADHD identified with specific EFA deficiencies. It may take longer for adults to notice the positive effects of EFA supplementation than it does for children because of the more rapid brain development in children. Monastra (2008) noted that the EFA deficiency observed in ADHD samples might be related to inefficient conversion of EFAs into long-chain polyunsaturated fatty acids, which is mediated by zinc. Considering the negative effects of ADHD on good health hygiene, lower levels of EFAs in ADHD samples might reflect an effect of the disorder on good dietary practices rather than a cause of symptoms.

Some adults with ADHD and comorbid mood problems may experience mild benefit from adjunctive use of EFAs (Martinez & Marangell, 2004; Stoll, 2001). Preliminary studies have found an imbalance of an excess of omega-6 in relation to omega-3 fatty acids in samples of adults with depression and indicate that increased supplemental or dietary omega-3 fatty acids result in improved mood (Arnold, 2001). Overall, however, EFA supplementation is not an adequate single treatment for ADHD for patients of any age, although it may be a complement to a treatment plan in cases of comorbid depression and to optimize good health practices.

Amino Acid Supplementation

Amino acid supplementation—amino acids being precursors of various neurotransmitters implicated in ADHD symptoms—is quite possibly the CAM treatment that has been most widely studied in adults with ADHD (Arnold, 2001). Lower than average levels of amino acids have been found in samples of individuals with ADHD (Baker et al., 1991; Bornstein et al., 1990). Studies of both adults and children indicate that short-term benefits are associated with supplementation of tryptophan, tyrosine, phenylalanine, and S-adenosylmethionine. Unfortunately, the benefits only last for 2 to 3 months, at which point tolerance develops (Arnold, 2001; Nemzer, Arnold, Votolato, & McConnell, 1986; Reimherr, Wender, Wood, & Ward, 1987; Shekim, Antun, Hanna, McCracken, & Hess, 1990; Wood, Reimherr, & Wender, 1985a, 1985b). Several other studies, however, have failed to show positive therapeutic effects, making it doubtful that amino acid supplementation is a fruitful approach apart from providing short-term relief in cases of documented deficiency (Arnold, 2002). Impurities in at least one amino acid supplement, L-tryptophan, was associated with an epidemic of eosinophilia-myalgia syndrome in 1989; thus, the risk associated with this CAM outweighs its potential to provide short-lived benefits (Arnold, 2006).

Mineral Supplementation

A variety of studies have reported decreased levels of iron, zinc, and magnesium in children with ADHD relative to control participants (Arnold, 2001, 2002). Thus, supplementation to ensure that individuals with ADHD meet recommended daily allowances (RDAs) of these minerals is thought to contribute to a mild degree of symptom improvement as well as representing a good health practice. It is important to remember, however, that although documented mineral deficiency is a cause for concern, toxicity may result from excessive mineral supplementation; thus, it should be undertaken only under medical supervision.

Studies of iron supplementation have reported improvements in cognitive functioning and hyperactivity in children identified with nonanemic iron deficiency, although these studies did not target children with ADHD (Bruner, Joffe, Duggan, Casella, & Brandt, 1996; Burattini et al., 1990). A preliminary study indicates that iron supplementation was associated with improvements in parent ratings (but not teacher ratings) in boys with ADHD (Sever, Ashkenazi, Tyano, & Weizman, 1997). A case study of supplementation for a young child with ADHD and iron deficiency reported improvements in parent and teacher ratings after 8 months (Konofal, Cortese, Lecendreux, Arnulf, & Mouren, 2005). Women with ADHD may benefit from iron supplementation, considering that women as a group are vulnerable to iron deficiency (Arnold, 2001), although this would represent a general health issue for women rather than an ADHD issue. Thus, no compelling evidence supports iron supplementation for adult ADHD.

Zinc is important for a number of bodily processes, such as neural metabolism, fatty acid absorption, and melatonin production (Arnold, 2001; DiGirolamo & Ramirez-Zea, 2009). As was mentioned earlier, zinc mediates EFA metabolism and thus may facilitate improvements observed in some studies of omega-3 fatty acid supplementation (Monastra, 2008). Although zinc levels have been found to be deficient in studies of children with ADHD, it is unclear whether these deficiencies necessarily correlate with higher symptom ratings. As zinc is a cofactor with various enzymatic processes, however, adequate zinc levels might influence stimulant response (Arnold, Votolato, Kleykamp, Baker, & Bornstein, 1990). Nevertheless, there are no prospective studies of the benefits of zinc supplementation for adult ADHD, although men as a group are vulnerable to zinc deficiency (Arnold, 2001), which is a general men's health issue rather than an ADHD issue.

A review of the research on zinc supplementation in children with ADHD revealed that the two studies reporting positive findings were conducted in Turkey and Iran, regions of the world in which zinc deficiency is suspected to be endemic (Arnold & DiSilvestro, 2005; DiGirolamo & Ramirez-Zea, 2009). Studies reporting positive findings associated with zinc supplementation for ADHD have been conducted on children concurrently treated with stimulant medications. Nonetheless, the potential benefit of zinc supplementation as an adjunctive treatment for ADHD remains investigational.

Finally, magnesium levels have been found to be deficient in some studies of children with ADHD, and supplementation targeting magnesium deficiency has been associated with improvements in parent and teacher ratings of symptoms (Arnold, 2001). However, toxicity is a risk of over-supplementation, and it should be undertaken only under medical supervision. Regarding adults with ADHD, pregnant women should consult their physician regarding magnesium supplementation, as magnesium is associated with eclampsia of pregnancy in some cases (Arnold, 2001).

In sum, although not explicitly studied in adult samples, iron, zinc, or magnesium supplementation, conducted under medical supervision, might provide some mild improvements to a small minority of adults with ADHD with documented mineral deficiencies. Moreover, these and other nutritional deficiencies may reflect impairments associated with adult ADHD insofar as its symptoms result in poor self-monitoring and poor health maintenance (i.e., healthy diet), although a pilot study documenting lower blood levels of EFAs in teens with ADHD when compared with control participants indicated that these differences were not explained by differences in dietary intake (Colter, Cutler, & Meckling, 2008). However, the authors noted that teens with ADHD ingested higher levels of fat than did control participants, which could interfere with the metabolism of EFAs. Hence, the supplementation would represent an intervention for symptoms of mineral deficiency and not for the core symptoms of ADHD. Although a reduction of the effects of such deficiency is desirable, the improvements would not approach the symptom relief provided by standard pharmacotherapy regimens for ADHD. Thus, mineral supplementation for ADHD remains investigational.

Vitamin and Nutritional Supplementation

The research support for the various forms of nutritional supplementation reviewed in this chapter is minimal, preliminary, and equivocal, at best (Arnold, 2001, 2007). Moreover, the preponderance of research has been conducted with children with ADHD, although one would suspect that similar equivocal effects of supplementation would be found in adult samples. Although supplementation for individuals with ADHD demonstrating insufficiencies of specific EFAs or minerals may be associated with greater benefits, maintaining the RDAs of various vitamins, minerals, and other nutrients is good health hygiene that optimizes standard treatments for ADHD by improving overall well-being.

In addition to the supplementation approaches mentioned earlier, several other nutritional supplements remain in the investigational phase, although there are significant flaws in extant research designs (Arnold, 2007). Among these agents are glyconutritional supplements containing basic saccharides involved in cell communication; carnitine, crucial for fatty acid metabolism (Van Oudheusden & Scholte, 2002); choline, a building block of the neurotransmitter acetylcholine, which affects memory and other cognitive functions (Yeo, Hill, Campbell, Vigil, & Brooks, 2000); and dimethylaminoethanol (DMAE), a precursor of choline, which is involved in acetylcholine synthesis and cell transmission and structure (Arnold, 2001). DMAE was originally available as a prescription drug for minimal brain dysfunction but was subsequently withdrawn because of lack of evidence of effectiveness, and it has not been approved by the FDA despite being one of the better-studied CAM treatments for ADHD (Arnold, 2007).

Vitamins and minerals are similarly involved in the synthesis of neurotransmitters and energy metabolism, and there has been interest in the potential benefits of megadoses of vitamins. However, on the basis of reviews of the systematic research, there is currently no evidence to support the use of vitamins and minerals in the treatment of ADHD (Arnold, 2002; NRC, 2007; Reiff & Tippins, 2004). In fact, taking megadoses of specific vitamins or megavitamins carries with it some risk of possible liver or nerve damage (Arnold, 2006), although these effects are reversible on discontinuation of the vitamin. Adhering to RDA guidelines for vitamins and minerals is a reasonable strategy, as is medically supervised treatment of documented deficiencies. However, isolated nutritional deficiencies do not cause the widespread and significant symptoms associated with ADHD. In fact, nutritional deficiencies might be a consequence of adult ADHD insofar as affected individuals are less likely to follow and maintain good health practices (Barkley, Murphy, & Fischer, 2008).

Dietary Restrictions

Said simply, there is no reliable evidence that poor diet, too much sugar, too much caffeine, or food additives are causal factors for the widespread symptoms and impairments characteristic of ADHD (Nigg, 2006; Reiff & Tippins, 2004; Rojas & Chan, 2005). Likewise, there is no compelling empirical evidence for the use of restriction diets in the treatment of ADHD (Rojas & Chan, 2005; Waschbusch & Hill, 2001). Regarding adult ADHD, existing food sensitivities tend to wane with age.

In fact, a study was performed in which mothers endorsing the belief that sugar consumption leads to disruptive behavior were observed during interactions with their children (Hoover & Milich, 1994). Before interacting with their mothers, all children in the study were given placebos. Half of the mothers were told their child was given a placebo; the other half of the mothers were told their child was given a "sugar pill." Mothers' subsequent ratings of their child's behavior during interactions were consistent with their expectancies about the influence of sugar on behavior. Mothers who thought their child had ingested sugar observed significantly higher levels of disruptive behavior (and were more critical of and directive with their children) than mothers who were told their child had ingested placebo. The point of the study is that expectancies create the appearance of associations where there are none.

Nonetheless, there may be small subgroups of individuals, not limited to those with ADHD, who experience allergic reactions or sensitivities to some chemicals or food additives for which elimination of the identified food item(s) could result in symptomatic improvements (Arnold, 2006; Nigg, 2006; Schab & Trinh, 2004; Stevens, 2000; Uhlig, Merkenschlager, Brandmaier, & Egger, 1997). Slight increases in activity level were noted after nonclinical samples of preschool and school-age children ingested food dye and a preservative (McCann et al., 2007). However, the modest change in activity did not reach levels that would be viewed as clinically significant. Thus, the association between diet and behavior, when it is evident, is small; consequently, the expected effects for dietary interventions would be commensurately small, except in cases in which there is an identified allergic reaction to a food item or additive. No available data suggest that individuals with ADHD are at a greater risk of demonstrating these food sensitivities than other individuals.

An interesting caveat regarding diet is that grapefruit juice may affect the way the body absorbs and metabolizes amphetamines. Consequently, ingestion of grapefruit juice could potentially interfere with the therapeutic effects of prescribed stimulant medications in children and adults with ADHD (Adesman & Sherman, 2007).

Single Photon Emission Tomography Scan

Single photon emission tomography (SPECT) is a functional neuroimaging procedure that provides a snapshot of the brain in action by measuring cerebral blood flow and metabolic activity. SPECT is not an intervention tool. However, some treatment programs are based on the use of SPECT as an assessment tool with which to identify ADHD subtype profiles (e.g., Amen, 2001).

The primary concern with the use of SPECT as part of a costly diagnostic assessment is that its primary use has been in research and its clinical use does not yet have reliable empirical support (Castellanos, 2002; Cook, 2004; Council on Children, Adolescents and Their Families, 2005; cf. Wu et al., 2006). Although the heterogeneous nature of ADHD and its comorbidity patterns suggest that there might be diverse subtype profiles (e.g., Monastra, 2008; Ramsay & Rostain, 2006b), these profiles have not yet been reliably demonstrated (see Solanto et al., 2007). Thus, claims made about the ability to discern clinically valid subtypes using SPECT and using these subtypes to improve treatment outcomes have not been demonstrated by research.

Herbal and Homeopathic Treatments

As thin as is the research support for supplementations, these CAM treatments are relatively noncontroversial, as they are guided by established nutritional standards. However, homeopathic and herbal treatments lack even this level of minimal research support (Rojas & Chan, 2005), with only some open pilot data showing positive results for some Chinese herbal combinations to children with ADHD (Arnold, 2001).

Herbal treatments, such as ginseng and ginkgo biloba, are alleged to improve memory and other cognitive functions, but their usefulness for symptoms of ADHD are anecdotal, with no research support. Likewise, hypericum perforatum, better known as St. John's wort, has no research support for its use with ADHD (Arnold, 2001; NRC, 2007; Weber et al., 2008). It is important to remember that many herbal treatments are crude drug preparations that are not regulated by the FDA, in terms of neither efficacy nor safety (Arnold, 2006). They may be mistakenly thought of as merely "nutritional" or "natural" and therefore benign. It is important to report herbal treatments to a prescribing physician or whenever providing an account of current medications to a health care professional, as they may interact negatively with prescription drugs.

Homeopathic treatment involving the principle of "similars," the notion that substances that cause symptoms in healthy people can cure similar symptoms in ill people, was subjected to a randomized controlled study in a sample of children with ADHD (Jacobs, Williams, Girard, Njike, & Katz, 2005). Participants (ages 6–12 years) received homeopathic consultation and 3 follow-up meetings occurring every 6 weeks for a total of 18 weeks. Participants were randomized to receive either individualized homeopathic remedy or placebo. Both groups improved significantly at outcome, but there were no significant differences between homeopathy and placebo, suggesting that improvements were associated with nonspecific factors. Consequently, no compelling evidence supports the use of herbal or homeopathic treatments for ADHD (Altunç, Pittler, & Ernst, 2007).

Other CAM Approaches

Finally, a host of other proposed treatments for ADHD symptoms include antifungal treatment for yeast overgrowth, purported to compromise immune functioning (Arnold, 2001; NRC, 2007); auditory treatment; thyroid treatment; sensory integration; optometric vision therapy (Ingersoll, 2007); oral flower essences (Horrigan, 2002); chelation therapy (i.e., deleading); and even tarantula venom (Dickerson, 2004). Although some of these therapies are associated with specific problems that may play a role in ADHD for some individuals, such as the connection between elevated blood lead levels and ADHD symptoms for some children (Arnold, 2007; Bustos & Goldstein, 2008; Nigg, 2006), the proposed interventions (e.g., chelation therapy) do not have research support for their use. Moreover, some problems, such as documented thyroid dysfunction or vision or auditory problems, may be associated with some circumscribed symptoms similar to those observed in ADHD and can coexist with ADHD for some individuals. These conditions, of course, should be evaluated and treated by competent health care professionals; however, these conditions alone fail to account for the core dysfunction and widespread impairments associated with ADHD. Thus, symptom improvement associated with treating, say, hypothyroidism, should not be confused with being a treatment for ADHD.

CONCLUSION

Comprehensive approaches are needed to effectively manage the myriad effects of ADHD (see Table 7.1). ADHD is a chronic condition requiring ongoing management. Thus, it is important to continue to search for effective treatment options, including approaches that are useful for a wide range

TABLE 7.1

Summary of Complementary and Alternative Medicine (CAM) Treatments for Adult Attention-Deficit/Hyperactivity Disorder (ADHD)

CAM treatment	Strengths	Limitations	Current status and future directions
Therapeutic interventions or exercises	Preliminary positive results for some approaches that warrant follow-up study May be helpful in cases of comorbidity and/or poor response to medications	Insufficient research support for most approaches Unclear whether therapies address ADHD, comorbid symptoms, or provide short-lived improved over-all well-being Better assessment strategies are needed to identify ADHD syndrome rather than "attention problems"	Much more research is needed, particularly randomized control designs with adults with ADHD It will be necessary to clarify mechanisms of action Future research may identify comorbidity patterns that might be responsive to these approaches
Supplementation and nutrition	May be helpful in cases of documented deficiency Some mildly positive results obtained in some studies of supplementation	Benefits limited to correcting documented deficiencies—not treatment of ADHD Deficiencies may be an effect of ADHD, not cause Potential negative effects of overuse Equivocal research results, at best Benefits likely do not exceed those from good health practices	It will be important to identify adults with ADHD with documented deficiencies Future studies must explain relevance of these interventions for ADHD as well as the efficacy of supplementation Clinicians can help patients recognize the effects of adult ADHD on overall nutrition and health hygiene behaviors
Homeopathy and miscellaneous	Other options for individuals seeking nonstandard treatments Easy access (e.g., no need for prescriptions)	No research support for their use Potential negative interactions with medications May delay more effective treatment if CAM sought out first No regulation of practitioner qualifications	It will be important to identify specific problems that might respond to these approaches and to determine the efficacy of these interventions in general, not just for adults with ADHD Future studies must explain the relevance, if any, of these interventions for ADHD in terms of existing scientific models of ADHD Better research designs are needed

of individuals with ADHD as well as those that might benefit identified subgroups, including individuals for whom pharmacotherapy is contraindicated.

Anecdotal accounts of potentially useful approaches should be subjected to clinical study. A handful of the treatments reviewed in this chapter have produced interesting preliminary results in pilot studies, and a few of them may eventually yield some clinically useful coping strategies or treatment options for some subgroups of patients with ADHD. A few of them may provide some circumscribed coping benefits or may address some coexisting difficulties, such as depression or nutritional deficiency. However, none of the treatments reviewed have demonstrated adequate efficacy to be recommended to patients as an effective, stand-alone treatment, particularly considering the time and cost associated with many of them.

The optimistic claims for untested and unorthodox treatments for ADHD are often inversely proportional to the available level of evidence for their effectiveness. Thus, referring clinicians and consumers should be careful and informed when considering the use or recommendation of CAM approaches for adult ADHD. Standard treatment options with demonstrable research evidence should always be the first line of treatment for individuals of all ages with ADHD.

8

IMPLICATIONS FOR CLINICIANS, CHALLENGES AND FUTURE DIRECTIONS IN RESEARCH, AND FINAL THOUGHTS

A practicing scientist sent a letter to *Time* Magazine, commenting on a report on the death of a prominent cancer researcher. The deceased researcher's groundbreaking work was at first met with skepticism by professional colleagues. The ensuing letter to the magazine provided a nice reminder about the role of the scientific method:

> Such skepticism is commonly portrayed as a flaw, when in fact it's the single most valuable skill we can bring to bear on our work. Contrary to popular belief, good scientists don't seek to prove a hypothesis true. We make every possible effort to prove it wrong by subjecting it to the most withering attacks we can dream up. (It's actually great fun.) This refusal to accept a new idea until it has run a gauntlet of testing is the very reason scientific "truth" is so reliable. (FitzGerald, 2008, p. 7)

It is through rigorous research, independent replication, dissemination, and ongoing peer review that scientific consensus is constructed.

Clinical outcome research is bound by the same scientific conditions mentioned above. In the case of the treatment of adult attention-deficit/hyperactivity disorder (ADHD), the end goal of outcome research is to supply mental health professionals and consumers with treatment guidelines composed of the interventions that have the greatest likelihood of being the greatest help to the greatest number of patients. As sound guidelines are formalized, recommendations for treating specific subgroups can also be developed (e.g., pharmacotherapy for adults with ADHD and substance use disorders). Such frameworks provide practicing clinicians with a starting point for administering treatment that represents the highest standards for the field.

Developing evidence-based clinical guidelines for adult ADHD is a challenging process. Nonmedication treatments have been systematically studied only over the past decade or so. Pharmacotherapy research for adult ADHD, although having a strong empirical foundation, does not yet approach the number of studies conducted with children with ADHD. Moreover, the heterogeneity of ADHD symptom profiles, comorbidity patterns, and functional impairments exhibited by this clinical population make it difficult to define the "standard" adult with ADHD for whom "standard" treatment will be beneficial. Thus, the simultaneous tasks of the practicing clinician are to select appropriate evidence-supported interventions from the available clinical research literature and to devise and implement a treatment plan that addresses a patient's distinct problems and impairments. The craft of clinical work involves carrying out treatment and modifying interventions to meet the needs of the patient.

The effectiveness of pharmacotherapy in the treatment of adult ADHD is well established. If an adult with ADHD can select only one treatment with the highest likelihood of providing the greatest relief from the widest range of symptoms, medication should be that choice. That being said, the craft of medication management involves many factors, such as selecting the appropriate medication on the basis of medical and comorbidity patterns, titration to therapeutic dose, dealing with side effects, and ongoing compliance issues.

Most adults with ADHD who are in treatment require more than pharmacotherapy alone. As is the case with other medical and psychiatric conditions, if first-line treatments are insufficient, ineffective, or refused, then other treatment approaches must be considered. Consequently, the purpose of this book has been to review the current nonmedication treatment options for adults with ADHD. Nonmedication treatments currently have much less empirical support than pharmacotherapy, making the selection of (or referral for) such treatments challenging.

Reviewing the evidence for nonmedication treatments for adult ADHD is further complicated by the multiple definitions of what constitutes adequate "evidence." *Evidence-based psychological practice* has been defined as "the integration of the best available research with clinical expertise in the context of patient characteristics, culture, and, preferences" (APA Presidential Task Force on Evidence-Based Practice, 2006, p. 273). This broad, guiding framework allows clinicians to consider multiple levels of research evidence in the absence of data from sophisticated studies, those with randomized control designs rated the best.

A subdomain of evidence-based practice is the development of empirically validated treatments, which represent specific treatments targeting specific disorders or clinical problems (Chambless & Hollon, 1998; Task Force on Promotion and Dissemination of Psychological Procedures, 1995). In fact, the case has been made that the focus should be on the development of evidence-based principles of change that can be implemented in psychosocial treatment, rather than specific treatment packages (G. M. Rosen & Davison, 2003). Although none of the nonmedication treatments reviewed in previous chapters could be considered a "well-established," empirically validated treatment for adult ADHD, some approaches may be nearing "probably efficacious" status and use sound principles of change. Various other professional organizations and task forces have established criteria for defining sufficient evidence with which to guide treatment selection within their professional domains.

The aim of these task forces is admirable: establishing standards to guide professional services. It is encouraging that a wide range of study designs are viewed as contributing potentially useful evidence, although greater weight is afforded those with stronger methodologies. From the standpoint of clinical practice, these standards provide a decision-making framework in which a comparative review of the available research evidence and a patient's individual circumstances allow the practitioner and patient to make informed decisions about treatment planning, even among treatment options based on less than optimal research support. A potential downside of these multiple standards, however, is clinical complacency: Practitioners may selectively pick and choose standards to justify their current practices and, at times, ignore evidence that contraindicates these practices. Consequently, the craft of clinical practice with adults with ADHD often involves developing treatment plans for patients for whom the standard approaches are insufficient, taking into account case-specific factors.

The purpose of this final chapter is to provide a brief summary of the clinical implications of the review of nonmedication treatments covered in this book. The next section of the chapter discusses some of the challenges inherent in outcome research for adult ADHD and future directions that will contribute to the eventual development of a solid empirical foundation for these clinical approaches. A final brief section presents some final thoughts on nonmedication treatments for adult ADHD.

IMPLICATIONS FOR CLINICIANS

The previous six chapters of this book have covered a wide range of clinical material in terms of a variety of treatment approaches for adult ADHD. One of the ongoing struggles in mental health professions is translating clinical outcome research into useful suggestions for clinical practice. The sections that follow provide a review of the clinical applications and implications of each of these therapies and how they might be used to help adults with ADHD who are in treatment.

Psychosocial Treatments

The study of psychosocial treatments for adult ADHD has accelerated, with the number of outcome studies doubling in the past few years. Several standard psychotherapy approaches have been modified for use with adults with ADHD and turned into manualized treatment programs, with more forthcoming. Consequently, practitioners working with adults with ADHD have some useful frameworks with which to carry out psychosocial treatment.

Although differing in various aspects of their approaches, the available psychosocial treatments for adult ADHD share many therapeutic components. A common starting point involves confirming the diagnosis of ADHD and providing psychoeducation. An accurate diagnosis of ADHD and an affirmation that the difficulties encountered by a patient result from a neurodevelopmental syndrome and are not evidence of a "character flaw" could be considered the foundational cognitive modification intervention in treatment. This recognition can be very powerful and emotionally overwhelming for patients, and a grief reaction is not uncommon. In fact, the patient's significant others (e.g., parents, spouse) may also have emotional reactions related to their misinterpretation of behaviors that are now understood as manifestations of a disorder or regrets that they did not seek help sooner.

Psychoeducation plays an important role in psychosocial treatment. In addition to providing information and resources regarding adult ADHD, it involves helping patients identify the effects of ADHD on their daily lives. Personal education and empowerment might also include bibliotherapy, experimentation with helpful organizational gadgets, and other forms of "environmental engineering" to make living and work environments relatively ADHD friendly. Identifying and understanding the various cognitive, behavioral, emotional, and functional manifestations of ADHD in a personalized way helps to demystify various life problems and to develop targets for treatment.

To this end, the importance of the therapeutic alliance has been underestimated in the ADHD treatment literature. Many adults with ADHD who seek treatment may have had repeated experiences of feeling they had let others down because of their behaviors and have developed views of themselves as failures. Consequently, they may be particularly sensitive, reacting to setbacks during treatment as evidence that "this is not working for me" or "I cannot do this." Helping patients normalize the trial-and-error aspect of the change process and viewing setbacks as an expected part of treatment can help challenge all-or-nothing views of therapeutic progress. Commonly difficulties that occur during treatment of adult ADHD—lateness to appointments, forgetting therapeutic homework, difficulty following through on tasks—can be used as opportunities to promote improvements rather than seen as evidence of "resistance," and so on, thus helping to foster a sense of resilience and a collaborative problem management approach in sessions. What is more, these factors work together to help foster a patient's sense of hope insofar as he or she is provided a framework within which to understand seemingly unpredictable behaviors, the notion that there is a plan for change, and a relationship with a supportive professional who understands adult ADHD.

Standard mechanisms of change in psychosocial treatments for adult ADHD include a focus on the development of coping strategies and metacognitive skills (e.g., organization, time management). It should be noted that what most adult patients with adult ADHD often require is not necessarily information about various skills but assistance with the effective and consistent implementation of these skills in their daily lives (e.g., at the point of performance). For example, a patient may recognize that it is important to keep to a schedule but may not follow through on reviewing and prioritizing a schedule each day or at various times throughout the day. Hence, it is important to maintain a focus on target problems throughout treatment.

Most psychosocial treatments for adult ADHD studied seem to follow a cognitive–behavioral therapy (CBT) framework. A focus on cognitive and behavioral modification supports the metacognitive skill training mentioned earlier insofar as negative thoughts, feelings of frustration, and procrastination behaviors often interfere with the implementation of coping skills. CBT strategies provide a coping scaffolding to counteract these tendencies. Moreover, CBT is an effective treatment approach with which to address the common comorbid mood, anxiety, or substance use problems. In fact, reducing comorbid symptoms may help improve overall functioning, foster resilience, and thereby allow patients to better focus on coping with ADHD.

Academic Support and Accommodations for Postsecondary Students With ADHD

Many adults with ADHD experience difficulties in the course of their postsecondary education. Although academic supports and accommodations are widely recommended for ADHD students of all ages, there is no research on the effectiveness of academic accommodations, and only three studies of academic support or coaching approaches for adults with ADHD (and one involving high school students with ADHD).

Clinicians working with adult ADHD students may not necessarily provide specific academic support services. However, many postsecondary students with ADHD may seek therapeutic support in dealing with academic stress and for developing effective coping strategies. Consequently, many of the clinical suggestions mentioned in the discussion of psychosocial treatments are relevant when working with adult students with ADHD, with their treatment objectives primarily centered on academic issues. For example, psychoeducation for a college student with ADHD might involve developing an understanding of his or her particular learning and studying style, which would inform choice of classes and specific instructors, daily class schedule (e.g., "What time of day is best for you to attend class? How many classes can you handle each day?"), daily study schedule (e.g., "When are some good blocks of time to do work?"), and study location (e.g., "Can you do work in your room without being distracted or is it better to go to the library?"). A personalized review of the myriad factors that influence academic performance helps students with ADHD make informed decisions about their education.

Considering the regular amount and type of work associated with most academic programs, students with ADHD face greater than average challenges related to issues of time management, organization, and procrastination. It can be useful to have students with ADHD monitor their reactions to various academic tasks that may affect follow-through and result in procrastination to identify and implement different coping approaches. It is often helpful for these students to break down larger projects that may seem overwhelming to them (e.g., study for a test, write a research paper) into specific, time-limited tasks (e.g., review class notes for 15 minutes, work on an outline for a paper during a break between classes). Managing distractions that serve as the source of procrastination is another common therapeutic issue. As mentioned before, developing discrete, manageable task goals and balancing them with sufficient recreational activities enhances overall well-being. As always, factors that affect the implementation of these plans usually provide the grist for the mill in therapy sessions.

Clinicians may also play a role in helping students with ADHD use available support resources. In many cases, students with ADHD may put off making an appointment with an academic support counselor or following through on an accommodation, such as priority class registration, as a manifestation of procrastination. However, some students may be ambivalent about seeking such accommodations or services because they are reticent to disclose their diagnosis. What is more, many college students with ADHD may have been evaluated at the urging of their parents but have not yet come to terms with the diagnosis or the coping efforts that might be required to get the most out of their educational experience. Consequently, treatment may be used to explore these issues and to help students with ADHD become advocates for themselves and their education. Clinicians may provide referrals for additional evaluation if they suspect the presence of learning problems not explained by ADHD or if testing is needed for accommodations for standardized examinations. Finally, other coping issues may affect students with ADHD, such as psychiatric comorbidity or substance use issues that are amenable to treatment.

Career Counseling and Workplace Support

Although recent research has documented the profound negative effects of ADHD on occupational functioning, there is no research guiding career counseling or workplace support interventions. However, clinicians treating adults with ADHD who have questions regarding their professional options may refer them for additional career counseling. The main focus of career counseling is the review of personal interests and various other factors, including features of ADHD that determine the goodness of fit of a particular job or career for an individual. Career counselors may administer various interest, vocational aptitude, and personality inventories that help workers make informed decisions about their job options. It is very likely that clinicians will find themselves in the position of addressing these sorts of issues in the course of helping patients with ADHD review the match between the demands of a job with their particular skill sets. Moreover, workers with ADHD who are otherwise qualified for a particular job may have to consider other workplace factors that might affect performance, such as flexibility in scheduling, the physical work environment (e.g., noise, distractions), amount of supervision, and so on. Of course, there are no perfect work situations; however, it is important to be informed of potential areas of difficulty so that they can be managed.

To this end, workplace coping issues can be addressed as part of a therapeutic agenda. ADHD coaching is an emerging field that also targets occupational functioning and the manner in which symptoms of ADHD create difficulties, such as disorganization, poor time management, and procrastination. Adults with ADHD often benefit from instituting informal accommodations and coping strategies in the workplace, such as using organizational tools, modifying work schedules or responsibilities, requesting written follow-up of verbal instructions, and so on. As with the time management and organizational strategies discussed in other sections, the effective and consistent implementation of these coping tools is usually most difficult for workers with ADHD. Many individuals with ADHD experience interpersonal difficulties at work, often related to the downstream effects of not following through on work or not following directions, but just as often because of interpersonal issues, such as interrupting during conversations, being forgetful, or poor frustration management, all of which can be addressed in treatment.

Relationships and Social Functioning

A growing research literature documents the negative effects of ADHD on social and interpersonal functioning throughout the life span. Adults with ADHD might experience functional difficulties in committed relationships, married and family life, and other settings requiring the appropriate use of social skills. The growing awareness of how adult ADHD affects relationships has yielded some anecdotal clinical approaches, but no formal treatment programs involving adults with ADHD have been studied, although most psychosocial treatments do address interpersonal issues.

That being said, family treatment involving parents with ADHD can be modified to address issues related to how the disorder may affect parenting behavior. That is, there are effective parenting strategies, such as positive attending and behavioral management principles. However, these strategies require effective monitoring of child behavior and implementation of the parenting strategies, both of which are more difficult for parents with ADHD than for those parents without ADHD. Thus, it is important to identify the influence of adult ADHD on parenting and, similar to other coping strategies, spend time identifying and addressing potential barriers to follow-through. The primary culprits in parental ADHD are likely disorganization—having difficulty establishing a behavior plan—and poor emotional regulation—being overwhelmed by frustration in the moment. Parents may also harbor self-critical thoughts about their parenting competence, which further interferes with follow-through.

Adult ADHD also can have negative effects in marital or other committed relationships. Forgetfulness, distractibility during conversations, and poor follow-through on promises and commitments can be interpreted as evidence of "not caring" by a partner without ADHD. There may be additional stressors with increasing severity of a partner's ADHD insofar as there may be financial problems related to overspending, employment difficulties, and the effects of psychiatric comorbidity on a relationship. Moreover, the partner without ADHD may struggle with personal issues that affect the relationship. Improvements in managing ADHD in the affected partner will likely improve functioning within the relationship; however, there may be built-up resentments and maladaptive relationship patterns that continue to cause problems. Relationship interventions often focus on having partners schedule time together performing joint activities, seeing as it is easy for partners to drift away from having positive interactions. Cognitive and behavioral change strategies may include monitoring and challenging common distorted thoughts, such as "mind reading" (e.g., "I just know he 'forgot' to run the errand on purpose" vs "He probably forgot to write

down the errand") and positive attending (e.g., notice something the partner does that is appreciated and tell him or her). These strategies are common to many relationship treatment approaches, but the partner with
ADHD may require assistance with implementation and the partner without ADHD may require psychoeducation about the partner's ADHD to
come to terms with it.

Finally, the symptoms of ADHD can interfere with the development
and implementation of effective social skills in adulthood. Specific coping
reminders and rehearsal may help improve social performance, but targeted
social skills training has not been studied in samples of adults with ADHD;
instead, social skills are often addressed as a component of psychosocial treatment. Again, it is usually not lack of awareness of appropriate social skills but
their timely and effective implementation.

Neurofeedback and Neurocognitive Training

Most of the nonmedication treatments for adult ADHD address the
functional impairments associated with the disorder. Neurofeedback and
neurocognitive training, in contrast, target the core symptoms of ADHD,
with the claim being that they intervene at the level of brain functioning.
Neurofeedback has a long and controversial history in the field of ADHD
but has been administered to both children and adults. Similarly, the adult
version of a computerized working memory training (WMT) program, the
most promising neurocognitive training approach, has been found to produce improvements in both targeted and nontargeted measures of working
memory performance in randomized control studies of children with
ADHD. Most practicing clinicians do not provide neurofeedback training
(NFT) or WMT but may have patients who have questions about these
treatment options.

Recent preliminary data in studies of children up to 18 years old indicate that quantitative electroencephalography may be helpful as a component of an assessment for ADHD. Although there are anecdotal reports of
the benefits of NFT, and it has been marketed as providing enduring symptom relief on par with medications, the limited studies with adults with
ADHD on which those claims are based are seriously flawed. Many practitioners who provide NFT may use it as part of a multimodal treatment
approach. Although recent studies of NFT have been much improved in
their quality and methodology, the current research base for NFT for adults
with ADHD provides only tentative support for its efficacy, and better
established treatments should be attempted before pursuing NFT as an
adjunctive treatment.

Similarly, although WMT has yielded some promising preliminary results, questions remain about the maintenance of gains and mechanisms of action of the procedure. Although working memory deficits are a common feature of ADHD, it is unclear whether these skills can be trained to the degree that they result in functional improvements in daily life. Moreover, WMT coaches provide support and encouragement, and increase adherence to the protocol, all of which could be considered therapeutic factors that might contribute to the positive outcomes obtained in extant studies. Although there are ongoing studies of WMT, a prudent recommendation is that patients should be encouraged to explore established treatments before pursuing WMT as an adjunctive treatment.

Complementary and Alternative Treatments

The assortment of complementary and alternative medicine (CAM) treatments spans a wide range of approaches, including various adjunctive nonmedication therapeutic strategies, such as mindfulness meditation training; nontraditional treatments, such as chiropractic treatment; and various nutritional or natural medicine supplementations. Most clinicians will not include these sorts of strategies or supplements as a part of their treatment plan. However, patients may inquire about the potential benefit of various treatments on the basis of what they have heard from other people, read online, seen or heard in the media, and so on.

As a group, CAM approaches are considered neither stand-alone treatments nor standard components of a treatment regimen for adult ADHD. In most cases, little or no research justifies their use, with most studies being marked by insufficient diagnostic procedures, poor research designs, unsupported hypotheses, and unsubstantiated theories of ADHD. Moreover, some herbal or nutritional supplementation approaches may carry some risk and should be used only under medical supervision. Hence, in the cases of supplementation, patients should be encouraged to discuss options with a primary care physician or a prescribing physician for patients who are taking other medications, are on other supplementation regimens, or both. In most cases, benefits of CAM approaches based on traditional health and medical principles (e.g., vitamin and mineral supplementation) address the downstream effects of ADHD (e.g., poor dietary habits) and do not treat primary symptoms.

Some standard health and therapeutic exercises, such as mindfulness meditation training or yoga, may provide some structured activities with which to gain some short-lived stress relief but may not provide true symptom relief. These sorts of activities may represent helpful coping strategies, but it is important to help patients understand these exercises as healthy coping strategies rather than as alternative treatments for ADHD.

Most CAM approaches, however, may be costly in terms of time, effort, money, or all three, for negligible (if any) improvements compared with standard treatments. Moreover, CAM practitioners may not specialize in diagnostic assessment strategies, which could result in a misdiagnosis of ADHD. Regardless of these limitations, some patients may decide to pursue some of these treatments hoping to gain some additional symptom relief or because they have not responded to, or cannot use, standard treatments because of some sort of contraindication (e.g., a cardiac health profile that obviates pharmacotherapy). Patients have the right of self-determination and to seek out treatments of their choice. However, clinicians can help patients be informed consumers of various treatments available for adult ADHD and differentiate standard treatment approaches, such as pharmacotherapy, psychosocial treatments modified for adult ADHD, and academic and workplace support, from approaches with limited or no clinical outcome research support.

CHALLENGES AND FUTURE DIRECTIONS IN RESEARCH

Clinical outcome research is hard work. Many factors complicate the design and completion of solid research in clinical settings. What is more, there is no perfect study; rather, questions are answered from the accumulated results of diverse studies and replications. In addition to providing information about existing treatments for adult ADHD, the studies reviewed heretofore also provide useful directions for future research that have implications for clinical practice.

Treatment Development

The past several years have seen the development of many promising treatment approaches. As they become more sophisticated, however, several factors must be addressed in ongoing treatment development and clinical outcome research.

Diagnostic Assessment

The first hurdle in providing treatment for adult ADHD is to ensure that patients are accurately diagnosed. Indeed, a limitation of several treatment studies of adult ADHD, particularly many neurofeedback and CAM approaches, is the use of questionable diagnostic procedures. Considering the high comorbidity rates among adults with ADHD, rigorous assessment strategies are paramount to ensure accurate identification of ADHD and coexisting diagnoses, including making sure other psychiatric or medical conditions are not mimicking ADHD symptoms. The presence of specific comorbidity patterns (including substance abuse) might alter treatment planning for both pharmacotherapy and nonmedication treatments.

Point of Performance

The negative effects of ADHD are pervasive, affecting an array of adult roles. Moreover, the functional problems associated with ADHD most often do not result from lack of coping knowledge but from implementation problems in the effective and consistent use of coping strategies. Thus, the true measure of the effectiveness of treatments for adult ADHD is their ability to have positive effects in real-world situations that have historically been difficult to manage, otherwise known as the *point of performance*.

The treatments reviewed in previous chapters are administered in settings that vary in their proximity to performance situations, from psychosocial treatments and neurofeedback conducted in consulting rooms, to testing accommodations for college students with ADHD that are implemented during actual exams. However, all treatments aim to have interventions reach real-life coping situations. Future outcome research should emphasize the effective application of therapeutic strategies in daily life to reduce the symptoms, the impairment, or both, associated with ADHD. It is likely that emerging portable technological tools will increasingly be integrated into treatment programs to provide organizational and time management frameworks, offer timely reminders of coping tools, provide a record of therapeutic interventions (e.g., adaptive responses to pessimistic cognitions), and provide a variety of possible services that together increase the timely implementation of coping strategies and the ability to record their use at the point of performance.

Treatment Compliance

All treatments, by definition, require that individuals engage in some sort of behavior change to experience therapeutic effects. Even if there existed the proverbial "magic pill" that was available as an over-the-counter medication, the steps of going to the store, purchasing the pill, and taking it as directed would require a minimal degree of follow-through. The nonmedication approaches for adult ADHD uniformly require adherence to specific treatment protocols to obtain optimal therapeutic effects. ADHD is a syndrome characterized by symptoms that interfere with the implementation of effective coping skills, meaning patients with ADHD will likely experience problems following through with treatment recommendations, even if all that would be required is showing up for a session.

To date, the vast majority of outcome studies of nonmedication treatments for adult ADHD have not used random assignment for the understandable reason that most have been clinic-based open studies for which there has been no external funding. It is difficult to ask patients who are paying for clinical services to agree to be randomly assigned to different treatment groups (or a waiting list). However, a limitation of these nonrandomized designs is that individuals who select particular treatments and who consent to participate in pre- and posttreatment evaluations are likely to be particularly motivated and treatment-compliant consumers. Thus, positive findings, although useful, might not be obtained from the clinical population at large.

It is common sense that there is a positive correlation of treatment compliance and outcome. However, nonmedication treatment development for adults with ADHD will have to be particularly sensitive to the fact that the disorder being treated makes treatment follow-through difficult. Thus, adherence factors are simultaneously a focus of intervention and an outcome measure. What is more, nonmedication intervention approaches could be developed and studied that target specific types of behavioral compliance, including medication compliance, general health care behaviors (e.g., dental care, physical exercise), or various administrative tasks (e.g., filing taxes, paying bills on time).

Treatment Availability and Quality

Despite the many promising nonmedication treatment options that are available to adults with ADHD, there are many barriers to their availability and the relative quality. Adult ADHD remains a clinical subspecialty for which few clinicians have received formalized training. Thus, it is difficult for consumers to find mental health professionals with a strong background in the assessment and treatment of ADHD, much less finding a team of experienced clinicians in cases requiring multimodal treatment.

The business market for the treatment of adult ADHD is growing. Thus, there is increased interest in developing pharmacological agents that obtain U.S. Food and Drug Administration approval for the treatment of adult ADHD, thereby allowing them to be marketed as such. However, there is corresponding skepticism about the business motives of pharmaceutical companies and their involvement in research and treatment.

Nonmedication treatments for adult ADHD also benefit from the aforementioned market forces. There is a growing submarket of individuals with ADHD who choose to bypass medications because of safety concerns reported in the mass media as well as in alternative media (i.e., Internet). Thus, in the desire for nonmedication treatments, a variety of "therapies" are being offered by individuals with what are, at best, questionable qualifications. In other cases, fully trained and licensed mental health or medical professionals might endorse a therapy on the basis of anecdotal information or extrapolate "preliminary" findings reported by competent researchers as "proof" of clinical effectiveness. What is more, some emerging fields, such as ADHD coaching, are still defining their requisite training and certification requirements. Thus, although promising treatments exist, there are no systematic guarantees of the qualifications of individual practitioners who are providing them in the community.

Apart from availability, the most prominent barrier to the availability of effective nonmedication treatments is probably cost. Insurance plans might not reimburse for certain nonmedication treatments. In cases in which the aforementioned treatments are covered for other conditions, such as psychotherapy for depression, these same treatments might not be covered for a primary diagnosis of ADHD. In cases in which there is a comorbid condition, however, a justification could be made for reimbursement for clinical services.

More distressing, however, is that the individuals most chronically and severely impaired by adult ADHD are the individuals most likely to have experienced academic, occupational, and other functional impairments to a degree that they are without adequate (if any) insurance coverage and cannot afford to pay for treatment, including medications. Thus, future nonmedication treatment development and research will have to address issues related to their cost-effectiveness and availability to consumers, particularly considering that nearly 90% of adults with ADHD in the United States do not receive specialized care (Kessler et al., 2006).

Research Development

Although not yet fulfilling criteria for being empirically validated treatments, the developing research foundation for some nonmedication treatments for adult ADHD, such as psychosocial treatments, is promising. Moreover, there are interesting pilot studies of potentially useful intervention approaches for adult ADHD, such as academic support or coaching and

WMT, although ongoing research is needed to establish their efficacy. Finally, several areas of clinical research have not yet been tapped, such as marital and family therapy involving adults with ADHD. Adult ADHD treatment outcome studies are on the rise, and several issues related to research designs and methodology need to be addressed, some of which are reviewed next.

Methodology

Despite a variety of limitations, such as lack of funding that has downstream effects on study design (e.g., random assignment, availability of trained, masked raters), some preliminary research on nonmedication treatments for adult ADHD is promising. However, these studies will have to be followed by research using increasingly sophisticated designs and control groups to establish the efficacy (i.e., whether it works) and effectiveness (i.e., whether it works in the community) of these treatments.

Randomized controlled designs comparing active treatments are the gold standard for empirical validation. Several treatments have been established as producing desired clinical improvements using open clinical studies and randomized designs with wait-list control groups. Future studies should be designed to compare active treatments to demonstrate efficacy, with the ultimate goal being to establish their effectiveness across community samples and over time (i.e., posttreatment follow-up assessments).

Medication Status

Most nonmedication treatment outcome studies have been conducted with participants who received concurrent pharmacotherapy for ADHD. The positive therapeutic effects of medications are achieved by improving many aspects of brain functioning. Downstream improvements in daily functioning result from reduced interference from inattention, impulsivity, and hyperactivity.

Although most nonmedication treatments intervene at the level of functional impairments, few studies of nonmedication treatments have been conducted on nonmedicated samples of adults with ADHD. These sorts of studies would provide important information about the range of benefits provided by these treatments and their relative contribution to overall functioning in the absence of medications. What is more, such studies, which could be performed using placebo-controlled, crossover designs, would provide data regarding the sequential introduction of treatments. That is, current clinical practice suggests that medications provide a foundation of symptom relief from which additional treatments are added, as needed. However, research on the contribution of individual treatments might provide guidelines for treatment introduction, either starting them concurrently or sequentially. Finally, potentially fruitful research could be conducted with samples of adults with ADHD with cardiac or medical risk profiles obviating the use of medications, who are medication nonresponders, who otherwise refuse medications, or who fit all of these criteria.

Mechanisms of Action

The information guides for prescription medications for adult ADHD include descriptions of their mechanisms of action on a synaptic level, pharmacokinetics, and pharmacodynamics. Although such neurochemical models may not directly translate to attempts to understand nonmedication treatments, such discussions of mechanisms of action in the clinical outcome literature are important in outlining precisely how and why different treatment approaches are helpful for adults with ADHD.

On the one hand, many nonmedication treatments, such as the psychosocial treatments, operate in a top-down fashion, intervening at the level of impairment and helping individuals better manage the effects of ADHD using some combination of metacognitive coping strategies, cognitive and behavioral modification, and exposure to avoided situations as well as reduction of interference from comorbid disorders (Ramsay, 2007). On the other hand, some treatment approaches, such as NFT and WMT, purport to operate in bottom-up fashion by intervening directly at the level of brain functioning. However, the precise mechanisms of action for nonmedication, brain-based treatments remain unclear, although some models have been proposed (e.g., Monastra, 2004). Explicating how nonmedication treatments work would be a useful objective for future research.

Negative Side Effects

Side effects are a principal drawback of pharmacotherapy. In a minority of cases, these side effects are severe enough to require discontinuation of treatment. Apart from physical side effects, other costs might be associated with pharmacotherapy, including monetary cost and inconvenience (e.g., planning and organization) of filling prescriptions, scheduling medication management appointments, and the inconvenience of taking a daily medication. Finally, some individuals may have medical or cardiac health profiles that preclude the use of medications.

Although a commonly cited benefit of nonmedication treatments for adult ADHD is that they do not have negative side effects, the issue might not be so straightforward. It is important to acknowledge that nonmedication treatment approaches are not completely risk free. Although the types of side effects of these treatments will be different from the physical effects commonly associated with medications (e.g., dry mouth, dizziness), aspects of treatment could create different forms of discomfort (e.g., Ramsay, in press).

Most nonmedication treatments for adult ADHD require at least a time-limited course of treatment for which negative side effects might include cost, time and travel for sessions, the inconvenience and difficulty of therapeutic homework and coping tasks, and short-term distress that might be involved in coming to terms with the effects of ADHD. Some CAM approaches, such as supplementation or herbal remedies, carry some risk of physical side effects or interactions with medications. Even in the case of NFT or WMT, equipment costs, boredom with tasks, and the inconvenience of daily training exercises are among the features that could interfere with follow-through. It is important to identify the potential difficulties inherent in treatment in order to reduce them and to allow consumers to make informed decisions about their treatment options.

Diversity Issues

Because most clinical outcome research on nonmedication treatments for adult ADHD has been the result of unfunded, clinic-based studies, the samples have been restricted to individuals able to find and afford specialized treatment. For the most part, participants have been Caucasian, well educated, and generally well functioning. However, studies of treatments provided to individuals with severe impairment and complex comorbidity patterns have not been conducted. Future studies should focus on recruiting individuals with a wider range of functional impairments as well as representing greater ethnic and racial diversity.

Studies of nonmedication treatments for adult ADHD are also relevant within distinct clinical populations, such as substance abuse treatment facilities, prison populations, and geriatric populations, to name a few possibilities. Research on identification and treatment of adult ADHD in these underserved populations will involve such factors as assessment, prevalence rates, pharmacotherapy, and comorbidity. However, interventions that provide psychoeducation and target impairments associated with adult ADHD hold the promise of reducing relapse rates in substance abuse treatment programs, decreasing recidivism in correctional facilities, and improving quality of life for seniors with ADHD.

Clinical Outcome Measures

An important aspect of clinical outcome research is the choice of outcome measures. Most treatment studies used ratings of ADHD symptoms, comorbid mood and anxiety symptoms, and life impairment. However, some studies used outcome measures with questionable associations with either ADHD symptoms or associated impairment (e.g., IQ scores). Thus, the selection of appropriate clinical outcome measures is crucial for nonmedication treatment studies.

Functional Outcomes

Most nonmedication treatments focus on domains of impairment associated with adult ADHD. Therefore, it is important to develop and use measures of functional outcomes, that is, domains of life functioning and adaptive behaviors that are impaired by ADHD and are responsive to intervention. In addition to self-report measures of these functional outcomes, adult ADHD research will benefit from obtaining observer ratings and objective measures of functioning. Academic grades or workplace performance evaluations provide useful measures of functioning. Other measures might include late fees paid on bills, performance in simulated academic and workplace settings, treatment session attendance, and follow-through on therapeutic tasks.

Some domains of life are difficult to measure, such as relationship functioning. Features of social interactions can be difficult to operationally define and measure. Moreover, observer ratings in some treatment situations are vulnerable to bias, such as a partner's ratings in a strained romantic relationship. However, family treatment programs for children and teens with ADHD have used performance on a structured family interaction task as an outcome measure that could be used in families with adults with ADHD. Qualitative research designs have also been used in studies of experiences of families affected by ADHD.

Although most nonmedication treatments for adult ADHD aim to achieve improvement in functioning by impairment reduction, it is still useful to use symptom measures. Although it could be argued that these treatments improve symptom management without reducing core symptoms per se, it is worthwhile measuring even mild effects on symptoms, including psychological symptoms (e.g., self-esteem). Moreover, because ADHD is at its core a neurobiological syndrome, it would be informative to use neuropsychological and neuroimaging outcome measures of nonmedication treatments. The use of neuroimaging technology in research on depression has provided important data on the distinct contribution of pharmacotherapy and CBT to treatment outcome (Goldapple et al., 2004). The use of similar functional imaging studies in the nonmedication treatment of adult ADHD would be groundbreaking (see McNab et al., 2009).

Readiness for Change

Although discussed in the adult ADHD literature as a clinical heuristic, formalized assessment of patients' readiness for change in treatment would be a useful measure of a potential moderator variable for outcome (e.g., Prochaska & Norcross, 2001). That is, it seems that greater ambivalence about treatment would be associated with lower compliance and, thus, less positive treatment outcomes. Moreover, readiness for change profiles could be used to individualize treatment by spending more time at the outset of treatment addressing ambivalence about, and enhancing motivation for, treatment. Thus, the use of such measures would make a potentially important contribution to clinical outcome studies.

Beliefs and Knowledge About ADHD

An issue related to readiness for change is the beliefs and knowledge about ADHD that individuals bring to treatment. The psychoeducation that is common across most nonmedication treatments for adult ADHD involves a combination of providing up-to-date scientific information about the nature of the disorder and its effects on personal functioning, as well as treatment and coping options. A clinical aspect of psychoeducation often involves providing accurate information and modifying beliefs about ADHD and its management. Moreover, various ethnic and cultural groups might be underrepresented in adult ADHD research in part because of skepticism about the diagnosis and treatment of ADHD in particular and about psychiatric and psychological treatment in general. Identifying areas of skepticism or misinformation would increase the likelihood of directly addressing them and increasing the likelihood of treatment follow-through.

Policy Issues

Although beyond the purview of a review of nonmedication treatments for adult ADHD, many research issues have implications for public policy that, in turn, affect treatment. Although adult ADHD has garnered increased attention in the public and mass media, there remains a great deal of misinformation and misunderstanding about the disorder. Moreover, many health care professionals who might be the first contact for consumers seeking help for ADHD may hold similar misconceptions. Consequently, there remains an important need for the dissemination of scientifically accurate information about adult ADHD and its treatment to the public, mental health and health care professionals (in practice and in training), postsecondary educators, employers, and legislators.

For example, insurance coverage for part-time college students is an adult ADHD issue. That is, many qualified students might compensate for their symptoms by taking lighter class loads and enrolling in summer classes, thus requiring more time to complete graduation requirements. However, these students risk losing insurance coverage under their parents' or colleges' insurance plans because they are not considered full time. Likewise, potentially useful workplace accommodations and therapeutic services at the point of performance might require reasonable and time-limited adjustments to workplace settings with only minor inconvenience but would ultimately benefit both employee and employer.

A variety of treatment approaches are needed to help adults with ADHD to develop adequate self-management strategies. Considering the prevalence of adult ADHD, medical and graduate training programs in mental health professions must at least introduce ADHD as a life-span developmental disorder likely to be encountered in the course of standard clinical practice. Professional organizations and referral networks should list qualified professionals who specialize in the diagnosis and treatment of ADHD. It is paramount that emerging therapeutic fields involved in helping adults with ADHD, such as ADHD coaching or WMT, verify that practitioners fulfill stringent training and certification requirements to safeguard consumers. That is, although various assessment and treatment protocols have evidence supporting their use, community mental health providers may not be trained or experienced in the administration of these protocols with adult ADHD patients seeking their services.

Although it is the responsibility of clinician–researchers to develop and research treatments, demonstrate their effectiveness, and disseminate findings to professionals, availability and access to these treatments is a policy matter. At least some, if not most, insurance companies in the United States do not reimburse adult patients seeking psychological therapy services with a primary diagnosis of ADHD (see Watkins, 2002). The situation might be similar for any adult manifestation of a life-span developmental disorder that cannot be treated to a "cure." However, the combination of pharmacotherapy and several adjunctive treatments for adult ADHD has demonstrated a degree of efficacy to justify third-party reimbursement.

Finally, the ongoing development of evidence-based, nonmedication treatments for adult ADHD requires that these interventions be targeted for funding by various agencies and foundations that provide research grants. There is adequate preliminary data for many of the treatments reviewed in previous chapters to warrant further study using randomized controlled designs to adequately test their effectiveness in comparison with other treatments and to explore combined treatment protocols. Treatment development grants for emerging therapies are also necessary to determine their potential contribution to functional improvements of adults with ADHD. Some therapeutic approaches might be found to be effective, stand-alone treatments for most adults with ADHD; others might provide circumscribed benefits to identifiable subpopulations of ADHD adults; and many treatments might not be effective. However, the purpose of clinical research is to gather data with which to make these determinations in the interest of providing mental health professionals and consumers with the best information possible to make informed treatment decisions.

FINAL THOUGHTS

Interest in the array of nonmedication treatments available for adults with ADHD is rising. ADHD is a chronic, neurodevelopmental syndrome with severe and wide-ranging negative effects on the lives of those affected and, by extension, the lives of their loved ones. Although medications are considered the first line of treatment, medications alone are insufficient in the majority of treated cases of adult ADHD. Moreover, some individuals choose to pursue nonmedication treatments alone, either by choice or by necessity because of an inability to use medications. The significant impairments experienced by adults with ADHD necessitate the development and dissemination of a range of therapeutic options to help individuals manage the myriad effects of ADHD on life functioning.

The desire for nonmedication treatment options for adult ADHD, however, does not negate the need for solid clinical research to establish the efficacy of these therapies. The treatments reviewed in earlier chapters run the gamut from those with a strong research foundation, to those that have not yet clearly demonstrated efficacy in clinical studies, as well as those interventions that have simply not yet been studied or that have not demonstrated any appreciable benefits (see Table 8.1). The coming decade will likely be a fertile one for the study of nonmedication treatments for adult ADHD. It is important to provide useful treatment frameworks to mental health professionals and educators who are on the front lines providing support to adults with ADHD. It is important to keep in mind that the ultimate goal is to provide hope and direction to people who seek help with managing and transcending the effects of ADHD in their lives.

TABLE 8.1
Summary of Nonmedication Treatments for Adult Attention-Deficit/Hyperactivity Disorder (ADHD)

Treatment	Strengths	Limitations	Current status and future directions
Psychosocial treatment	Good assessment protocols used in studies Variety of modalities and research methodologies Improvements in symptoms and impairments Treatment is well tolerated and acceptable Targets impairments related to ADHD	Participants may not be representative of adult ADHD population at large Diverse treatment protocols must be replicated Requires adherence Cost and availability	Psychosocial treatments are the most widely studied nonmedication treatment for adult ADHD More studies needed on ADHD coaching Need for more randomized studies with active treatment controls Need for studies of participants who are not taking medications Need for greater diversity in study samples Cognitive–behavioral therapy–oriented approaches seem to be most effective
Academic intervention			
Academic accommodations	Designed to address the effects of disability Personalized support Administered at point of performance	No research support for recommendations Disclosure and documentation are required for legal protection	Legally protected, accepted modifications Accommodations make pragmatic sense, but there is no research Outcome research is needed to further guide accommodation selection
Academic support or coaching	Promising pilot research Personalized support Direct relevance for academic impairments Targets important skills	No formal protocols Preliminary research Requires adherence Limited availability	Encouraging preliminary results Need randomized controlled studies Future studies to determine essential elements of academic support and whether they outperform standard approaches

Workplace intervention Career counseling	Systematic approach for exploring aptitudes, interests, and job options Available at most postsecondary schools	No research Hard to quantify outcomes Cost for adults seeking private career counseling	Useful service Research might identify areas of concern in occupational settings that are particularly relevant for adults with ADHD Studies might also assess whether career counseling outperforms standard job or career search behaviors
Workplace accommodations	Personalized Designed to address specific work impairments Administered at point of performance Many useful informal accommodations	Hard to secure legally mandated work accommodations Unclear whether workplace approaches are effectively used without medications No outcome research	Workplace coping strategies are pragmatic and acceptable Target an important area of impairment Systematic research of accommodations and related interventions (e.g., ADHD coaching) is needed
Relationship treatment Family therapy	Targets area of impairment, particularly considering heritability of ADHD Personalized treatment Accepted treatment approach	Existing treatments focus on children and teens with ADHD Difficult to quantify outcomes Limited availability of family specialists in ADHD	Family treatments are acceptable and address a common source of stress Existing family treatments can be modified to address parental ADHD Future outcome studies might consider parental ADHD as a moderator variable and as a focus of intervention
Marital therapy	ADHD is a common source of marital stress Personalized treatment Accepted treatment	No outcome research Difficult to quantify outcomes Limited availability of marital specialists in ADHD	Marital therapy is viewed as acceptable Preliminary outcome research is needed for marital therapy for couples with at least one partner diagnosed with ADHD

(continues)

TABLE 8.1

Summary of Nonmedication Treatments for Adult Attention-Deficit/Hyperactivity Disorder (ADHD)   (Continued)

Treatment	Strengths	Limitations	Current status and future directions
Social skills training	Targets of impairment relevant for many areas of life Personalized treatment Accepted treatment	No outcome research No formalized, stand-alone intervention approach Problems may result from ineffective use of skills rather than skill deficit	Social skills training is viewed as an acceptable approach, although it is unclear whether adults with ADHD seek it as a stand-alone treatment Preliminary research of the efficacy of social skills training for adult ADHD is needed Elements of social skills training might be integrated with existing psychosocial approaches
Neurocognitive treatment Neurofeedback training (NFT)	Tentative positive results for adults with ADHD Anecdotal support Potential usefulness in assessment	Few studies of adults with ADHD Significant flaws in most studies Unclear whether NFT outperforms standard assessments or treatments	Randomized control designs with adults with ADHD Control for therapeutic time and support Measure functional outcomes Clarify mechanisms of action
Working memory training	Positive results in studies of children and teens with ADHD Strong research designs Generalized gains in working memory	No studies of adults with ADHD Unclear whether positive outcomes include improved daily functioning	Randomized control designs with adults with ADHD Measure functional outcomes Clarify mechanisms of action

Complementary and alternative medicine (CAM)			
Therapeutic interventions or exercises	Promising initial results for some approaches May be helpful in cases of comorbidity, poor response to medications, or both	Insufficient research support for most approaches Unclear whether therapies address ADHD or comorbid symptoms Better assessment strategies are needed	Much more research is needed Randomized control designs with adults with ADHD Clarify mechanisms of action Identify comorbidity patterns that might be responsive to these approaches
Supplementation and nutrition	May be helpful in cases of documented deficiency Some positive results obtained in some studies of supplementation	Benefits limited to correcting documented insufficiency Potential negative effects of overuse Equivocal research results, at best Benefits likely do not exceed those from good health practices	Identification of individuals with documented deficiencies Future studies must explain relevance of these interventions for ADHD Recognition of effects of ADHD on overall nutrition and health hygiene behaviors
Homeopathy and miscellaneous CAM	Options for individuals seeking nonstandard treatments Easy access (e.g., no need for prescriptions)	No research support for their use Potential negative interactions with medications May delay more effective treatment if CAM sought out first No regulation of practitioner qualifications	Identify specific problems that might respond to these approaches Future studies must explain relevance of these interventions for ADHD Better research designs

APPENDIX A: RESOURCES

This resource list has been compiled to provide interested readers with sources of information about various topics addressed in this volume. Inclusion in this list, however, should not necessarily be considered an endorsement by the author.

GENERAL INFORMATION AND RESOURCES

Attention Deficit Disorder Association (ADDA)	http://www.add.org
National Resource Center for ADHD	http://www.help4add.org
Children and Adults with ADHD (CHADD)	http://www.chadd.org
ADD Resources	http://www.ADDresources.org
ADD Warehouse	http://www.ADDwarehouse.com
National Center for Gender Issues and ADHD	http://www.ncgiadd.org
ADDvance	http://www.ADDvance.com
ADDconsults	http://www.ADDconsults.com
Attention Research Update	http://www.helpforadd.com
National Attention Deficit Disorder Information and Support Service (ADDISS)	http://www.addiss.co.uk
Canadian Attention Deficit Hyperactivity Disorder Resource Alliance (CADDRA)	http://www.caddra.ca
ADHD Foundation of Canada	http://www.adhdfoundation.ca/

ADULT ADHD TREATMENT PROGRAMS

Arizona State University (Tempe) Clinical Psychology Center (AZ)
Cambridge Health Alliance—Center for Child and Adolescent Development (MA)
Chesapeake ADHD Center of Maryland (MD)
Duke University Medical Center ADHD Program (NC)
Fairleigh Dickinson University Adult ADHD Clinic (NJ)
The Hallowell Center (MA)
Kahi Mohala Behavioral Health (HI)

Massachusetts General Hospital (MA)
Mt. Sinai School of Medicine ADHD Center (NY)
New York University (NY)
State University of New York Upstate Medical University (Syracuse) ADHD Program (NY)
University of California, Los Angeles (UCLA), ADHD Clinic (CA)
University of California, San Diego (UCSD), Adult Attention Deficit Program (CA)
University of Connecticut Medical School-Neuropsychology Service-Adult ADHD Clinic (CT)
University of Illinois at Chicago Adult ADHD Clinic (IL)
University of Iowa (Iowa City) Center for Disabilities and Development (IA)
University of Missouri—Columbia Psychological Services Clinic (MO)
University of North Carolina at Greensboro ADHD Clinic (NC)
University of Pennsylvania Adult ADHD Treatment and Research Program (PA)
West Virginia University Health Sciences Center ADHD Treatment Clinic (WV)

PROFESSIONAL JOURNALS OR NEWSLETTERS

The ADHD Report	http://www.guilford.com
Editor, Russell Barkley, PhD	
Current Attention Disorders Reports	http://www.current-reports.com
Editor, Anthony L. Rostain, MD	
Journal of ADHD & Related Disorders	http://www.apsard.org
Editors, Joseph Biederman, MD,	
and Stephen V. Faraone, PhD	
Journal of Attention Disorders	http://www.jad.sagepub.com
Editor, Sam Goldstein, PhD	

ADHD MAGAZINES

ADDitude Magazine	http://www.additudemag.com
Attention	http://www.chadd.org

ADHD COACHING

ADD Coach Academy	http://www.addca.org
ADHD Coaches Organization	http://www.adhdcoaches.org

American Coaching Association	http://www.americoach.org
Institute for the Advancement of ADHD Coaching	http://www.adhdcoachinstitute.org
International Coach Federation	http://www.coachfederation.org
Optimal Functioning Institute	http://www.addcoach.com

ACADEMIC SUPPORT AND ACCOMMODATIONS

Association of Higher Education and Disability (AHEAD)	http://www.ahead.org
Georgia Assistive Technology Project	http://www.gatfl.org
LD Online	http://www.ldonline.org
Learning Disabilities Association of America	http://www.ldnatl.org
Weingarten Learning Resources Center (PENN)	http://www.vpul.upenn.edu/lrc/
Landmark College	http://www.landmark.edu
University of Arizona Strategic Alternative Learning Techniques (SALT) Center	http://www.salt.arizona.edu/
Muskingum College PLUS Program	http://www.muskingum.edu/home/cal/plus

CAREER COUNSELING AND WORKPLACE SUPPORT

Job Accommodation Network	http://www.jan.wvu.edu
Job Application and the Americans With Disabilities Act	http://www.eeoc.gov
National Career Development Association	http://www.ncda.org

ADULT ADHD AND MARRIAGE

Thoughts on ADHD and Marriage	http://www.adhdmarriage.com
Is It You, Me, Or Adult A.D.D.?	http://www.adhdrollercoaster.org

ADULT ADHD, SOCIAL SKILLS, AND RELATIONSHIPS

Various articles by Dr. Michele Novotni	http://www.michelenovotni.com/articles/

NEUROFEEDBACK

Association for Applied Psychophysiology and Biofeedback	http://www.aapb.org
Biofeedback Certification Institution of America	http://www.bcia.org
International Society for Neurofeedback and Research	http://www.isnr.org

WORKING MEMORY TRAINING

Cogmed	http://www.cogmed.com

COMPLEMENTARY AND ALTERNATIVE TREATMENTS

The ADD/ADHD Online Newsletter	http://www.youradhdnewsletter.com/
Dore Program	http://www.dorecenters.com

APPENDIX B: MEDICATIONS FOR ADULT ATTENTION-DEFICIT/ HYPERACTIVITY DISORDER (ADHD)

TABLE B.1
U.S. Food and Drug Administration–Approved Medications
for the Treatment of Adult ADHD

Generic name (class)	Trade name	Daily dose range for adults (mg)
Mixed salts of a single-entity amphetamine (stimulant—long acting)	Adderall XR	10–70
Dexmethylphenidate (stimulant—long acting)	Focalin XR	10–40
Atomoxetine (nonstimulant)	Strattera	40–120
Lisdexamfetamine dimesylate (prodrug stimulant—long acting)	Vyvanse	30–70
Methylphenidate (stimulant—long acting)	Concerta	18–108

TABLE B.2
Other Medications Used in the Treatment of Adult ADHD (Off-Label)

Generic name (class)	Trade name	Daily dose range for adults (mg)
Methylphenidate (stimulant—short acting)	Ritalin Metadate	20–80
(stimulant—long acting)	Ritalin LA, SR Metadate CD, ER	10–80
(transdermal patch)	Daytrana	15–30
Dextromethlyphenidate (stimulant—short acting)	Focalin	30–70
Dextroamphetamine (stimulant—short acting)	Dexedrine DextroStat	10–60
(stimulant—intermediate acting)	Dexedrine Spansule	10–60
Mixed salts of a single-entity amphetamine (stimulant—short acting)	Adderall	10–70
Modafinil (stimulant)	Provigil Sparlon	100–400
Buproprion (antidepressant)	Wellbutrin SR Wellbutrin XL	150–400 150–450
Venlafaxine (antidepressant)	Effexor Effexor XR	75–225
Desipramine (tricyclic antidepressant)	Norpramin	100–300
Imipramine (tricyclic antidepressant)	Tofranil	100–300
Nortriptyline (tricyclic antidepressant)	Pamelor	50–150
Clonidine (α_2-adrenergic agonist)	Catapres	0.1–0.4
Guanfacine (α_2-adrenergic agonist)	Tenex	0.5–4

Note. Data are from Adler and Florence (2006); Prince, Wilens, Spencer, & Biederman (2006); Ramsay and Rostain (2008a); and Rostain and Ramsay (2006a).

REFERENCES

Aberson, B., Shure, M. B., & Goldstein, S. (2007). Social problem-solving intervention can help children with ADHD. *Journal of Attention Disorders, 11*, 4–7.

Abi-Saab, W., Wilens, T. E., Apostol, G., Kratochvil, C. J., Robieson, W. Z., Pritchett, Y. L., et al. (2008, May). *Efficacy and safety of ABT-089 in adults with attention-deficit/hyperactivity disorder*. Paper presented at the 161st Annual Meeting of the American Psychiatric Association, Washington, DC.

Able, S. L., Johnston, J. A., Adler, L. A., & Swindle, R. W. (2006). Functional and psychosocial impairment in adults with undiagnosed ADHD. *Psychological Medicine, 37*, 97–107.

The ADDA Subcommittee on AD/HD Coaching. (2002). *The ADDA guiding principles for coaching individuals with attention deficit disorder*. Retrieved February 3, 2008, from http://www.add.org/articles/coachingguide.html

Adesman, A., & Sherman, C. (2007, February/March). Does nutrition make a difference? *ADDitude Magazine, 7*(4), 11–12.

Adler, L., & Florence, M. (2006). *Scattered minds*. New York: Putnam.

Adler, L., Goodman, D. W., Kollins, S. H., Weisler, R., Krishnan, S., Zhang, Y., et al. (2007, October). *Efficacy and safety of lisdexamfetamine dimesylate in adults with attention-deficit/hyperactivity disorder*. Paper presented at the 54th Annual Meeting of the American Academy of Child and Adolescent Psychiatry, Boston, MA.

Adler, L., Spencer, T. J., Brown, T. E., Holdnack, J., Saylor, K., Schuh, K., et al. (2009). Once-daily atomoxetine for adult attention-deficit/hyperactivity disorder: A 6-month, double-blind trial. *Journal of Clinical Psychopharmacology, 29*, 44–50.

Adler, L., Spencer, T. J., Williams, D. W., Moore, R. J., & Michelson, D. (2008). Long-term, open-label safety and efficacy of atomoxetine in adults with ADHD: Final report of a 4-year study. *Journal of Attention Disorders, 12*, 248–253.

Allsopp, D. H., Minskoff, E. H., & Bolt, L. (2005). Individualized course-specific strategy instruction for college students with learning disabilities and ADHD: Lessons learned from a model demonstration program. *Learning Disabilities Research & Practice, 20*, 103–118.

Alpert, J. E., Maddocks, A., Nierenberg, A. A., O'Sullivan, R., Pava, J. A., Worthington III, J. J., et al. (1996). Attention deficit hyperactivity disorder in childhood among adults with major depression. *Psychiatry Research, 62*, 213–219.

Alster, E. H. (1997). The effects of extended time on algebra test scores for college students with and without learning disabilities. *Journal of Learning Disabilities, 30*, 222–227.

Altunç, U., Pittler, M. H., & Ernst, E. (2007). Homeopathy for childhood and adolescence ailments: Systematic review of randomized clinical trials. *Mayo Clinic Proceedings, 82*, 69–75.

Amen, D. G. (2001). *Healing ADD: The breakthrough program that allows you to see and heal the 6 types of ADD.* New York: Putnam.

American Academy of Child and Adolescent Psychiatry. (1997). Practice parameters for the assessment and treatment of children, adolescents, and adults with attention-deficit/hyperactivity disorder. *Journal of the American Academy of Child & Adolescent Psychiatry, 36*(Suppl. 10), 85–121.

American Academy of Child and Adolescent Psychiatry. (2002). Practice parameters for the use of stimulant medications in the treatment of children, adolescents, and adults. *Journal of the American Academy of Child & Adolescent Psychiatry, 41*(Suppl. 2), 26–49.

American Academy of Child and Adolescent Psychiatry. (2007). Practice parameter for the assessment and treatment of children and adolescents with attention-deficit/hyperactivity disorder. *Journal of the American Academy of Child & Adolescent Psychiatry, 46*, 894–921.

American Academy of Pediatrics. (2001). Clinical practice guideline: Treatments of the school-aged child with attention-deficit/hyperactivity disorder. *Pediatrics, 108*, 1033–1044.

American Psychiatric Association. (1968). *Diagnostic and statistical manual of mental disorders* (2nd ed.). Washington, DC: Author.

American Psychiatric Association. (1980). *Diagnostic and statistical manual of mental disorders* (3rd ed.). Washington, DC: Author.

American Psychiatric Association. (1987). *Diagnostic and statistical manual of mental disorders* (3rd ed., rev.). Washington, DC: Author.

American Psychiatric Association. (1994). *Diagnostic and statistical manual of mental disorders* (4th ed.). Washington, DC: Author.

American Psychiatric Association. (2000). *Diagnostic and statistical manual of mental disorders* (4th ed., text rev.). Washington, DC: Author.

Americans With Disabilities Act of 1990. Pub. L. No. 101–336, 42 U.S.C. § 12101 et seq. (2008).

Antalis, C. J., Stevens, L. J., Campbell, M., Pazdro, R., Ericson, K., & Burgess, J. R. (2006). Omega-3 fatty acid status in attention-deficit/hyperactivity disorder. *Prostaglandins, Leukotrienes & Essential Fatty Acids, 75*, 299–308.

Antshel, K. M., & Barkley, R. A. (2008). Psychosocial interventions in attention deficit hyperactivity disorder. *Child and Adolescent Psychiatric Clinics of North America, 17*, 421–437.

Antshel, K. M., & Remer, R. (2003). Social skills training in children with attention deficit hyperactivity disorder: A randomized-controlled clinical trial. *Journal of Clinical Child and Adolescent Psychology, 32*, 153–165.

APA Presidential Task Force on Evidence-Based Practice. (2006). Evidence-based practice in psychology. *American Psychologist, 61*, 271–285.

Appelbaum, K. L. (2008). Assessment and treatment of correctional inmates with ADHD. *American Journal of Psychiatry, 165*, 1520–1524.

Arnold, L. E. (2001). Alternative treatments for adults with attention-deficit hyperactivity disorder (ADHD). *Annals of the New York Academy of Sciences, 931*, 310–341.

Arnold, L. E. (2002). Treatment alternatives for attention deficit hyperactivity disorder. In P. J. Jensen & J. R. Cooper (Eds.), *Attention deficit hyperactivity disorder: State of science—best practices* (pp. 13-1–13-29). Kingston, NJ: Civic Research Institute.

Arnold, L. E. (2006, August). Alternative and complementary treatments for AD/HD. *Attention Magazine, 13*(4), 30–34.

Arnold, L. E. (2007, November). *The place of complementary interventions in comprehensive care: Grandma was right all along?* Paper presented at the 19th Annual International Conference of Children and Adults With Attention Deficit Hyperactivity Disorder, Crystal City, VA.

Arnold, L. E., & DiSilvestro, R. A. (2005). Zinc in attention-deficit/hyperactivity disorder. *Journal of Child and Adolescent Psychopharmacology, 15*, 619–627.

Arnold, L. E., Votolato, N. A., Kleykamp, D., Baker, G. B., & Bornstein, R. A. (1990). Does hair zinc predict amphetamine improvement of ADHD/hyperactivity? *International Journal of Neuroscience, 50*, 103–107.

Attention Deficit Disorder Association. (2006a). *ADHD in the workplace: A survey of adults in 14 common professions*. Mt. Laurel, NJ: Author.

Attention Deficit Disorder Association. (2006b). *Guiding principles for the diagnosis and treatment of attention deficit/hyperactivity disorder*. Mt. Laurel, NJ: Author.

Aviram, R. B., Rhum, M., & Levin, F. R. (2001). Psychotherapy of adults with comorbid attention-deficit/hyperactivity disorder and psychoactive substance use disorder. *Journal of Psychotherapy Practice and Research, 10*, 179–186.

Baijal, S., & Gupta, R. (2008). Meditation-based training: A possible intervention for attention deficit hyperactivity disorder. *Psychiatry, 5*(4), 48–55.

Baker, G. B., Bornstein, R. A., Rouget, A. C., Ashton, S. E., van Muyden, J. C., & Coutts, R. T. (1991). Phenylethylaminergic mechanisms in attention-deficit disorder. *Biological Psychiatry, 29*, 15–22.

Banaschewski, T., Besmens, F., Zieger, H., & Rothenberger, A. (2001). Evaluation of sensorimotor training in children with ADHD. *Perceptual and Motor Skills, 92*, 137–149.

Barkley, R. A. (1997a). *ADHD and the nature of self-control*. New York: Guilford Press.

Barkley, R. A. (1997b). Behavioral inhibition, sustained attention, and executive functions: Constructing a unifying theory of ADHD. *Psychological Bulletin, 121*, 65–94.

Barkley, R. A. (Ed.). (1998). *Attention-deficit hyperactivity disorder: A handbook for diagnosis and treatment* (2nd ed.). New York: Guilford Press.

Barkley, R. A. (2001). The executive functions and self-regulation: An evolutionary neuropsychological perspective. *Neuropsychology Review, 11*, 1–29.

Barkley, R. A. (2002a). Major life activity and health outcomes associated with attention-deficit/hyperactivity disorder. *Journal of Clinical Psychiatry, 63* (Suppl. 12), 10–15.

Barkley, R. A. (2002b). Psychosocial treatments for attention-deficit/hyperactivity disorder in children. *Journal of Clinical Psychiatry, 63*(Suppl. 12), 36–43.

Barkley, R. A. (Ed.). (2006a). *Attention-deficit hyperactivity disorder: A handbook for diagnosis and treatment* (3rd ed.). New York: Guilford Press.

Barkley, R. A. (2006b). Driving risks in adults with ADHD: Yet more evidence and a personal story. *The ADHD Report, 14*(5), 1–9.

Barkley, R. A. (2006c). Editorial commentary: Issues in working memory training in ADHD. *The ADHD Report, 14*(1), 9–11.

Barkley, R. A. (2007). What may be in store for *DSM–V*. *The ADHD Report, 15*(4), 1–7.

Barkley, R. A., & Cox, D. (2007). A review of driving risks and impairments associated with attention-deficit/hyperactivity disorder and the effects of stimulant medication on driving performance. *Journal of Safety Research, 38*, 113–128.

Barkley, R. A., Edwards, G., Laneri, M., Fletcher, K., & Metevia, L. (2001). The efficacy of problem-solving communication training alone, behavior management training alone, and their combination for parent–adolescent conflict in teenagers with ADHD and ODD. *Journal of Consulting and Clinical Psychology, 69*, 926–941.

Barkley, R. A., Fischer, M., Smallish, L., & Fletcher, K. (2002). The persistence of attention-deficit/hyperactivity disorder into young adulthood as a function of reporting source and definition of disorder. *Journal of Abnormal Psychology, 111*, 279–289.

Barkley, R. A., Fischer, M., Smallish, L., & Fletcher, K. (2006). Young adult outcome of hyperactive children: Adaptive functioning in major life areas. *Journal of the American Academy of Child & Adolescent Psychiatry, 45*, 192–202.

Barkley, R. A., Guevremont, D. G., Anastopoulos, A. D., & Fletcher, K. F. (1992). A comparison of three family therapy programs for treating family conflicts in adolescents with attention deficit hyperactivity disorder. *Journal of Consulting and Clinical Psychology, 60*, 450–462.

Barkley, R. A., & Murphy, K. R. (2006a). *Attention-deficit hyperactivity disorder: A clinical workbook* (3rd ed.). New York: Guilford Press.

Barkley, R. A., & Murphy, K. R. (2006b). Identifying new symptoms for diagnosing ADHD in adulthood. *The ADHD Report, 14*(4), 7–11.

Barkley, R. A., Murphy, K. R., Du Paul, G. J., & Bush, T. (2002). Driving in young adults with attention deficit hyperactivity disorder: Knowledge, performance, adverse outcomes, and the role of executive functioning. *Journal of the International Neuropsychological Society, 8*, 655–672.

Barkley, R. A., Murphy, K. R., & Fischer, M. (2008). *ADHD in adults: What the science says*. New York: Guilford Press.

Beauregard, M., & Lévesque, J. (2006). Functional magnetic resonance imaging investigation of the effect of neurofeedback training on the neural bases of selective attention and response inhibition in children with attention-deficit/hyperactivity disorder. *Applied Psychophysiology and Biofeedback, 31,* 3–20.

Beck, A. T. (1976). *Cognitive therapy and the emotional disorders.* New York: Meridian.

Bellak, L. (1977). Psychiatric states in adults with minimal brain dysfunction. *Psychiatric Annals, 7,* 575–589.

Bemporad, J. (2001). Aspects of psychotherapy with adults with attention deficit disorder. *Annals of the New York Academy of Sciences, 931,* 302–309.

Bemporad, J., & Zambenedetti, M. (1996). Psychotherapy of adults with attention-deficit disorder. *Journal of Psychotherapy Practice and Research, 5,* 228–237.

Berman, W. H., & Bradt, G. (2006). Executive coaching and consulting: "Different strokes for different folks." *Professional Psychology: Research and Practice, 37,* 244–253.

Bernier, J. C., & Siegel, D. H. (1994). Attention-deficit hyperactivity disorder: A family and ecological systems perspective. *Families in Society, 75,* 142–151.

Berry, S. A., Orman, C., Cooper, K., Votto, D., Starr, H. L., & Adler, L. (2007, October). *Safety and efficacy of OROS methylphenidate in adults with ADHD.* Poster session presented at the 54th Annual Meeting of the American Academy of Child and Adolescent Psychiatry, Boston, MA.

Betchen, S. J. (2003). Suggestions for improving intimacy in couples in which one partner has attention-deficit/hyperactivity disorder. *Journal of Sex and Marital Therapy, 29,* 103–124.

Biederman, J. (2004). Impact of comorbidity in adults with attention-deficit/hyperactivity disorder. *Journal of Clinical Psychiatry, 65*(Suppl. 3), 3–7.

Biederman, J., & Faraone, S. V. (2004). Attention deficit hyperactivity disorder: A worldwide concern. *The Journal of Nervous and Mental Disease, 192,* 453–454.

Biederman, J., & Faraone, S. V. (2005, October). *Economic impact of adult ADHD.* Poster session presented at the 17th Annual International Conference of Children and Adults With Attention Deficit Hyperactivity Disorder, Dallas, TX.

Biederman, J., Faraone, S. V., & Monuteaux, M. C. (2002). Impact of exposure to parental attention-deficit hyperactivity disorder on clinical features and dysfunction in the offspring. *Psychological Medicine, 32,* 817–827.

Biederman, J., Faraone, S. V., Monuteaux, M. C., Bober, M., & Cadogen, E. (2004). Gender effects on attention-deficit/hyperactivity disorder in adults, revisited. *Biological Psychiatry, 55,* 692–700.

Biederman, J., Faraone, S. V., Spencer, T. J., Mick, E., Monuteaux, M. C., & Aleardi, M. (2006). Functional impairments in adults with self-reports of diagnosed ADHD: A controlled study of 1,001 adults in the community. *Journal of Clinical Psychiatry, 67,* 524–540.

Biederman, J., Kwon, A., Aleardi, M., Chouinard, V. A., Marino, T., Cole, H., et al. (2005). Absence of gender effects on attention deficit hyperactivity disorder: Findings in nonreferred subjects. *American Journal of Psychiatry, 162,* 1083–1089.

Biederman, J., Mick, E., & Faraone, S. V. (2000). Age-dependent decline of symptoms of attention deficit hyperactivity disorder: Impact of remission definition and symptom type. *American Journal of Psychiatry, 157*, 816–818.

Biederman, J., Mick, E., Faraone, S. V., Braaten, E., Doyle, A., Spencer, T., et al. (2002). Influence of gender on attention deficit hyperactivity disorder in children referred to a psychiatric clinic. *American Journal of Psychiatry, 159*, 36–42.

Biederman, J., Mick, E., Fried, R., Aleardi, M., Potter, A., & Herzig, K. (2005). A simulated workplace experience for nonmedicated adults with and without ADHD. *Psychiatric Services, 56*, 1617–1620.

Biederman, J., Wilens, T., Mick, E., Faraone, S. V., & Spencer, T. (1998). Does attention-deficit hyperactivity disorder impact the developmental course of drug and alcohol dependence? *Biological Psychiatry, 44*, 269–273.

Biederman, J., Wilens, T., Mick, E., Spencer, T., & Faraone, S. V. (1999). Pharmacotherapy of attention-deficit hyperactivity disorder reduces risk for substance abuse disorder. *Pediatrics, 104*, 20–25.

Birnbaum, H. G., Kessler, R. C., Lowe, S. W., Secnik, K., Greenberg, P. E., Leong, S. A., et al. (2005). Costs of attention deficit-hyperactivity disorder (ADHD): Excess costs of person with ADHD and their family members in 2000. *Current Medical Research and Opinion, 21*, 195–205.

Boonstra, A. M., Kooij, J. J. S., Oosterlaan, J., Sergeant, J. A., Buitelaar, J. K., & Van Someren, J. W. (2007). Hyperactive night and day? Actigraphy studies in adult ADHD: A baseline comparison and the effect of methylphenidate. *Sleep, 30*, 433–442.

Bornstein, R. A., Baker, G. B., Carroll, A., King, G., Wong, J. T., & Douglass, A. B. (1990). Plasma amino acids in attention deficit disorder. *Psychiatry Research, 33*, 301–306.

Bower, J. M., & Parsons, L. M. (2003). Rethinking the "lesser brain." *Scientific American, 289*(2), 50–57.

Bramham, J., Young, S., Bickerdike, A., Spain, D., McCartan, D., & Xenitidis, K. (2009). Evaluation of group cognitive behavioral therapy for adults with ADHD. *Journal of Attention Disorders, 12*, 434–441.

Brattberg, G. (2006). PTSD and ADHD: Underlying factors in many cases of burnout. *Stress and Health, 22*, 305–313.

Brody, G. H. (2004). Sibling's direct and indirect contributions to child development. *Current Directions in Psychological Science, 13*, 124–126.

Brown, T. E. (1996). *Brown Attention Deficit Disorder Scales.* San Antonio, TX: Psychological Corporation.

Brown, T. E. (2000). Psychosocial interventions for attention-deficit disorders and comorbid conditions. In T. E. Brown (Ed.), *Attention deficit disorders and comorbidities in children, adolescents, and adults* (pp. 537–568). Washington, DC: American Psychiatric Press.

Brown, T. E. (2005). *Attention deficit disorder: The unfocused mind in children and adults.* New Haven, CT: Yale University Press.

Brown, T. E. (2006). Executive functions and attention deficit hyperactivity disorder: Implications of two conflicting views. *International Journal of Disability, Development and Education, 53,* 35–46.

Bruner, A. B., Joffe, A., Duggan, A., Casella, J. F., & Brandt, J. (1996). Randomized study of cognitive effects of iron supplementation in non-anemic iron-deficient girls. *The Lancet, 347,* 992–998.

Burattini, M. G., Amendola, F., Aufiero, T., Spano, M., Di Bitonto, G., Del Vecchio, G. C., et al. (1990). Evaluation of the effectiveness of gastro-protected proteoferrin in therapy of sideropenic anemia in childhood. *Minerva Pediatrics, 42,* 343–347.

Busch, B., Biederman, J., Cohen, L. G., Sayer, J. M., Monuteaux, M. C., Mick, E., et al. (2002). Correlates of ADHD among children in pediatric and psychiatric clinics. *Psychiatric Services, 53,* 1103–1111.

Bustos, R. R., & Goldstein, S. (2008). Including blood lead levels of all immigrant children when evaluating for ADHD. *Journal of Attention Disorders, 11,* 425–426.

Canu, W. H. (2007). Vocational safety preference of college men with and without attention-deficit/hyperactivity disorder: An exploratory study. *Journal of College Counseling, 10,* 54–63.

Canu, W. H., & Carlson, C. L. (2003). Differences in heterosocial behavior and outcomes of ADHD-symptomatic subtypes in a college sample. *Journal of Attention Disorders, 6,* 123–133.

Canu, W. H., & Carlson, C. L. (2004). ADHD and social adaptation: From childhood to adulthood. *The ADHD Report, 12*(2), 1–6.

Canu, W. H., & Carlson, C. L. (2007). Rejection sensitivity and social outcomes of young adult men with ADHD. *Journal of Attention Disorders, 10,* 261–275.

Canu, W. H., Newman, M. L., Morrow, T. L., & Pope, D. L. (2008). Social appraisal of adult ADHD: Stigma and influences of the beholder's Big Five personality traits. *Journal of Attention Disorders, 11,* 700–710.

Carlson, C. L., & Mann, M. (2002). Sluggish cognitive tempo predicts a different pattern of impairment in the attention deficit hyperactivity disorder, predominantly inattentive type. *Journal of Clinical Child and Adolescent Psychology, 31,* 123–129.

Carney, J. K. (2002). Self- and interactive regulation: Treating a patient with AD/HD. *Psychoanalytic Inquiry, 22,* 355–371.

Carroll, C. B., & Ponterotto, J. G. (1998). Employment counseling for adults with attention-deficit/hyperactivity disorder: Issues without answers. *Journal of Employment Counseling, 35,* 79–95.

Castellanos, F. X. (2002). Proceed, with caution. SPECT cerebral blood flow studies of children and adolescents with attention deficit hyperactivity disorder. *The Journal of Nuclear Medicine, 43,* 1630–1633.

Castellanos, F. X., Giedd, J. N., Berquin, P. C., Walter, J. M., Sharp, W., Tran, T., et al. (2001). Quantitative brain magnetic resonance imaging in girls with attention-deficit/hyperactivity disorder. *Archives of General Psychiatry, 58,* 289–295.

Cephalon, Inc. (2006). *Cephalon reports no benefit from Provigil in a study of adults with ADHD*. Retrieved November 30, 2006, from http://phx.corporate-ir.net/phoenix.zhtml?c=81709&p=irol-newsArticle&ID=18727&highlight=adhd

Chamberlain, S. R., del Campo, N., Dowson, J., Müller, U., Clark, L., Robbins, T. W., et al. (2007). Atomoxetine improved response inhibition in adults with attention deficit/hyperactivity disorder. *Biological Psychiatry, 62,* 977–984.

Chambless, D. L., & Hollon, S. D. (1998). Defining empirically supported therapies. *Journal of Consulting and Clinical Psychology, 66,* 7–18.

Chan, E. (2002). The role of complementary and alternative medicine in attention-deficit hyperactivity disorder. *Journal of Developmental & Behavioral Pediatrics, 23*(Suppl. 1), 37–45.

Chan, E., Rappaport, L. A., & Kemper, K. J. (2003). Complementary and alternative therapies in childhood attention and hyperactivity problems. *Journal of Developmental & Behavioral Pediatrics, 24,* 4–8.

Chronis, A. M., Chacko, A., Fabiano, G. A., Wymbs, B. T., & Pelham, W. E. (2004). Enhancements to the behavioral parent training paradigm for families of children with ADHD: Review and future directions. *Clinical Child and Family Psychology Review, 7,* 1–27.

Chronis, A. M., Gamble, S. A., Roberts, J. E., & Pelham, W. E. (2006). Cognitive-behavioral depression treatment for mothers of children with attention-deficit/hyperactivity disorder. *Behavior Therapy, 37,* 143–158.

Chronis, A. M., Jones, H. A., & Raggi, V. L. (2006). Evidence-based psychosocial treatments for children and adolescents with attention-deficit/hyperactivity disorder. *Clinical Psychology Review, 26,* 486–502.

Chronis, A. M., Lahey, B. B., Pelham, W. E., Williams, S. H., Baumann, B. L., Kipp, H., et al. (2007). Maternal depression and early positive parenting predict future conduct problems in young children with attention-deficit/hyperactivity disorder. *Developmental Psychology, 43,* 70–82.

Clark, D. L., Arnold, L. E., Crowl, L., Bozzolo, H., Peruggia, M., Ramadan, Y., et al. (2008). Vestibular stimulation for ADHD: Randomized controlled trial of comprehensive motion apparatus. *Journal of Attention Disorders, 11,* 599–611.

Cogmed America Inc. (2008). *Cogmed FAQs*. Retrieved March 25, 2008, from http://www.cogmed.com/articles/en/109.aspx

Colter, A. L., Cutler, C., & Meckling, K. A. (2008, February 14). Fatty acid status and behavioural symptoms of attention deficit hyperactivity disorder in adolescents: A case-control study. *Nutrition Journal (7/8)*. doi: 10.1186/1475-2891-708.

Conners, C. K. (2000). Attention-deficit/hyperactivity disorder—Historical development and overview. *Journal of Attention Disorders, 3,* 173–191.

Conners, C. K. (2001). *Conners' Rating Scales—Revised*. North Tonawanda, NY: Multi-Health Systems.

Conners, C. K., Erhardt, D., & Sparrow, E. (1999). *Conners' Adult ADHD Rating Scales*. North Tonawanda, NY: Multi-Health Systems.

Conway, A. R. A., Kane, M. J., & Engle, R. W. (2003). Working memory capacity and its relation to general intelligence. *Trends in Cognitive Sciences, 7*, 547–552.

Cook, I. A. (2004). *Guideline watch: Practice guideline for the psychiatric evaluation of adults.* Arlington, VA: American Psychiatric Association. Retrieved July 2, 2007, from http://www.psych.org/psych_pract/treatg/pg/prac_guide.cfm

Corcoran, J., & Dattalo, P. (2006). Parent involvement in treatment for ADHD: A meta-analysis of the published studies. *Research on Social Work Practice, 16*, 561–570.

Council on Children, Adolescents and Their Families. (2005). *Brain imaging and child and adolescent psychiatry with special emphasis on single photon emission computed tomography (SPECT): Resource document.* Arlington, VA: American Psychiatric Association. Retrieved July 2, 2007, from http://www.psych.org/edu/other_res/lib_archives/archives/200501.pdf

Counts, C. A., Nigg, J. T., Stawicki, J. A., Rappley, M. D., & von Eye, A. (2005). Family adversity in *DSM–IV* ADHD combined and inattentive subtypes and associated disruptive behavior problems. *Journal of the American Academy of Child & Adolescent Psychiatry, 44*, 690–698.

Crawford, R., & Crawford, V. (2002). Career impact: Finding the key to issues facing adults with ADHD. In S. Goldstein & A. T. Ellison (Eds.), *Clinician's guide to adult ADHD: Assessment and intervention* (pp. 187–204). New York: Academic Press.

Crichton, A. (2008). An inquiry into the nature and origin of mental derangement: On attention and its diseases. *Journal of Attention Disorders, 12*, 200–204. (Original work published 1798)

Crisp, J., Brown II, J., Sheets, J., & Reilley, S. P. (2005, January). *The differential contributions of depression and anxiety symptoms to misdiagnosis of AD/HD on the Brown ADD Scales.* Poster session presented at the 4th Annual Posters at the Capitol, Frankfort, KY.

Cunningham, C. E. (2007). A family-centered approach to planning and measuring the outcome of interventions for children with attention-deficit/hyperactivity disorder. *Journal of Pediatric Psychology, 32*, 676–694.

Curran, S., & Fitzgerald, M. (1999). Attention deficit hyperactivity disorder in the prison population. *American Journal of Psychiatry, 156*, 1664–1665.

da Silva, M. A., & Louza, M. (2008). Letter to the editor. *Journal of Attention Disorders, 11*, 623.

Davidson, M. A. (2008). ADHD in adults: A review of the literature. *Journal of Attention Disorders, 11*, 628–641.

De Boo, G. M., & Prins, P. J. M. (2007). Social incompetence in children with ADHD: Possible moderators and mediators in social-skills training. *Clinical Psychology Review, 27*, 78–97.

de Graaf, R., Kessler, R. C., Fayyad, J., ten Have, M., Alonso, J., Angermeyer, M., et al. (2008). The prevalence and effects of adult attention-deficit/hyperactivity disorder (ADHD) on the performance of workers: Results from the WHO World

Mental Health Survey Initiative. *Occupational and Environmental Medicine, 65*, 835–842.

Demos, J. N. (2005). *Getting started with neurofeedback*. New York: Norton.

Derksen, M. T. H., & Ritmeijer, I. J. M. (2007, October 15). *The effects of behavioural-cognitive group therapy for adults with ADHD*. Poster session presented at the 20th European College of Neuropsychopharmacology Congress, Vienna, Austria.

Diamond, G., & Josephson, A. (2005). Family-based treatment research: A 10-year update. *Journal of the American Academy of Child & Adolescent Psychiatry, 44*, 872–887.

Dickerson, J. (2004). Tarantula venom could be a new source for healing. *USA Today*. Retrieved December 17, 2007, from http://www.usatoday.com/news/health/2004-12-14-tarantula-inside_x.htm

DiGirolamo, A. M., & Ramirez-Zea, M. (2009). Role of zinc in maternal and child mental health. *American Journal of Clinical Nutrition, 89*(Suppl. 3), 940–945.

Dodson, W. W. (2005). Pharmacotherapy of adult ADHD. *Journal of Clinical Psychology, 61*, 589–606.

Dooling-Litfin, J. K., & Rosén, L. A. (1997). Self-esteem in college students with a childhood history of attention deficit hyperactivity disorder. *Journal of College Student Psychotherapy, 11*, 69–82.

Dore. (2007). *How does it work? The science behind Dore*. Retrieved April 16, 2009, from http://www.doreusa.com/how.aspx

Douglas, V. I. (1999). Cognitive control processes in attention-deficit/hyperactivity disorder. In H. C. Quay & A. E. Hogan (Eds.), *Handbook of disruptive disorders* (pp. 105–138). New York: Kluwer Academic.

Douglas, V. I. (2005). Cognitive deficits in children with attention deficit hyperactivity disorder: A long-term follow-up. *Canadian Psychology, 46*, 23–31

DuPaul, G. J., Schaughency, E. A., Weyandt, L. L., Tripp, G., Kiesner, J., Ota, K., et al. (2001). Self-report of ADHD symptoms in university students: Cross-gender and cross-national prevalence. *Journal of Learning Disabilities, 34*, 370–379.

Eakin, L., Minde, K., Hechtman, L., Ochs, E., Krane, R., Bouffard, B., et al. (2004). The marital and family functioning of adults with ADHD and their spouses. *Journal of Attention Disorders, 8*, 1–10.

Edwards, G., Barkley, R. A., Laneri, M., Fletcher, K., & Metevia, L. (2001). Parent–adolescent conflict in teenagers with ADHD and ODD. *Journal of Abnormal Child Psychology, 29*, 557–572.

Erikson, E. H. (1963). *Childhood and society* (2nd Ed.). New York: Norton.

Everett, C. A., & Everett, S. V. (1999). *Family therapy for ADHD: Treating children, adolescents, and adults*. New York: Guilford Press.

Eyestone, L. L., & Howell, R. J. (1994). An epidemiological study of attention-deficit hyperactivity disorder and major depression in a male prison population. *Bulletin of the American Academy of Psychiatry & the Law, 22*, 181–193.

Faraone, S. V. (2005). The scientific foundation for understanding attention-deficit/hyperactivity disorder as a valid psychiatric disorder. *European Child and Adolescent Psychiatry, 14,* 1–10.

Faraone, S. V., & Biederman, J. (2005a, October). *Adolescent predictors of functional outcome in adult ADHD: A population survey.* Poster session presented at the 17th Annual International Conference of Children and Adults With Attention Deficit Hyperactivity Disorder, Dallas, TX.

Faraone, S. V., & Biederman, J. (2005b). What is the prevalence of adult ADHD? Results of a population screen of 966 adults. *Journal of Attention Disorders, 9,* 384–391.

Faraone, S. V., Biederman, J., & Mick, E. (2006). The age-dependent decline of attention deficit hyperactivity disorder: A meta-analysis of follow-up studies. *Psychological Medicine, 36,* 159–165.

Faraone, S. V., Sergeant, J., Gillberg, C., & Biederman, J. (2003). The worldwide prevalence of ADHD: Is it an American condition? *World Psychiatry, 2,* 104–113.

Fayyad, J., de Graaf, R., Kessler, R., Alonso, J., Angermeyer, M. Demyttenaere, K., et al. (2007). Cross-national prevalence and correlates of adult attention-deficit hyperactivity disorder. *British Journal of Psychiatry, 190,* 402–409.

Fellman, W. R. (2006). *Finding a career that works for you* (2nd ed.). Plantation, FL: Specialty Press.

Field, T. M., Quintino, O., Hernandez-Reif, M., & Koslovsky, G. (1998). Adolescents with attention-deficit hyperactivity disorder benefit from massage therapy. *Adolescence, 33,* 103–108.

Fischer, M., Barkley, R. A., Smallish, L., & Fletcher, K. (2002). Young adult follow-up of hyperactive children: Self-reported psychiatric disorders, comorbidity, and the role of childhood conduct problems and teen CD. *Journal of Abnormal Child Psychology, 30,* 463–475.

FitzGerald, P. G. (2008, February 25). Healthy skepticism: Letter from a scientist. *Time, 171*(8), 7.

Flory, K., Molina, B. G., Pelham, W. E., Gnagy, E., & Smith, B. (2006). Childhood ADHD predicts risky sexual behavior in young adulthood. *Journal of Clinical Child and Adolescent Psychology, 35,* 571–577.

Friars, P. M., & Mellor, D. J. (2007). Drop out from behavioral management training programs for ADHD: A prospective study. *Journal of Child and Family Studies, 16,* 427–441.

Fried, R., Petty, C. R., Surman, C. B., Reimer, B., Aleardi, M., Martin, J. M., et al. (2006). Characterizing impaired driving in adults with attention-deficit/hyperactivity disorder: A controlled study. *Journal of Clinical Psychiatry, 67,* 567–574.

Friedman, S. R., Rapport, L. J., Lumley, M., Tzelepis, A., VanVoorhis, A., Stettner, L., et al. (2003). Aspects of social and emotional competence in adult attention-deficit/hyperactivity disorder. *Neuropsychology, 17,* 50–58.

Garvey, M. A., Kaczynski, K. J., Becker, D. A., & Bartko, J. J. (2001). Subjective reactions of children to single-pulse transcranial magnetic stimulation. *Journal of Child Neurology, 16,* 891–894.

Gau, S. S. F., Kessler, R. C., Tseng, W. L., Wu, Y. Y., Chiu, Y. N., Yeh, C. B., et al. (2007). Association between sleep problems and symptoms of attention-deficit/hyperactivity disorder in young adults. *Sleep, 30,* 195–201.

Gentile, J. P., Atiq, R., & Gillig, P. M. (2006). Psychotherapy for the patient with adult ADHD. *Psychiatry, 3*(8), 31–35.

Gevensleben, H., Holl, B., Albrecht, B., Vogel, C., Schlamp, D., Kratz, O., et al. (2009). Is neurofeedback an efficacious treatment for ADHD? A randomized controlled clinical trial. *The Journal of Child Psychology and Psychiatry.* Advance online publication. Retrieved January 12, 2009. doi: 10.1111/j.1469-7610.2008.02033.x

Gibson, B. S., Seroczynski, A., Gondoli, D. M., Braungart-Reiker, J., & Grundy, A. (2007, March). *Working memory training for early adolescents with attention-deficit hyperactivity disorder.* Poster session presented at the biennial meeting of the Society for Research in Child Development, Boston, MA.

Gilmore, K. (2000). A psychoanalytic perspective on attention-deficit/hyperactivity disorder. *Journal of the American Psychoanalytic Association, 48,* 1259–1293.

Gingerich, K. J., Turnock, P., Litfin, J. K., & Rosén, L. A. (1998). Diversity and attention deficit hyperactivity disorder. *Journal of Clinical Psychology, 54,* 415–426.

Goad, C. J., & Robertson, J. M. (2000). How university counseling centers serve students with disabilities: A status report. *Journal of College Student Psychotherapy, 14*(3), 13–22.

Goldapple, K., Segal, Z., Garson, C., Lau, M., Bieling, P., Kennedy, S., et al. (2004). Modulation of cortical-limbic pathways in major depression. *Archives of General Psychiatry, 61,* 34–41.

Goldstein, S. (2005). Coaching as a treatment for ADHD. *Journal of Attention Disorders, 9,* 379–381.

Goossensen, M. A., van de Glind, G., Carpentier, P. J., Wijsen, R. M. A., van Duin, G., Kooij, J. J. S. (2006). An intervention program for ADHD in patients with substance use disorders: Preliminary results of a field trial. *Journal of Substance Abuse Treatment, 30,* 253–259.

Gordon, M. (2000). Letter to the editor: College students and the diagnosis of attention deficit hyperactivity disorder. *Journal of American College Health, 49,* 46–47.

Gottman, J. M. (1998). Psychology and the study of marital processes. *Annual Review of Psychology, 49,* 169–197.

Granet, D. B., Gomi, C. F., Ventura, R., & Miller-Scholte, A. (2005). The relationship between convergence insufficiency and ADHD. *Strabismus, 13,* 163–168.

Greco, L. A., & Eifert, G. H. (2004). Treating parent–adolescent conflict: Is acceptance the missing link for an integrative family therapy? *Cognitive and Behavioral Practice, 11,* 305–314.

Greene, R. W., Biederman, J., Faraone, S. V., Monuteaux, M. C., Mick, E., DuPre, E., et al. (2001). Social impairment in girls with ADHD: Patterns, gender comparisons, and correlates. *Journal of the American Academy of Child & Adolescent Psychiatry, 40,* 704–710.

Greene, R. W., Biederman, J., Faraone, S. V., Sienna, M., & Garcia-Jetton, J. (1997). Adolescent outcome of boys with attention-deficit/hyperactivity disorders and social disability: Results from a 4-year longitudinal follow-up study. *Journal of Consulting and Clinical Psychology, 65,* 758–767.

Greenhill, L. L. (2001). Clinical effects of stimulant medication in ADHD. In M. V. Solanto, A. F. T. Arnsten, & F. X. Castellanos (Eds.), *Stimulant drugs and ADHD: Basic and clinical neuroscience* (pp. 31–71). New York: Oxford University Press.

Greenhill, L. L., Abikoff, H. B., Arnold, L. E., & Cantwell, D. P. (1996). Medication treatment strategies in the MTA study: Relevance to clinicians and researchers. *Journal of the American Academy of Child & Adolescent Psychiatry, 35,* 1304–1313.

Gross-Tsur, V. (2003). Use of complementary medicine in children with ADHD and epilepsy. *Pediatric Neurology, 29,* 53–55.

Grossberg, B. (2005) *Making ADD work.* New York: Perigee Books.

Gualtieri, C. T., & Johnson, L. G. (2008). Medications do not necessarily normalize cognition in ADHD patients. *Journal of Attention Disorders, 11,* 459–469.

Hallowell, E. M. (1995). Psychotherapy of adult attention deficit disorder. In K. G. Nadeau (Ed.), *A comprehensive guide to attention deficit disorder in adults: Research, diagnosis, and treatment* (pp. 146–167). New York: Brunner/Mazel.

Hallowell, E. M., & Ratey, J. J. (1994). *Driven to distraction.* New York: Touchstone.

Hallowell, E. M., & Ratey, J. J. (2005). *Delivered from distraction.* New York: Ballantine.

Halverstadt, J. S. (1998). *ADD & romance: Finding fulfillment in love, sex, & relationships.* Lanham, MD: Taylor Trade Publishing.

Hamazaki, T., Sawazaki, S., Itomura, M., Asaoka, E., Nagao, Y., Nishimura, N., et al., (1996). The effect of docosahexaenoic acid on aggression in young adults: A placebo-controlled double-blind study. *Journal of Clinical Investigation, 97,* 1129–1133.

Hammer, C. A., & Ferrari, J. R. (2002). Differential incidence of procrastination between blue- and white-collar workers. *Current Psychology, 21,* 333–338.

Harrison, A. G. (2004). An investigation of reported symptoms of ADHD in a university population. *The ADHD Report, 12*(6), 8–11.

Harrison, A. G. (2006). Adults faking ADHD: You must be kidding! *The ADHD Report, 14*(4), 1–7.

Harrison, A. G., Edwards, M. J., & Parker, K. C. H. (2007). Identifying students faking ADHD: Preliminary findings and strategies for detection. *Archives of Clinical Neuropsychology, 22,* 577–588.

Harrison, L. J., Manocha, R., & Rubia, K. (2004). Sahaja yoga meditation as a family treatment programme for children with attention deficit-hyperactivity disorder. *Clinical Child Psychology and Psychiatry, 9,* 479–497.

Hartman, C. A., Willcutt, E. G., Rhee, S. H., & Pennington, B. F. (2004). The relation between sluggish cognitive tempo and *DSM–IV* ADHD. *Journal of Abnormal Child Psychology, 32,* 491–503.

Harvey, E., Danforth, J. S., McKee, T. E., Ulaszek, W. R., & Friedman, J. L. (2003). Parenting of children with attention-deficit/hyperactivity disorder (ADHD): The role of parental ADHD symptomatology. *Journal of Attention Disorders, 7,* 31–42.

Hayes, S. C., Strosahl, K. D., & Wilson, K. G. (1999). *Acceptance and commitment therapy: An experiential approach to behavior change.* New York: Guilford Press.

Heiligenstein, E., Conyers, L. M., Berns, A. R., & Smith, M. A. (1998). Preliminary normative data on *DSM–IV* attention deficit hyperactivity disorder in college students. *Journal of American College Health, 46,* 185–188.

Heiligenstein, E., Guenther, G., Levy, A., Savino, F., & Fulwiler, J. (1999). Psychological and academic functioning in college students with attention deficit hyperactivity disorder. *Journal of American College Health, 47,* 181–185.

Heiligenstein, E., & Keeling, R. P. (1995). Presentation of unrecognized attention deficit hyperactivity disorder in college students. *Journal of American College Health, 43,* 226–228.

Henker, C. K., & Whalen, B. (1999). The child with attention-deficit/hyperactivity disorder in school and peer settings contexts. In H. C. Quay & A. E. Hogan (Eds.), *Handbook of disruptive behavior disorders* (pp. 157–178). New York: Kluwer Academic/Plenum Publishers.

Hesslinger, B., van Elst, L. T., Nyberg, E., Dykierek, P., Richter, H., Berner, M., et al. (2002). Psychotherapy of attention deficit hyperactivity disorder in adults: A pilot study using a structured skills training program. *European Archives of Psychiatry and Clinical Neuroscience, 252,* 177–184.

Hill, J. C., & Schoener, E. P. (1996). Age-dependent decline of attention deficit hyperactivity disorder. *American Journal of Psychiatry, 153,* 1143–1146.

Hines, A. M., & Shaw, G. A. (1993). Intrusive thoughts, sensation seeking, and drug use in college students. *Bulletin of the Psychonomic Society, 31,* 541–544.

Hirshberg, L. M. (2007). Place of electroencephalographic biofeedback for attention-deficit/hyperactivity disorder. *Expert Review of Neurotherapeutics, 7,* 315–319.

Hirshberg, L. M., Chiu, S., & Frazier, J. A. (2005). Emerging brain-based interventions for children and adolescents: Overview and clinical perspective. *Child and Adolescent Psychiatric Clinics of North America, 14,* 1–19.

Hoover, D. W., & Milich, R. (1994). Effects of sugar ingestion expectancies on mother–child interactions. *Journal of Abnormal Child Psychology, 22,* 501–515.

Horrigan, J. P. (2002). Oral flower essences for ADHD. *Journal of the American Academy of Child & Adolescent Psychiatry, 41,* 895–896.

Hoza, B., Mrug, S., Gerdes, A. C., Hinshaw, S. P., Bukowski, W. M., Gold, J. A., et al. (2005). What aspects of peer relationships are impaired in children with attention-deficit/hyperactivity disorder? *Journal of Consulting and Clinical Psychology, 73,* 411–423.

Huband, N., McMurran, M., Evans, C., & Duggan, C. (2007). Social problem-solving plus psychoeducation for adults with personality disorder. *British Journal of Psychiatry, 190,* 307–313.

Hurley, D. (2007). Evidence-based standards should apply to dietary supplements, too. *Medscape General Medicine, 9*(3), 23.

Hurley, P. J., & Eme, R. (2004). *ADHD and the criminal justice system: Spinning out of control.* Charleston, SC: Book Surge.

Individuals With Disabilities Education Act of 1990, Pub. L. No. 101–476, 104 Stat. 1142 (1990).

Individuals With Disabilities Education Improvement Act of 2004, Pub. L. No. 108–446, 118 Stat. 2647 (2004).

Ingersoll, B. (2007, November 8). *Complementary and alternative treatments for AD/HD.* Workshop presented at the 19th Annual International Conference of Children and Adults With Attention Deficit Hyperactivity Disorder, Crystal City, VA.

International Coaching Federation. (2008). *Frequently asked questions about coaching.* Retrieved February 3, 2008, from http://www.coachfederation.org/ICF/For+Coaching+Clients/What+is+a+Coach/FAQs/

Jackson, B., & Farrugia, D. (1997). Diagnosis and treatment of adults with attention deficit hyperactivity disorder. *Journal of Counseling and Development, 75,* 312–319.

Jacobs, J., Williams, A., Girard, C., Njike, V., & Katz, D. (2005). Homeopathy for attention-deficit/hyperactivity disorder: A pilot randomized-controlled trial. *The Journal of Alternative and Complementary Medicine, 11,* 799–806.

Jamison, K. R. (1999). *Night falls fast: Understanding suicide.* New York: Knopf.

Jastrowski, K. E., Berlin, K. S., Sato, A. F., & Davies, W. H. (2007). Disclosure of attention-deficit/hyperactivity disorder may minimize risk of social rejection. *Psychiatry: Interpersonal & Biological Processes, 70,* 274–282.

Jensen, P. S., & Kenny, D. T. (2004). The effects of yoga on the attention and behavior of boys with attention-deficit/hyperactivity disorder (ADHD). *Journal of Attention Disorders, 7,* 205–216.

Jensen, P. S., Arnold, L. E., Swanson, J. M., Vitiello, B., Abikoff, H. B., Greenhill, L. L., et al. (2007). 3-year follow-up of the NIMH MTA study. *Journal of the American Academy of Child & Adolescent Psychiatry, 46,* 989–1002.

Jha, A. P., Krompinger, J., & Baime, M. J. (2007). Mindfulness training modifies subsystems of attention. *Cognitive, Affective, & Behavioral Neuroscience, 7,* 109–119.

Johnson, S. (2004). *Mind wide open: Your brain and the neuroscience of everyday life.* New York: Scribner.

Johnston, C., & Jassy, J. S. (2007). Attention-deficit/hyperactivity disorder and opposition/conduct problems: Links to parent–child interactions. *Canadian Child Psychiatric Review, 16,* 74–79.

Johnston, C., & Mash, E. J. (2001). Families of children with attention-deficit/hyperactivity disorder: Review and recommendations for future research. *Clinical Child and Family Psychology Review, 4,* 183–207.

Kabat-Zinn, J. (1994). *Wherever you go, there you are: Mindfulness meditation in everyday life*. New York: Hyperion.

Kahn, M. (2002). *Basic Freud: Psychoanalytic thought for the 21st century*. New York: Basic Books.

Kaiser, D. A. (1997). *Efficacy of neurofeedback on adults with attentional deficit and related disorders*. Retrieved March 27, 2008, from http://www.eegspectrum.com/ Applications/ADHD-ADD/AdultsAttDefRelDis-Intro/

Kaiser, D. A., & Othmer, S. (1997). *Efficacy of SMR-beta neurofeedback for attentional processes*. Retrieved March 27, 2008, from http://www.eegspectrum.com/ Applications/ADHD-ADD/EfficacySMR-BetaIntro2/

Kaufman-Scarborough, C., & Cohen, J. (2004). Unfolding consumer impulsivity: An existential phenomenological study of consumers with attention deficit disorder. *Psychology & Marketing, 21*, 637–669.

Kelleher, K. J. (2002). Use of services and costs for youth with ADHD and related conditions. In P. J. Jensen & J. R. Cooper (Eds.), *Attention deficit hyperactivity disorder: State of science—best practices* (pp. 27-1–27-14). Kingston, NJ: Civic Research Institute.

Kelly, K. M. (1995). Adult ADD support groups. In K. G. Nadeau (Ed.), *A comprehensive guide to attention deficit disorder in adults: Research, diagnosis, and treatment* (pp. 352–374). New York: Brunner/Mazel.

Kendall, J. (1999). Sibling accounts of attention deficit hyperactivity disorder (ADHD). *Family Process, 38*, 117–136.

Kennemer, K., & Goldstein, S. (2005). Incidence of ADHD in adults with severe mental health problems. *Applied Neuropsychology, 12*, 77–82.

Kepley, H. O., & Ostrander, R. (2007). Family characteristics of anxious ADHD children. *Journal of Attention Disorders, 10*, 317–323.

Kessler, R. C., Adler, L. A., Ames, M., Barkley, R. A., Birnbaum, H., Greenberg, P., et al. (2005). The prevalence and effects of adult attention deficit/hyperactivity disorder on work performance in a nationally representative sample of workers. *Journal of Occupational and Environmental Medicine, 47*, 565–572.

Kessler, R. C., Adler, L. A., Ames, M., Demler, O., Faraone, S., Hiripi, E., et al. (2005). The World Health Organization adult ADHD self-report scale (ASRS): A short screening scale for use in the general population. *Psychological Medicine, 35*, 245–256.

Kessler, R. C., Adler, L. A., Barkley, R. A., Biederman, J., Conners, C. K., Demler, O., et al. (2006). The prevalence and correlates of adult ADHD in the United States: Results from the national comorbidity survey replication. *American Journal of Psychiatry, 163*, 716–723.

Kessler, R. C., Adler, L. A., Barkley, R. A., Biederman, J., Conners, C. K., Faraone, S. V., et al. (2005). Patterns and predictors of attention-deficit/ hyperactivity disorder persistence into adulthood: Results from the national comorbidity survey replication. *Biological Psychiatry, 57*, 1442–1451.

Kessler, R. C., Adler, L. A., Gruber, M. J., Spencer, T., & Van Brunt, D. L. (2007). Validity of the World Health Organization Adult Symptom Rating Scale (ASRS) screener in a representative sample of health plan members. *International Journal of Methods in Psychiatric Research, 16*, 52–65.

Kessler, R. C., Lane, M., Stang, P. E., & Van Brunt, D. L. (2009). The prevalence and workplace costs of adult attention deficit hyperactivity disorder in a large manufacturing firm. *Psychological Medicine, 39*, 137–147.

Khilnani, S., Field, T., Hernandez-Reif, M., & Schanberg, S. (2003). Massage therapy improves mood and behavior of students with attention-deficit/hyperactivity disorder. *Adolescence, 38*, 623–638.

Kilcarr, P. (2002). Making marriages work for individuals with ADHD. In S. Goldstein & A. T. Ellison (Eds.), *Clinician's guide to adult ADHD: Assessment and intervention* (pp. 220–240). San Diego, CA: Academic Press.

Klingberg, T. (2006). Training working memory. *The ADHD Report, 14*(1), 6–8.

Klingberg, T., Fernell, E., Olesen, P. J., Johnson, M., Gustafsson, P., Dahlström, K., et al. (2005). Computerized training of working memory in children with ADHD—A randomized, controlled trial. *Journal of the American Academy of Child & Adolescent Psychiatry, 44*, 177–186.

Klingberg, T., Forssberg, H., & Westerberg, H. (2002). Training of working memory in children with ADHD. *Journal of Clinical and Experimental Neuropsychology, 24*, 781–791.

Knouse, L. E., Cooper-Vince, C., Sprich, S., & Safren, S. A.(2008). Recent developments in the psychosocial treatment of adult ADHD. *Expert Review of Neurotherapeutics, 8*, 1537–1548.

Ko, C. H., Yen, J. Y., Chen, C. S., Chen, C. C., & Yen, C. F. (2008). Psychiatric comorbidity of Internet addiction in college students: An interview study. *CNS Spectrums, 13*, 147–153.

Kolar, D., Keller, A., Golfinopoulos, Cumyn, L., Syer, C., & Hechtman, L. (2008). Treatment of adults with attention-deficit/hyperactivity disorder. *Neuropsychiatric Disease and Treatment, 4*, 107–121.

Konofal, E., Cortese, S., Lecendreux, M., Arnulf, I., & Mouren, M. C. (2005). Effectiveness of iron supplementation in a young child with attention-deficit/hyperactivity disorder. *Pediatrics, 116*, e732–e734.

Koocher, G. P. (2008, July 31). *Ethics and risk management update for experienced therapists.* Continuing education workshop, sponsored by J&K Seminars, Lancaster, PA.

Krain, A. L., & Castellanos, F. X. (2006). Brain development and ADHD. *Clinical Psychology Review, 26*, 433–444.

Kubik, J. A. (2007, November 8). *Efficacy of ADHD coaching for adults with attention deficit disorder.* Poster session presented at the 19th Annual International Conference of Children and Adults With Attention Deficit Hyperactivity Disorder, Crystal City, VA.

Kubik, J. A. (2009). Efficacy of ADHD coaching for adults with ADHD. *Journal of Attention Disorders OnlineFirst*. Advance online publication. Retrieved March 10, 2009. doi: 10.1177/1087054708329960

Kumar, R. (2008). Approved and investigational uses of modafinil: An evidence-based review. *Drugs, 68*, 1803–1839.

Labauve, B. J. (2003). Systemic treatment of attention deficit hyperactivity disorder. *Journal of Systemic Therapies, 22*, 45–55.

Lange, G., Sheerin, D., Carr, A., Dooley, B., Barton, V., Marshall, D., et al. (2005). Family factors associated with attention deficit hyperactivity disorder and emotional disorders in children. *Journal of Family Therapy, 27*, 76–96.

Latham, P. S., & Latham, P. H. (2002). What clinicians need to know about legal issues relevant to ADHD. In S. Goldstein & A. T. Ellison (Eds.), *Clinician's guide to adult ADHD: Assessment and intervention* (pp. 205–218). New York: Academic Press.

Latham, P. S., & Latham, P. H. (2007). *Learning disabilities, ADHD and the law in higher education and employment.* Washington, DC: JKL Communications.

Leibson, C. L., Katusic, S. K., Barbaresi, W. J., Ransom, J., & O'Brien, P. C. (2001). Use and costs of medical care for children and adolescents with and without attention-deficit/hyperactivity disorder. *Journal of the American Medical Association, 285*, 60–66.

Lewandowski, L. J., Lovett, B. J., Codding, R. S., & Gordon, M. (2008). Symptoms of ADHD and academic concerns in college students with and without ADHD diagnoses. *Journal of Attention Disorders, 12*, 156–161.

Lewandowski, L. J., Lovett, B. J., Parolin, R., Gordon, M., & Codding, R. S. (2007). Extended time accommodations and the mathematics performance of students with and without ADHD. *Journal of Psychoeducational Assessment, 25*, 17–28.

Lifford, K. J., Harold, G. T., & Thapar, A. (2008). Parent–child relationships and ADHD symptoms: A longitudinal analysis. *Journal of Abnormal Child Psychology, 36*, 285–296.

Lindstrom, J. H., & Gregg, N. (2007). The role of extended time on the SAT for students with learning disabilities and/or attention-deficit/hyperactivity disorder. *Learning Disabilities Research & Practice, 22*, 85–95.

Linehan, M. M. (1993). *Cognitive-behavioral treatment of borderline personality disorder.* New York: Guilford Press.

Linterman, I., & Weyandt, L. (2001). Divided attention skills in college students with ADHD: Is it advantageous to have ADHD? *The ADHD Report, 9*(5), 1–10.

Long, A. B. (2008). Introducing the new and improved Americans With Disabilities Act: Assessing the ADA Amendments Act, published online ahead of print September 25, 2008. *Northwestern University Law Review Colloquy, 103*, 217–229.

Loo, S. K. (2003). EEG and neurofeedback findings in ADHD. *The ADHD Report, 11*(3), 1–9.

Loo, S. K., & Barkley, R. A. (2005). Clinical utility of EEG in attention deficit hyper-activity disorder. *Applied Neuropsychology, 12,* 64–76.

Loo, S., & Smalley, S. (2008). ADHD in the northern Finnish birth cohort. *The ADHD Report, 16*(2), 1–5.

Makris, N., Biederman, J., Valera, E. M., Bush, G., Kaiser, J., Kennedy, D. N., et al. (2007). Cortical thinning of the attention and executive function networks in adults with attention-deficit/hyperactivity disorder. *Cerebral Cortex, 17,* 1364–1375.

Mann, H. B., & Greenspan, S. I. (1976). The identification and treatment of adult brain dysfunction. *American Journal of Psychiatry, 133,* 1013–1017.

Mannuzza, S., & Klein, R. G. (1999). Adolescent and adult outcome in attention-deficit hyperactivity disorder. In H. C. Quay & A. E. Hogan (Eds.), *Handbook of disruptive behavior disorders* (pp. 279–294). New York: Kluwer Academic.

Mannuzza, S., Klein, R. G., Bessler, A., Malloy, P., & LaPadula, M. (1998). Adult psychiatric status of hyperactive boys grown up. *American Journal of Psychiatry, 155,* 493–498.

Mannuzza, S., Klein, R. G., Konig, P. H., & Giampino, T. L. (1989). Hyperactive boys almost grown up: IV. Criminality and its relationship to psychiatric status. *Archives of General Psychiatry, 46,* 1073–1079.

Mapou, R. L. (2009). *Adult learning disabilities and ADHD: Research informed assessment.* New York: Oxford University Press.

Martinez, J. M., & Marangell, L. B. (2004). Omega-3 fatty acids: Do "fish oils" have a therapeutic role in psychiatry? *Current Psychiatry, 3*(1), 25–26, 35–37, 41–42, 52.

McCann, D., Barrett, A., Cooper, A., Crumpler, D., Dalen, L., Grimshaw, K., et al. (2007). Food additives and hyperactive behaviour in 3-year-old and 8/9-year-old children in the community: A randomised, double-blinded, placebo-controlled trial. *The Lancet, 370,* 1560–1567.

McCormick, L. H. (2004). Adult outcome of child and adolescent attention deficit hyperactivity disorder in a primary care setting. *Southern Medical Journal, 97,* 823–826.

McDermott, S. P. (2000) Cognitive therapy for adults with attention-deficit/hyperactivity disorder. In T. E. Brown (Ed.), *Attention deficit disorders and comorbidities in children, adolescents, and adults* (pp. 569–606). Washington, DC: American Psychiatric Press.

McDermott, S. P. (2009) Cognitive therapy for adults with attention-deficit/hyperactivity disorder. In T. E. Brown (Ed.), *ADHD comorbidities: Handbook for ADHD complications in children and adults* (pp. 399–414). Washington, DC: American Psychiatric Press.

McGough, J. J., & Barkley, R. A. (2004). Diagnostic controversies in adult attention deficit hyperactivity disorder. *American Journal of Psychiatry, 161,* 1948–1956.

McGough, J. J., Smalley, S. L., McCracken, J. T., Yang, M., Del'Homme, M., Lynn, D. E., et al. (2005). Psychiatric comorbidity in adult attention deficit hyperactivity disorder: Findings from multiplex families. *American Journal of Psychiatry, 162,* 1621–1627.

McNab, F., & Klingberg, T. (2008). Prefrontal cortex and basal ganglia control access to working memory. *Nature Neuroscience, 11,* 103–107.

McNab, F., Varrone, A., Farde, L., Jucaite, A., Bystritsky, P., Forssberg, H., et al. (2009, February 6). Changes in cortical dopamine D1 receptor binding associated with cognitive training, *Science, 323,* 800–802.

Medori, R., Ramos-Quiroga, J. A., Casas, M., Kooij, J. J. S., Niemelä, A., Trott, G., et al. (2008). A randomized, placebo-controlled trial of three fixed dosages of prolonged-release OROS methylphenidate in adults with attention-deficit/hyperactivity disorder. *Biological Psychiatry, 63,* 981–989.

Merriman, D. E., & Codding, R. S. (2008). The effects of coaching on mathematics homework completion and accuracy of high school students with attention-deficit/hyperactivity disorder. *Journal of Behavioral Education, 17,* 339–355.

Michelson, D., Adler, L., Spencer, T., Reimherr, F. W., West, S. A., Allen, A. J., et al. (2003). Atomoxetine in adults: Two randomized, placebo-controlled studies. *Biological Psychiatry, 58,* 125–131.

Mick, E., Faraone, S. V., & Biederman, J. (2004). Age-dependent expression of attention-deficit/hyperactivity disorder symptoms. *Psychiatric Clinics of North America, 27,* 215–224.

Mikami, A. Y., & Hinshaw, S. P. (2006). Resilient adolescent adjustment among girls: Buffers of childhood peer rejection and attention-deficit/hyperactivity disorder. *Journal of Abnormal Child Psychology, 34,* 825–839.

Mikami, A. Y., & Pfiffner, L. J. (2008). Sibling relationships among children with ADHD. *Journal of Attention Disorders, 11,* 482–492.

Miller, T. W., Nigg, J. T., & Faraone, S. V. (2007). Axis I and Axis II comorbidity in adults with ADHD. *Journal of Abnormal Psychology, 116,* 519–528.

Millstein, R. B., Wilens, T. E., Biederman, J., & Spencer, T. J. (1997). Presenting ADHD symptoms and subtypes in clinically referred adults with ADHD. *Journal of Attention Disorders, 2,* 159–166.

Minde, K., Eakin, L., Hechtman, L., Ochs, E., Bouffard, R., Greenfield, B., et al. (2003). The psychosocial functioning of children and spouses of adults with ADHD. *Journal of Child Psychology and Psychiatry, 44,* 637–646.

Mitchell, E. A., Aman, M. G., Turbott, S. H., & Manku, M. (1987). Clinical characteristics and serum essential fatty acid levels in hyperactive children. *Clinical Pediatrics, 26,* 406–411.

Mitchell, E. A., Lewis, S., & Cutler, D. R. (1983). Essential fatty acids and maladjusted behavior in children. *Prostaglandins, Leukotrienes and Medicine, 12,* 281–287.

Monastra, V. J. (2004). EEG and neurofeedback findings in ADHD: An empirical response. *The ADHD Report, 12*(1), 5–9.

Monastra, V. J. (2008). *Unlocking the potential of patients with ADHD: A model for clinical practice.* Washington, DC: American Psychological Association.

Monastra, V. J., Lubar, J. F., & Linden, M. (2001). The development of a quantitative electroencephalographic scanning process for attention-deficit hyperactivity disorder: Reliability and validity studies. *Neuropsychology, 15,* 136–144.

Monastra, V. J., Lubar, J. F., Linden, M., VanDeusen, P., Green, G., Wing, W., et al. (1999). Assessing attention deficit hyperactivity disorder via quantitative electroencephalography: An initial validation study. *Neuropsychology, 13,* 424–433

Monastra, V. J., Monastra, D. M., & George, S. (2002). The effects of stimulant therapy, EEG biofeedback, and parenting style on the primary symptoms of attention-deficit/hyperactivity disorder. *Applied Psychophysiology and Biofeedback, 27,* 231–249.

Montes, L. G. A., García, A. O. H., & Ricardo-Garcell, J. (2007). ADHD prevalence in adult outpatients with nonpsychotic psychiatric illnesses. *Journal of Attention Disorders, 11,* 150–156.

Morales, O. G., Henry, M. E., Nobler, M. S., Wassermann, E. M., & Lisanby, S. H. (2005). Electroconvulsive therapy and repetitive transcranial magnetic stimulation in children and adolescents: A review and report of two cases of epilepsies partialis continua. *Child and Adolescent Psychiatric Clinics of North America, 14,* 193–210.

Morgan, W. D. (2000). Adult attention deficit disorder. In J. R. White & A. S. Freeman (Eds.), *Cognitive-behavioral group therapy for specific problems and populations* (pp. 211–232). Washington, DC: American Psychological Association.

Moyer, P. (2007a, October 19). *Doctor's guide: Personal edition: Adults with ADHD benefit from cognitive behavioural group therapy: Presented at ECNP.* Retrieved May 6, 2008, from http://www.pslgroup.com/dg/215F9E.htm

Moyer, P. (2007b, May 22). *Doctor's guide: Personal edition: Treatment shows promise for adult comorbid ADHD and bipolar disorder: Presented at APA.* Retrieved April 16, 2009, from http://www.docguide.com/news/content.nsf/news/852571020057 CCF6852572E300643D1F?OpenDocument&id=48DDE4A73E09A969852568 880078C249&c=Psychiatry%20Other&count=10

The MTA Cooperative Group (1999). A 14-month randomized clinical trial of treatment strategies for attention-deficit/hyperactivity disorder. Multimodal Treatment Study of Children with ADHD. *Archives of General Psychiatry, 56,* 1073–1086.

Murphy, K. R. (2005). Psychosocial treatments for ADHD in teens and adults: A practice-friendly review. *Journal of Clinical Psychology: In Session, 61,* 607–619.

Murphy, K. R., & Barkley, R. A. (1996a). Attention deficit hyperactivity disorder adults: Comorbidities and adaptive impairments. *Comprehensive Psychiatry, 37,* 393–401.

Murphy, K. R., & Barkley, R. A. (1996b). Prevalence of DSM–IV symptoms of ADHD in adult licensed drivers: Implications for clinical diagnosis. *Journal of Attention Disorders, 1,* 147–161.

Murphy, K. R., Barkley, R. A., & Bush, T. (2002). Young adults with ADHD: Subtype differences in comorbidity, educational, and clinical history. *Journal of Nervous and Mental Disease, 190,* 147–157.

Murphy, K. R., & Gordon, M. (2006). Assessment of adults with ADHD. In R. A. Barkley (Ed.), *Attention-deficit hyperactivity disorder: A handbook for diagnosis and treatment* (3rd ed., pp. 425–450). New York: Guilford Press.

Murphy, P., & Schachar, R. (2000). Use of self-ratings in the assessment of symptoms of attention deficit hyperactivity disorder in adults. *American Journal of Psychiatry, 157,* 1156–1159.

Nadeau, K. G. (2005). Career choices and workplace challenges for individuals with ADHD. *Journal of Clinical Psychology: In Session, 61,* 549–563.

Nadeau, K. G., & Quinn, P. O. (2002). *Understanding women with AD/HD.* Silver Spring, MD: Advantage Books.

Nash, J. K. (2005). Neurotherapy with adults. *Journal of Adult Development, 12,* 105–112.

National Resource Center on AD/HD. (2003a). *What we know: Coaching for adults with AD/HD.* Landover, MD: Children and Adults With Attention Deficit Hyperactivity Disorder.

National Resource Center on AD/HD. (2003b). *What we know: Social skills in adults with AD/HD.* Landover, MD: Children and Adults With Attention Deficit Hyperactivity Disorder.

National Resource Center on AD/HD. (2003c). *What we know: Succeeding in the workplace.* Landover, MD: Children and Adults With Attention Deficit Hyperactivity Disorder.

National Resource Center on AD/HD. (2007). *What we know: Complementary and alternative treatments* (rev. ed.). Landover, MD: Children and Adults With Attention Deficit Hyperactivity Disorder.

National Resource Center on AD/HD. (2008a). *What we know: AD/HD and neurofeedback: A review of eight studies.* Landover, MD: Children and Adults With Attention Deficit Hyperactivity Disorder. Retrieved March 31, 2008, from http://chadd.informz.net/admin31/content/template.asp?sid=7519&brandid=3090&uid=752577386&mi=284360&ptid=99

National Resource Center on AD/HD. (2008b). *What we know: Complementary and alternative treatment: Neurofeedback (EEG biofeedback) and AD/HD.* Landover, MD: Children and Adults With Attention Deficit Hyperactivity Disorder.

Neenan, M., & Dryden, W. (2002). *Life coaching: A cognitive-behavioural approach.* New York: Routledge.

Nemzer, E., Arnold, L. E., Votolato, N. A., & McConnell, H. (1986). Amino acid supplementation as therapy for attention deficit disorder (ADD). *Journal of the American Academy of Child & Adolescent Psychiatry, 25,* 509–513.

Nicolson, R. I., & Reynolds, D. (2003). Science, sense and synergy: Response to commentators. *Dyslexia, 9,* 167–176.

Nierenberg, A. A., Miyahara, S., Spencer, T., Wisniewski, S. R., Otto, M. W., Simon, N., et al. (2005). Clinical and diagnostic implications of lifetime attention-deficit/hyperactivity disorder comorbidity in adults with bipolar disorder: Data from the first 1,000 STEP-BD participants. *Biological Psychiatry, 57,* 1467–1473.

Nigg, J. T. (2006). *What causes ADHD? Understanding what goes wrong and why*. New York: Guilford Press.

Norcross, J. C., Koocher, G. P., & Garofalo, A. (2006). Discredited psychological treatments and tests: A Delphi Poll. *Professional Psychology: Research and Practice, 37*, 515–522.

Novotni, M., & Petersen, R. (1999). *What does everybody else know that I don't? Social skills help for adults with attention deficit/hyperactivity disorder (AD/HD)*. Plantation, FL: Specialty Press.

Ohlmeier, M. D., Peters, K., Kordon, A., Seifert, J., Wildt, B. T., Wiese, B., et al. (2007). Nicotine and alcohol dependence in patients with comorbid attention-deficit/hyperactivity disorder (ADHD). *Alcohol and Alcoholism, 42*, 539–543.

Olesen, P., Westerberg, H., & Klingberg, T. (2004). Increased prefrontal and parietal brain activity after training of working memory. *Nature Neuroscience, 7*, 75–79.

Orr, J. M., Miller, R. B., & Polson, D. M. (2005). Toward a standard of care for child ADHD: Implications for marriage and family therapists. *Journal of Marital and Family Therapy, 31*, 191–205.

Parker, D. R., & Byron, J. (1998). Differences between college students with AD/HD and LD: Practical implications for service providers. In P. Quinn & A. McCormick (Eds.), *Re-thinking AD/HD: A guide for fostering success in students with AD/HD at the college level* (pp. 14–30). Bethesda, MD: Advantage Books.

Pauli, Y. (2007). Improvement in attention in patients undergoing network spinal analysis: A case series using objective measures of attention. *Journal of Vertebral Subluxation Research, August 23, 2007*, 1–9.

Pelham, W. E., Gnagy, E. M., Greiner, A. R., Hoza, B., Hinshaw, S. P., Swanson, J. P., et al. (2000). Behavioral versus behavioral and pharmacological treatment in ADHD children attending a summer treatment program. *Journal of Abnormal Child Psychology, 28*, 507–525.

Pelham, W. E., Wheeler, T., & Chronis, A. (1998). Empirically supported psychosocial treatments for attention deficit hyperactivity disorder. *Journal of Clinical Child Psychology, 27*, 190–205.

Pera, G. (2008). *Is it you, me, or adult ADD?* San Francisco: 1201 Alarm Press.

Phelan, T. W. (2002). Families and ADHD. In S. Goldstein & A. T. Ellison (Eds.), *Clinician's guide to adult ADHD: Assessment and intervention* (pp. 241–260). San Diego, CA: Academic Press.

Philipsen, A., Richter, H., Peters, J., Alm, B., Sobanski, E., Colla, M., et al. (2007). Structured group psychotherapy in adults with attention deficit hyperactivity disorder. *The Journal of Nervous and Mental Disease, 195*, 1013–1019.

Pliszka, S. R. (2003). *Neuroscience for the mental health clinician*. New York: Guilford Press.

Power, T. J., Karustis, J. L., & Habboushe, D. F. (2001). *Homework success for children with ADHD: A family–school intervention program*. New York: Guilford Press.

Pressman, L. J., Loo, S. K., Carpenter, E. M., Asarnow, J. R., Lynn, D., McCracken, J. T., et al. (2006). Relationship of family environment and parent psychiatric diagnosis to impairment in ADHD. *Journal of the American Academy of Child & Adolescent Psychiatry, 45,* 346–354.

Prince, J. B., Wilens, T. E., Spencer, T. J., & Biederman, J. (2006). Pharmacotherapy of ADHD in adults. In R. A. Barkley (Ed.), *Attention-deficit hyperactivity disorder: A handbook for diagnosis and treatment* (pp. 704–736). New York: Guilford Press.

Prochaska, J. O., & Norcross, J. C. (2001). Stages of change. *Psychotherapy: Theory, Research, Practice, Training, 47,* 443–448.

Psychogiou, L., Daley, D. M., Thompson, M. J., & Sonuga-Barke, E. J. S. (2008). Do maternal attention-deficit/hyperactivity disorder symptoms exacerbate or ameliorate the negative effect of child attention-deficit/hyperactivity disorder symptoms on parenting? *Development and Psychopathology, 20,* 121–137.

Quintana, H., Snyder, S. M., Purnell, W., Aponte, C., & Sita, J. (2007). Comparison of a standard psychiatric evaluation to rating scales and EEG in the differential diagnosis of attention-deficit/hyperactivity disorder. *Psychiatry Research, 152,* 211–222.

Rabiner, D. L., Anastopoulos, A. D., Costello, J., Hoyle, R. H., & Swartzwelder, H. S. (2008). Adjustment to college in students with ADHD. *Journal of Attention Disorders, 11,* 689–699.

Rachal, K. C., Daigle, S., & Rachal, W. S. (2007). Learning problems reported by college students: Are they using learning strategies? *Journal of Instructional Psychology, 34,* 191–199.

Rafalovich, A. (2001). Psychodynamic and neurological perspectives on ADHD: Exploring strategies for defining a phenomenon. *Journal for the Theory of Social Behavior, 31,* 397–418.

Ramsay, J. R. (2007). Current status of cognitive behavioral therapy as a psychosocial treatment for adult attention-deficit/hyperactivity disorder. *Current Psychiatry Reports, 9,* 427–433.

Ramsay, J. R. (in press). Evidence-based psychosocial treatments for adult ADHD: A review. *Current Attention Disorders Reports.*

Ramsay, J. R., & Rostain, A. L. (2003). A cognitive therapy approach for adult attention-deficit/hyperactivity disorder. *Journal of Cognitive Psychotherapy: An International Quarterly, 17,* 319–334.

Ramsay, J. R., & Rostain, A. L. (2005a). Adapting psychotherapy to meet the needs of adults with attention-deficit/hyperactivity disorder. *Psychotherapy: Theory, Research, Practice, Training, 42,* 72–84.

Ramsay, J. R., & Rostain, A. L. (2005b). Girl, repeatedly interrupted: The case of a young adult woman with ADHD. *Clinical Case Studies, 4,* 329–346.

Ramsay, J. R., & Rostain, A. L. (2006a). Cognitive behavior therapy for college students with attention-deficit/hyperactivity disorder. *Journal of College Student Psychotherapy, 21,* 3–20.

Ramsay, J. R., & Rostain, A. L. (2006b). Issues in ADHD in adults. *The ADHD Report, 14*(6), 5–8.

Ramsay, J. R., & Rostain, A. L. (2007a, November). Clinical outcome of five adults with ADHD receiving CBT without medications. In S. Safren (Chair), *Issues in CBT outcome research for ADHD across the lifespan*. Symposium conducted at the 41st Annual Convention of the Association for Behavioral and Cognitive Therapies, Philadelphia, PA.

Ramsay, J. R., & Rostain, A. L. (2007b). Psychosocial treatments for attention-deficit/hyperactivity disorder in adults: Current evidence and future directions. *Professional Psychology: Research and Practice, 38*, 338–346.

Ramsay, J. R., & Rostain, A. L. (2008a). Adult ADHD research: Current status and future directions. *Journal of Attention Disorders, 11*, 624–627.

Ramsay, J. R., & Rostain, A. L. (2008b). *Cognitive behavioral therapy for adult ADHD: An integrative psychosocial and medical approach*. New York: Routledge.

Ranseen, J. D. (1998). Lawyers with ADHD: The special test accommodation controversy. *Professional Psychology: Research and Practice, 29*, 450–459.

Rasmussen, K., Almvik, R., & Levander, S. (2001). Attention deficit hyperactivity disorder, reading disability, and personality disorders in a prison population. *Journal of the American Academy of Psychiatry and the Law, 29*, 186–193.

Rasmussen, P., & Gillberg, C. (2000). Natural outcome of ADHD with developmental coordination disorder at age 22 years: A controlled, longitudinal, community-based sample. *Journal of the American Academy of Child & Adolescent Psychiatry, 39*, 1424–1431.

Ratey, J. J. (2008). *Spark: The revolutionary new science of exercise and the brain*. New York: Little, Brown.

Ratey, J. J., Greenberg, M. S., Bemporad, J. R., & Lindem, K. J. (1992). Unrecognized attention-deficit hyperactivity disorder in adults presenting for outpatient psychotherapy. *Journal of Child and Adolescent Psychopharmacology, 2*, 267–275.

Ratey, J. J., Hallowell, E., & Miller, A. (1997). Psychosocial issues and psychotherapy in adults with attention deficit disorder. *Psychiatric Annals, 27*, 582–587.

Ratey, N. A. (2002). Life coaching for adult ADHD. In S. Goldstein & A. T. Ellison (Eds.), *Clinician's guide to adult ADHD: Assessment and intervention* (pp. 261–277). San Diego, CA: Academic Press.

Ratey, N. A. (2008). *The disorganized mind: Coaching your ADHD brain to take control of your time, tasks, and talents*. New York: St. Martin's Press.

Ratey, N. A., Maynard, S., & Sleeper-Triplett, J. (2007, November 8). *Mastering AD/HD coaching challenges*. Workshop presented at the 19th Annual International Conference of Children and Adults With Attention Deficit/Hyperactivity Disorder, Crystal City, VA.

Reaser, A., Prevatt, F., Petscher, Y., & Proctor, B. (2007). The learning and study strategies of college students with ADHD. *Psychology in the Schools, 44*, 627–638.

Rehabilitation Act of 1973. Pub. L. No. 93-112.87 Stat. 355.

Reiff, M. I., & Tippins, S. (2004). *ADHD: A complete and authoritative guide*. Elk Grove Village, IL: American Academy of Pediatrics.

Reilley, S. P. (2005). Empirically informed attention-deficit/hyperactivity disorder evaluation with college students. *Journal of College Counseling, 8,* 153–164.

Reilley, S. P., Charles, D., & Smith, T. D. (2004, May). *Depression masquerading as adult AD/HD on the Brown ADD Scales.* Poster session presented at the 16th Annual Meeting of the American Psychological Society, Chicago, IL.

Reimherr, F. W., Marchant, B. K., Strong, R. E., Hedges, D. W., Adler, L., Spencer, T. J., et al. (2005). Emotional dysregulation in adult ADHD and response to atomoxetine. *Biological Psychiatry, 58,* 125–131.

Reimherr, F. W., Wender, P. H., Wood, D. R., & Ward, M. (1987). An open trial of *l*-tryrosine in the treatment of attention deficit disorder, residual type. *American Journal of Psychiatry, 144,* 1071–1073.

Resnick, R. J. (2000). *The hidden disorder: A clinician's guide to attention deficit hyperactivity disorder in adults.* Washington, DC: American Psychological Association.

Reynolds, D., Nicolson, R. I., & Hambly, H. (2003). Evaluation of an exercise-based treatment for children with reading difficulties. *Dyslexia, 9,* 48–71.

Riccio, C. A., & French, C. L. (2004). The status of empirical support for treatments of attention deficits. *The Clinical Neuropsychologist, 18,* 528–558.

Richards, I. L., Moores, E., Witton, C., Reddy, P. A., Rippon, G., Rochelle, K. S. H., et al. (2003). Science, sophistry and "commercial sensitivity": Comments on "Evaluation of an exercise-based treatment for children with reading difficulties," by Reynolds, Nicolson, and Hambly. *Dyslexia, 9,* 146–150.

Richards, T. L., Rosen, L. A., & Ramirez, C. A. (1999). Psychological functioning differences among college students with confirmed ADHD, ADHD by self-report only, and without ADHD. *Journal of College Student Development, 40,* 299–304.

Richardson, A. J., & Montgomery, P. (2005). The Oxford–Durham study: A randomized controlled trial of dietary supplementation with fatty acids in children with developmental coordination disorder. *Pediatrics, 115,* 1360–1366.

Richardson, A. J., & Puri, B. K. (2002). A randomized double-blind, placebo-controlled study of the effects of supplementation with highly unsaturated fatty acids on ADHD-related symptoms in children with specific learning disabilities. *Progress in Neuro-Psychopharmacology & Biological Psychiatry, 26,* 233–239.

Robbins, C. A. (2005). ADHD couple and family relationships: Enhancing communication and understanding through imago relationship therapy. *Journal of Clinical Psychology: In Session, 61,* 565–577.

Robbins, J. (2000). *A symphony in the brain: The evolution of the new brain wave biofeedback.* New York: Atlantic Monthly Press.

Robin, A. L. (2006). Training families with adolescents with ADHD. In R. A. Barkley (Ed.), *Attention-deficit hyperactivity disorder: A handbook for diagnosis and treatment* (3rd ed., pp. 499–546). New York: Guilford Press.

Robin, A. L., & Payson, E. (2002). The impact of ADHD on marriage. *The ADHD Report, 10*(3), 9–11, 14.

Rojas, N. L., & Chan, E. (2005). Old and new controversies in the alternative treatment of attention-deficit hyperactivity disorder. *Mental Retardation and Development Disabilities Research Reviews, 11,* 116–130.

Root, R. W. (1996). The gestalt cycle of experience as a theoretical framework for conceptualizing the attention deficit disorder. *The Gestalt Journal, 19*(2), 9–50.

Root, R. W., & Resnick, R. J. (2003). An update on the diagnosis and treatment of attention-deficit/hyperactivity disorder in children. *Professional Psychology: Research and Practice, 34,* 34–41.

Rosen, G. M., & Davison, G. C. (2003). Psychology should list empirically supported principles of change (ESPs) and not credential trademarked therapies or other treatment packages. *Behavior Modification, 27,* 300–312.

Rosen, Z. B., Baime, M. J., Ramsay, J. R., Rostain, A., Screenivasan, K. K., & Jha, A. P. (2008, June). *Mindfulness training improves working memory performance in adults with ADHD.* Poster session presented at the 2008 Mind and Life Summer Research Institute, Garrison, NY.

Rosenfield, B., Ramsay, J. R., & Rostain, A. L. (2008). Extreme makeover: The case of an adult man with severe ADHD. *Clinical Case Studies, 7,* 471–490.

Rossiter, T. R., & La Vaque, T. J. (1995). A comparison of EEG biofeedback and psychostimulants in treating attention deficit/hyperactivity disorders. *Journal of Neurotherapy, 1,* 48–59.

Rössler, W., Lauber, C., Angst, J., Haker, H., Gamma, A., Eich, D., et al. (2006). The use of complementary and alternative medicine in the general population: Results from a longitudinal community study. *Psychological Medicine, 37,* 73–84.

Rostain, A. L., & Ramsay, J. R. (2006a). Adult with ADHD? Try medication + psychotherapy. *Current Psychiatry, 5*(2), 13–16, 21–24, 27.

Rostain, A. L., & Ramsay, J. R. (2006b). College and high school students with attention-deficit/hyperactivity disorder: New directions in assessment and treatment. In American College Health Association (Ed.), *Use and misuse of stimulants: A guide for school health professionals* (pp. 7–16). Englishtown, NJ: Princeton Media Associates.

Rostain, A. L., & Ramsay, J. R. (2006c). A combined treatment approach for adults with attention-deficit/hyperactivity disorder: Results of an open study of 43 patients. *Journal of Attention Disorders, 10,* 150–159.

Rucklidge, J. J., & Kaplan, B. J. (1997). Psychological functioning of women identified in adulthood with attention-deficit/hyperactivity disorder. *Journal of Attention Disorders, 2,* 167–176.

Rucklidge, J. J., & Kaplan, B. J. (2000). Attributions and perceptions of childhood in women with ADHD symptomatology. *Journal of Clinical Psychology, 56,* 711–722.

Rugsaken, K. T., Robertson, J. A., & Jones, J. A. (1998). Using the learning and study strategies inventory scores as additional predictors of student academic performance. *NACADA Journal, 18,* 20–26.

Runyan, M. K. (1991). The effect of extra time on reading comprehension scores for university students with and without learning disabilities. *Journal of Learning Disabilities, 24,* 104–108.

Rutherford, R., Nicolson, R., & Arnold, E. (2006, August). *Significant reduction in symptoms of attention-deficit in learning-disabled children and adults following exercise-based treatment.* Poster session presented at the 114th Annual Convention of the American Psychological Association, New Orleans, LA. Retrieved January 30, 2008, from http://www.dorecenters.com/research/adhdstudy.aspx

Rybak, Y. E., McNeely, H. E., Mackenzie, B. E., Jain, U. R., & Levitan, R. D. (2006). An open trial of light therapy in adult attention-deficit/hyperactivity disorder. *Journal of Clinical Psychiatry, 67,* 1527–1535.

Rybak, Y. E., McNeely, H. E., Mackenzie, B. E., Jain, U. R., & Levitan, R. D. (2007). Seasonality and circadian preference in adult attention-deficit/hyperactivity disorder: Clinical and neuropsychological correlates. *Comprehensive Psychiatry, 48,* 562–571.

Safren, S. A. (2006). Cognitive-behavioral approaches to ADHD treatment in adulthood. *Journal of Clinical Psychiatry, 67*(Suppl. 8), 46–50.

Safren, S. A., Lanka, G. D., Otto, M. W., & Pollack, M. H. (2001). Prevalence of childhood ADHD among patients with generalized anxiety disorder and a comparison condition, social phobia. *Depression and Anxiety, 13,* 190–191.

Safren, S. A., Otto, M. W., Sprich, S., Winett, C. L., Wilens, T. E., & Biederman, J. (2005). Cognitive-behavior therapy for ADHD in medication-treated adults with continued symptoms. *Behaviour Research and Therapy, 43,* 831–842.

Safren, S. A., Perlman, C. A., Sprich, S., & Otto, M. W. (2005). *Mastering your adult ADHD: A cognitive-behavioral treatment program—Therapist guide.* Oxford, England: Oxford University Press.

Satterfield, J. H., Faller, K. J., Crinella, F. M., Schell, A. M., Swanson, J. M., & Homer, L. D. (2007). A 30-year prospective follow-up study of hyperactive boys with conduct problems: Adult criminality. *Journal of the American Academy of Child & Adolescent Psychiatry, 46,* 601–610.

Satterfield, J. H., & Schell, A. (1997). A prospective study of hyperactive boys with conduct problems and normal boys: Adolescent and adult criminality. *Journal of the American Academy of Child & Adolescent Psychiatry, 36,* 1726–1735.

Scarr, S., & McCartney, K. (1983). How people make their own environments: A theory of genotype → environment effects. *Child Development, 54,* 424–435.

Schab, D. W., & Trinh, N. T. (2004). Do artificial food colors promote hyperactivity in children with hyperactive syndromes? A meta-analysis of double-blind placebo-controlled trials. *Journal of Developmental & Behavioral Pediatrics, 25,* 423–434.

Schatz, D. B., & Rostain, A. L. (2006). ADHD with comorbid anxiety: A review of the current literature. *Journal of Attention Disorders, 10,* 141–149.

Schulenberg, S. E., Melton, A. M. A., & Foote, H. L. (2006). College students with ADHD: A role for logotherapy in treatment. *The International Forum for Logotherapy, 29,* 37–45.

Schwiebert, V. L., Sealander, K. A., & Dennison, J. L. (2002). Strategies for counselors working with high school students with attention-deficit/hyperactivity disorder. *Journal of Counseling and Development, 80,* 23–10.

Seitler, B. N. (2008). Successful child psychotherapy of attention deficit/hyperactive disorder: An agitated depression explanation. *American Journal of Psychoanalysis, 68,* 276–294.

Seligman, M. E. P., & Csikszentmihalyi, M. (2000). Positive psychology: An introduction. *American Psychologist, 55,* 5–14.

Sever, Y., Ashkenazi, A., Tyano, S., & Weizman, A. (1997). Iron treatment in children with ADHD: A preliminary report. *Neuropsychobiology, 35,* 178–180.

Shaffer, R. J., Jacokes, L. E., Cassily, J. F., Greenspan, S. I., Tuchman, R. F., & Stemmer, Jr., P. J. (2001). Effect of interactive metronome training on children with ADHD. *American Journal of Occupational Therapy, 55,* 155–162.

Shaw, G., & Giambra, L. (1993). Task-unrelated thoughts of college students diagnosed as hyperactive in childhood. *Developmental Neuropsychology, 9,* 17–30.

Shaw, P., Eckstrand, K., Sharp, W., Blumenthal, J., Lerch, J. P., Greenstein, D., et al. (2007). Attention-deficit/hyperactivity disorder is characterized by a delay in cortical maturation. *Proceedings of the National Academy of Sciences, 104,* 19649–19654.

Shaw-Zirt, B., Popali-Lehane, L., Chaplin, W., & Bergman, A. (2005). Adjustment, social skills, and self-esteem in college students with symptoms of ADHD. *Journal of Attention Disorders, 8,* 109–120.

Shekim, W. O., Antun, F., Hanna, G. L., McCracken, J. T., & Hess, E. B. (1990). S-Adenosyl-l-methionine (SAM) in adults with ADHD, RS: Preliminary results from an open trial. *Psychopharmacology Bulletin, 26,* 249–253.

Shire Pharmaceutical. (2008a). *How Vyvanse works.* Retrieved May 8, 2008, from http://www.vyvanse.com/hcp/works/vyvanse_works.asp

Shire Pharmaceutical. (2008b). *Press release: FDA approves Vyvanse (lisdexamfetamine dimesylate), the first and only once-daily prodrug stimulant to treat ADHD in adults.* Retrieved May 8, 2008, from http://www.vyvanse.com/pdf/adult_approval_2008.pdf

Sinha, D., & Efron, D. (2005). Complementary and alternative medicine use in children with attention deficit hyperactivity disorder. *Journal of Paediatric Child Health, 41,* 23–26.

Slagter, H. A., Lutz, A., Greischar, L. L., Francis, A. D., Nieuwenhuis, S., Davis, J. M., et al. (2007). Mental training affects distribution of limited brain resources. *PLoS Biology, 5,* 1228–1235.

Smith, A. J., Brown, R. T., Bunke, V., Blount, R. L., & Christopherson, E. (2002). Psychosocial adjustment and peer competence of siblings of children with attention-deficit/hyperactivity disorder. *Journal of Attention Disorders, 5,* 165–177.

Smith, B. H., Cole, W. R., Ingram, A. H., & Bogle, K. E. (2004). Screening for ADHD among first-year college students. *The ADHD Report, 12*(2), 6–10.

Snowling, M. J., & Hulme, C. (2003). A critique of claims from Reynolds, Nicolson & Hambly (2003) that DDAT is an effective treatment for children with reading difficulties—"Lies, damned lies and (inappropriate) statistics?" *Dyslexia, 9*, 127–133.

Snyder, S. M., Quintana, H., Sexson, S. B., Knott, P., Haque, A. F. M., & Reynolds, D. A. (2008). Blinded, multi-center validation of EEG and rating scales in identifying ADHD within a clinical sample. *Psychiatry Research, 159*, 346–358.

Snyder, T. D., Dillow, S. A., & Hoffman, C. M. (2007). *Digest of education statistics 2006* (NCES 2007-017: National Center for Education Statistics, Institute of Education Sciences, U.S. Department of Education). Washington, DC: U.S. Government Printing Office.

Sobanski, F. (2006). Psychiatric comorbidity in adults with attention-deficit/hyperactivity disorder (ADHD). *European Archive of Psychiatry and Clinical Neuroscience, 256*(Suppl. 1), i26–i31.

Sohlberg, M. M., & Mateer, C. A. (2001). Improving attention and managing attention problems: Adapting rehabilitation techniques to adults with ADD. *Annals of the New York Academy of Sciences, 931*, 359–375.

Solanto, M. V., Gilbert, S. N., Ray, A., Zhu, J., Pope-Boyd, S., Stepak, B., et al. (2007). Neurocognitive functioning in AD/HD, predominantly inattentive and combined subtypes. *Journal of Abnormal Child Psychology, 35*, 729–744.

Solanto, M. V., Marks, D. J., Mitchell, K. J., Wasserstein, J., & Kofman, M. D. (2008). Development of a new psychosocial treatment for adults with AD/HD. *Journal of Attention Disorders, 11*, 728–736.

Solden, S. (1995). *Women with attention deficit disorder*. Grass Valley, CA: Underwood Books.

Sparks, R. L., Javorsky, J., & Philips, L. (2005). Comparison of the performance of college students classified as ADHD, LD, and LD/ADHD in foreign language courses. *Language Learning, 55*, 151–177.

Spencer, T., Adler, L. A., McGough, J. J., Muniz, R., Jiang, H., Pestreich, L., et al. (2007). Efficacy and safety of dexmethylphenidate extended-release capsules in adults with attention-deficit/hyperactivity disorder. *Biological Psychiatry, 61*, 1380–1387.

Spencer, T., Biederman, J., & Wilens, T. (2004a). Nonstimulant treatment of adult attention-deficit/hyperactivity disorder. *Psychiatric Clinics of North America, 27*, 373–384.

Spencer, T., Biederman, J., & Wilens, T. (2004b). Stimulant treatment of adult attention-deficit/hyperactivity disorder. *Psychiatric Clinics of North America, 27*, 361–372.

Spinella, M., & Miley, W. M. (2003). Impulsivity and academic achievement in college students. *College Student Journal, 37*, 545–549.

Sporn, A., & Lisanby, S. H. (2006). Non-pharmacological treatment modalities in children and adolescents: A review of electroconvulsive therapy, transcranial magnetic stimulation, vagus nerve stimulation, magnetic seizure therapy, and deep brain stimulation. *Clinical Neuropsychiatry, 3*, 230–244.

Stein, J. (2003). Evaluation of an exercise-based treatment for children with reading difficulties. *Dyslexia, 9*, 122–126.

Stevens, L. J. (2000). *Twelve effective ways to help your ADD/ADHD child: Drug-free alternatives for attention-deficit disorders.* New York: Penguin.

Stevens, L. J., Zhang, W., Peck, L., Kuczek, T., Grevstad, N., Mahon, A., et al. (2003). EFA supplementation in children with inattention, hyperactivity, and other disruptive behaviors. *Lipids, 38*, 1007–1021.

Stevens, L. J., Zentall, S. S., Deck, J. L., Abate, M. L., Watkins, B. A., Lipp, S. R., et al. (1995). Essential fatty acid metabolism in boys with attention-deficit hyperactivity disorder. *American Journal of Clinical Nutrition, 62*, 761–768.

Stevenson, C. S., Stevenson, R. J., & Whitmont, S. (2003). A self-directed psychosocial intervention with minimal therapist contact for adults with attention deficit hyperactivity disorder. *Clinical Psychology and Psychotherapy, 10*, 93–101.

Stevenson, C. S., Whitmont, S., Bornholt, L., Livesey, D., & Stevenson, R. J. (2002). A cognitive remediation programme for adults with attention deficit hyperactivity disorder. *Australian and New Zealand Journal of Psychiatry, 36*, 610–616.

Still, G. F. (2006). Some abnormal psychical conditions in children: Excerpts from three lectures. *Journal of Attention Disorders, 10*, 126–136. (Original work published 1902)

Stoll, A. L. (2001). *The omega-3 connection.* New York: Fireside Books.

Strehl, U., Leins, U., Goth, G., Klinger, C., Hinterberger, T., & Birbaumer, N. (2006). Self-regulation of slow cortical potentials: A new treatment for children with attention-deficit/hyperactivity disorder. *Pediatrics, 118*, e1530–e1540.

Stubberfield, T., & Parry, T. (1999). Utilization of alternative therapies in attention-deficit hyperactivity disorder. *Journal of Paediatrics and Child Health, 35*, 450–453.

Swartz, S. L., Prevatt, F., & Proctor, B. E. (2005). A coaching intervention for college students with attention deficit/hyperactivity disorder. *Psychology in the Schools, 46*, 647–656.

Swensen, A. R., Birnbaum, H. G., Secnik, K., Marynchenko, M., Greenberg, P., & Claxton, A (2003). Attention-deficit/hyperactivity disorder: Increased costs for patients and their families. *Journal of the American Academy of Child & Adolescent Psychiatry, 42*, 1415–1423.

Task Force on Promotion and Dissemination of Psychological Procedures. (1995). Training in and dissemination of empirically-validated psychological treatments: Report and recommendations. *Clinical Psychologist, 48*, 3–23.

Taylor, F. B., & Russo, J. (2000). Efficacy of modafinil compared to dextroamphetamine for the treatment of attention deficit hyperactivity disorder in adults. *Journal of Child and Adolescent Psychiatry, 10*, 311–320.

Teplin, L. A., Abram, K. M., McClelland, G. M., Dulcan, M. K., & Mericle, A. A. (2002). Psychiatric disorders in youth in juvenile detention. *Archives of General Psychiatry, 59*, 1133–1143.

Thompson, A. L., Molina, B. S. G., Pelham, W., & Gnagy, E. M. (2007). Risky driving in adolescents and young adults with childhood ADHD. *Journal of Pediatric Psychology, 32*, 745–759.

Thompson, L., & Thompson, M. (1998). Neurofeedback combined with training in metacognitive strategies: Effectiveness in students with ADD. *Applied Psychophysiology and Biofeedback, 23,* 243–263.

Treacy, L., Tripp, G., & Baird, A. (2005). Parent stress management training for attention-deficit/hyperactivity disorder. *Behavior Therapy, 36,* 223–233.

Tripp, G., Schaughency, E. A., Langlands, R., & Mouat, K. (2007). Family interactions in children with and without ADHD. *Journal of Child and Family Studies, 16,* 385–400.

Tuckman, A. (2007). *Integrative treatment for adult ADHD: A practical, easy-to-use guide for clinicians.* Oakland, CA: New Harbinger.

Tuckman, A. (2009). *More attention, less deficit: Success strategies for adults with ADHD.* Plantation, FL: Specialty Press.

Tudisco, R. M. (2007a). Accommodations for post-secondary students under the ADA. *Attention Magazine, 14*(3), 24–27.

Tudisco, R. M. (2007b). Coping with AD/HD on the job: Strategies for the workplace. *Attention Magazine, 14*(2), 26–31.

Turnock, P., Rosén, L. A., & Kaminski, P. L. (1998). Differences in academic coping strategies of college students who self-report high and low symptoms of attention deficit hyperactivity disorder. *Journal of College Student Development, 39,* 484–493.

Uhlig, T., Merkenschlager, A., Brandmaier, R., & Egger, J. (1997). Topographic mapping of brain electrical activity in children with food-induced attention deficit hyperkinetic disorder. *Neuropediatrics, 156,* 557–561.

van den Hoofdakker, B. J., van der Veen-Mulders, L., Sytema, S., Emmelkamp, P. M. G., Minderaa, R. B., & Nauta, M. H. (2007). Effectiveness of behavioral parent training for children with ADHD in routine clinical practice: A randomized controlled study. *Journal of the American Academy of Child & Adolescent Psychiatry, 46,* 1263–1271.

Van Oudheusden, L. J., & Scholte, H. R. (2002). Efficacy of carnitine in the treatment of children with attention-deficit hyperactivity disorder. *Prostaglandins, Leukotrienes and Essential Fatty Acids, 6,* 33–38.

Virta, M., Vedenpaa, A., Gronroos, N., Chydenius, E., Partinen, M., Vataja, R., et al. (2008). Adults with ADHD benefit from cognitive-behaviorally oriented group rehabilitation: A study of 29 participants. *Journal of Attention Disorders, 12,* 218–226.

Voigt, R. G., Llorente, A. M., Jensen, C. L., Fraley, J. K., Berretta, M. C., & Heird, W. C. (2001). A randomized, double-blind, placebo-controlled trial of docosahexaenoic acid supplementation in children with attention-deficit/hyperactivity disorder. *Journal of Pediatrics, 139,* 189–196.

Wakefield, J. C. (1992). Disorder as harmful dysfunction: A conceptual critique of DSM–III–R's definition of mental disorder. *Psychological Review, 99,* 232–247.

Ward, M. F., Wender, P. H., & Reimherr, F. W. (1993). The Wender Utah Rating Scale: An aid in the retrospective diagnosis of childhood attention deficit hyperactivity disorder. *American Journal of Psychiatry, 150,* 885–890.

Waschbusch, D. A., & Hill, G. P. (2001). Alternative treatments for children with attention-deficit/hyperactivity disorder: What does the research say? *The Behavior Therapist, 24,* 161–171.

Wasserstein, J., & Lynn, A. (2001). Metacognitive remediation in adult ADHD: Treating executive function deficits via executive functions. *Annals of the New York Academy of Sciences, 931,* 376–384.

Watkins, C. (2002). CareFirst BlueCross BlueShield of Maryland denies psychotherapy services to individuals with AD/HD. *Maryland Medicine, 3,* 8–9.

Weafer, J., Camarillo, D., Fillmore, M. T., Milich, R., & Marczinski, C. A. (2008). Simulated driving performance of adults with ADHD: Comparisons with alcohol intoxication. *Experimental and Clinical Psychopharmacology, 16,* 251–263.

Weaver, L., Mace, W., Akhtar, U. W., Rostain, A. L., & O'Reardon, J. P. (2008, May). *Safety & efficacy of rTMS in the treatment of ADHD in adolescents & young adults.* Poster session presented at the annual meeting of the Association of Convulsive Therapy, Washington, DC.

Weber, W., Stoep, A. V., McCarty, R. L., Weiss, N. S., Biederman, J., & McClellan, J. (2008). Hypericum perforatum (St John's wort) for attention-deficit/hyperactivity disorder in children and adolescents: A randomized controlled trial. *Journal of the American Medical Association, 299,* 2633–2641.

Wedlake, M. (2002). Cognitive remediation therapy for undergraduates with ADHD. *The ADHD Report, 10*(5), 11–13, 16.

Weinstein, C. E., Palmer, D. R., & Schulte, A. C. (2002). *The learning and study strategies inventory.* Clearwater, FL: H&H.

Weinstein, C. S. (1994). Cognitive remediation strategies: An adjunct to the psychotherapy of adults with attention-deficit hyperactivity disorder. *Journal of Psychotherapy Practice and Research, 3,* 44–57.

Weisler, R. H., Biederman, J., Spencer, T. J., Wilens, T. E., Faraone, S. V., Chrisman, A. K., et al. (2006). Mixed amphetamine salts extended release in the treatment of adult ADHD: A randomized, controlled trial. *CNS Spectrums, 11,* 625–639.

Weiss, G., & Hechtman, L. T. (1993). *Hyperactive children grown up* (2nd ed.). New York: Guilford Press.

Weiss, M., Hechtman, L. T., & The Adult ADHD Research Group (2006). A randomized double-blind trial of paroxetine and/or dextroamphetamine and problem-focused therapy for attention-deficit/hyperactivity disorder in adults. *Journal of Clinical Psychiatry, 67,* 611–619.

Weiss, M., Hechtman, L. T., & Weiss, G. (1999). *ADHD in adulthood: A guide to current theory, diagnosis, and treatment.* Baltimore: Johns Hopkins University Press.

Weiss, M., Hechtman, L. T., & Weiss, G. (2000). ADHD in parents. *Journal of the American Academy of Child & Adolescent Psychiatry, 39,* 1059–1061.

Weiss, M., Murray, C., & Weiss, G. (2002). Adults with attention-deficit/hyperactivity disorder: Current concepts. *Journal of Psychiatric Practice, 8,* 99–111.

Weiss, M., Safren, S. A., Solanto, M., Hechtman, L., Rostain, A. L., Ramsay, J. R., et al. (2008). Research forum on psychological treatment of adults with ADHD. *Journal of Attention Disorders, 11,* 642–651.

Wells, K. C., Pelham, W. E., Kotkin, R. A., Hoza, B., Abikoff, H. B., Abramowitz, A., et al. (2000). Psychosocial treatment strategies in the MTA study: Rationale, methods, and critical issues in design and implementation. *Journal of Abnormal Child Psychology, 28,* 483–505.

Wender, P. H. (1975). The minimal brain dysfunction syndrome. *Annual Review of Medicine, 26,* 45–62.

Wender, P. H., & Reimherr, F. W. (1990). Bupropion treatment of attention deficit hyperactivity disorder in adults. *American Journal of Psychiatry, 147,* 1018–1020.

Wender, P. H., Reimherr, F. W., & Wood, D. R. (1981). Attention deficit disorder ("minimal brain dysfunction") in adults: A replication study of diagnosis and drug treatment. *Archives of General Psychiatry, 38,* 449–456.

Westerberg, H., Brehmer, Y., D'Hondt, N., Söderlund, D., & Bäckman, L. (2007, April). *Computerized training of working memory—A new method for improving cognition in aging.* Poster session presented at the annual meeting of the Cognitive Neuroscience Society, San Francisco.

Westerberg, H., Jacobaeus, H., Hirvikoski, T., Clevberger, P., Östensson, M. L., Bartfai, A., et al. (2007). Computerized working memory training after stroke—A pilot study. *Brain Injury, 21,* 21–29.

Westerberg, H., & Klingberg, T. (2007). Changes in cortical activity after training of working memory—A single-subject analysis. *Physiology and Behavior, 92,* 186–192.

Weyandt, L. L., & DuPaul, G. (2006). ADHD in college students. *Journal of Attention Disorders, 10,* 9–19.

Weyandt, L. L., Iwaszuk, W., Fulton, K., Ollerton, M., Beatty, M., Fouts, H., et al. (2003). The Internal Restlessness Scale: Performance of college students with and without ADHD. *Journal of Learning Disabilities, 36,* 382–389.

Weyandt, L. L., Linterman, I., & Rice, J. A. (1995). Reported prevalence of attention difficulties in a general sample of college students. *Journal of Psychopathology and Behavioral Assessment, 17,* 293–304.

Weyandt, L. L., Rice, J. A., Linterman, I., Mitzlaff, L., & Emert, E. (1998). Neuropsychological performance of a sample of adults with ADHD, developmental reading disorder, and controls. *Developmental Neuropsychology, 14,* 643–656.

Whalen, B., & Henker, C. K. (1999). The child with attention-deficit/hyperactivity disorder in family contexts. In H. C. Quay & A. E. Hogan (Eds.), *Handbook of disruptive behavior disorders* (pp. 139–155). New York: Kluwer Academic/Plenum Publishers.

Wiggins, D., Singh, K., Getz, H. G., & Hutchins, D. E. (1999). Effects of brief group intervention for adults with attention deficit/hyperactivity disorder. *Journal of Mental Health Counseling, 21,* 82–92.

Wilens, T. E. (2003). Drug therapy for adults with attention-deficit/hyperactivity disorder. *Drugs, 63*, 2395–2411.

Wilens, T. E. (2007). Prevalence, diagnosis, and issues of comorbidity. *CNS Spectrums, 12*(4, Suppl. 6), 3–5.

Wilens, T. E., Biederman, J., Mick, E., & Spencer, T. J. (1995). A systematic assessment of tricyclic antidepressants in the treatment of adult attention deficit/hyperactivity disorder. *Journal of Nervous and Mental Disorders, 183*, 48–50.

Wilens, T. E., Biederman, J., Prince, J., Spencer, T. J., Faraone, S. V., Warburton, R., et al. (1996). Six-week, double-blind, placebo-controlled study of desipramine for adult attention deficit hyperactivity disorder. *American Journal of Psychiatry, 159*, 1147–1153.

Wilens, T. E., Biederman, J., & Spencer, T. J. (2002). Attention deficit/hyperactivity disorder across the lifespan. *Annual Review of Medicine, 53*, 113–131.

Wilens, T. E., & Decker, M. W. (2007). Neuronal nicotinic receptor agonists for the treatment of attention-deficit/hyperactivity disorder: Focus on cognition. *Biochemical Pharmacology, 74*, 1212–1223.

Wilens, T. E., Haight, B. R., Horrigan, J. P., Hudziak, J. J., Rosenthal, N. E., Connor, D. F., et al. (2005). Bupropion XL in adults with attention-deficit/hyperactivity disorder: A randomized, placebo-controlled study. *Biological Psychiatry, 57*, 793–801.

Wilens, T. E., McDermott, S. P., Biederman, J., Abrantes, A., Hahesy, A., & Spencer, T. (1999). Cognitive therapy in the treatment of adults with ADHD: A systematic chart review of 26 cases. *Journal of Cognitive Psychotherapy: An International Quarterly, 13*, 215–226.

Wilens, T. E., Spencer, T. J., Biederman, J., Girard, K., Doyle, R., Prince, J., et al. (2001). A controlled clinical trial of bupropion for attention deficit hyperactivity disorder in adults. *American Journal of Psychiatry, 158*, 282–288.

Wilens, T. E., Verlinden, M. H., Adler, L. A., Wozniak, P. J., & West, S. A. (2006). ABT-089, a neuronal nicotinic receptor partial agonist, for the treatment of attention-deficit disorder in adults: Results of a pilot study. *Biological Psychiatry, 59*, 1065–1070.

Wingo, A. P., & Ghaemi, S. N. (2007). ADHD—Only half the diagnosis in an adult with inattention? Overlapping symptoms may obscure comorbid bipolar illness. *Current Psychiatry, 6*(6), 46–48, 51–54, 59–61.

Wolf, L. E. (2001). College students with ADHD and other hidden disabilities. *Annals of the New York Academy of Sciences, 931*, 385–395.

Wood, D. R., Reimherr, F. W., & Wender, P. H. (1985a). Amino acid precursors for the treatment of attention-deficit disorder, residual type. *Psychopharmacology Bulletin, 26*, 249–253.

Wood, D. R., Reimherr, F. W., & Wender, P. H. (1985b). Treatment of attention-deficit disorder with *d, l*-phenylalanine. *Psychiatry Research, 16*, 21–26.

Wood, D. R., Reimherr, F. W., Wender, P. H., & Johnson, G. E. (1976). Diagnosis and treatment of minimal brain dysfunction in adults. *Archives of General Psychiatry, 33,* 1453–1460.

Wright, J. L. (2006). Psychoanalysis in conjunction with medication: A clinical research opportunity. *Journal of the American Psychoanalytic Association, 54,* 833–855.

Wu, J. C., Blinder, B., Maguire, G., Pavel, D., Alters, D., Best, S. D., et al. (2006). *Formal response to January 2005 American Psychiatric Association Council on Children, Adolescents and Their Families resource document.* Retrieved July 2, 2007, from http://amenclinics.com/ac/articles_detail.php?articleID=18

Yeo, R. A., Hill, D., Campbell, R., Vigil, J., & Brooks, W. M. (2000). Developmental instability and working memory ability in children: A magnetic resonance spectroscopy investigation. *Developmental Neuropsychology, 17,* 143–159.

Young, G. S. (2004). Blood phospholipid fatty acid analysis of adults with and without attention-deficit/hyperactivity disorder. *Lipids, 39,* 117–123.

Young, J. L., & Giwerc, D. (2003, December). Just what is coaching? *Attention Magazine, 10*(6), 36–41.

Young, S., & Bramham, J. (2007). *ADHD in adults: A psychological guide to practice.* Chichester, England: Wiley.

Zabarenko, L. M. (2002). AD/HD, psychoanalysis, and neuroscience: A survey of recent findings and their applications. *Psychoanalytic Inquiry, 22,* 413–432.

Zentall, S. S., Hall, A. M., & Lee, D. L. (1998). Attentional focus of student with hyperactivity during a word-search task. *Journal of Abnormal Child Psychology, 26,* 335–343.

Ziegler, R., & Holden, L. (1988). Family therapy for learning disabled and attention-deficit disordered children. *American Journal of Orthopsychiatry, 58,* 196–210.

Zwart, L. M., & Kallemeyn, L. M. (2001). Peer-based coaching for college students with ADHD and learning disabilities. *Journal of Postsecondary Education and Disability, 15,* 5–20.

Zylowska, L., Ackerman, D. L., Yang, M. H., Futrell, J. L., Horton, N. L., Hale, T. S., et al. (2008). Mindfulness meditation training in adults and adolescents with ADHD: A feasibility study. *Journal of Attention Disorders, 11,* 737–746.

INDEX

ABOUT THE AUTHOR

J. Russell ("Russ") Ramsay, PhD, is a licensed psychologist and assistant professor of psychology in psychiatry at the University of Pennsylvania (PENN) School of Medicine. He earned his doctorate in clinical psychology from the Pacific Graduate School of Psychology and completed a postdoctoral fellowship at PENN's Center for Cognitive Therapy. In addition to continuing to work as a senior staff psychologist at the Center for Cognitive Therapy, in 1999 he cofounded and still serves as the codirector of PENN's Adult Attention-Deficit/Hyperactivity Disorder (ADHD) Treatment and Research Program.

Dr. Ramsay has authored numerous professional articles and book chapters and has lectured internationally on various issues related to adult ADHD as well as the principles of cognitive behavioral therapy. He is coauthor of *Cognitive Behavioral Therapy for Adult ADHD: An Integrative Psychosocial and Medical Approach* and serves on the editorial boards of the *Journal of Attention Disorders* and the *Journal of Psychotherapy Integration*. He also serves on the professional advisory boards of the Attention Deficit Disorder Association (ADDA) and the Bucks County, Pennsylvania, chapter of Children and Adults with Attention-Deficit/Hyperactivity Disorder (CHADD).

Dr. Ramsay is active in community education and has presented at regional meetings of mental health organizations and CHADD chapters; been interviewed for numerous magazine, newspaper, and online articles; and served as an invited guest on public radio, television, and America Online. He also provides psychotherapy supervision to psychiatric residents and other trainees at PENN and was the recipient of the 2008 Martin P. Szuba Award for excellence in clinical teaching and research in the Department of Psychiatry at the PENN School of Medicine.